50 WALKS IN
Shropshire

50 Walks in Shropshire

Published by AA Publishing (a trading name of AA Media Limited, whose registered office is Grove House, Lutyens Close, Lychpit, Basingstoke, Hampshire RG24 8AG; registered number 06112600)

Mapping in this book is derived from the following products:
OS Landranger 126 (walks 2, 22–33, 36)
OS Landranger 127 (walks 1, 3–7)
OS Landranger 137 (walks 34, 35, 37–50)
OS Landranger 138 (walks 8–21)

© Crown copyright and database rights 2024 Ordnance Survey. 100021153.

Maps contain data available from openstreetmap.org © under the Open Database License found at opendatacommons.org

ISBN: 978-0-7495-8375-0
ISBN: 978-0-7495-8384-2 (SS)

A CIP catalogue record for this book is available from the British Library.

AA Media would like to thank the following contributors in the preparation of this guide:
Clare Ashton, Tracey Freestone, Lauren Havelock, Nicky Hillenbrand, Lin Hutton, Graham Jones, Ian Little, Richard Marchi, Nigel Phillips and Victoria Samways.

Cover design by
berkshire design company

Printed and bound in the UK by Oriental Press, Dubai.

A05851

We would like to thank the following photographers, companies and picture libraries for their assistance in the preparation of this book. Abbreviations for the picture credits are as follows:
Alamy = Alamy Stock Photo
Trade Cover, Christopher Nicholson/Alamy
Special Cover, Allan Hartley/Alamy
Back Cover Advert, SolStock/istockphoto; 9, Jon Lewis/Alamy; 12/13, SIMON STAPLEY/Alamy; 26/27, Allan Hartley/Alamy; 43, SPK/Alamy; 53, Edward Dyer/Alamy; 75, Richard O'Donoghue/Alamy; 94/95, John Keates/Alamy; 111, John Hayward/Alamy; 124/125, John Keates/Alamy; 141, Countrywide Images/Alamy; 169, Graham Johns/Alamy; 176, SolStock/istockphoto

The contents of this book are believed correct at the time of printing. Nevertheless, the publishers cannot be held responsible for any errors or omissions or for changes in the details given in this book or for the consequences of any reliance on the information it provides. This does not affect your statutory rights. We have tried to ensure accuracy in this book, but things do change and we would be grateful if readers would advise us of any inaccuracies they may encounter by emailing walks@aamediagroup.co.uk

We have done our best to make sure that these walks are safe and achievable by walkers with a basic level of fitness. However, we can accept no responsibility for any loss or injury incurred while following the walks. Advice on walking safely can be found on pages 10–11.

Some of the walks may appear in other AA books and publications.

Discover and book AA-rated places to stay at www.RatedTrips.com.

AA

50 WALKS IN
Shropshire

CONTENTS

How to use this book	6
Exploring the area	8
Walking in safety	10

The walks

WALK		GRADIENT	DISTANCE	PAGE
1	The Wrekin	▲▲	8.5 miles (13.7km)	14
2	Whixall Moss	Negligible	10 miles (16.1km)	17
3	Market Drayton	Negligible	5.25 miles (8.4km)	20
4	Wistanswick	▲	5.5 miles (8.9km)	23
5	An Ironbridge Circuit	▲▲	4.5 miles (7.2km)	28
6	Coalport	▲	5 miles (8km)	31
7	Coalbrookdale	▲▲	5 miles (8km)	34
8	Up Jacob's Ladder	▲▲	6.5 miles (10.4km)	37
9	Bridgnorth	▲▲	4 miles (6.4km)	40
10	Hampton Loade	▲	5 miles (8km)	44
11	Alveley	▲	5 miles (8km)	47
12	Severn Vale	▲	5.5 miles (8.8km)	50
13	A Wyre Forest Circuit	▲	5 miles (8km)	54
14	Bagginswood	▲▲	6.3 miles (10.1km)	57
15	Cleobury Mortimer	▲	4.8 miles (7.7km)	60
16	Brown Clee	▲▲▲	7 miles (11.3km)	63
17	Clee Hill	▲▲▲	8.25 miles (13.3km)	66
18	Diddlebury	▲	6.25 miles (10.1km)	69
19	Wenlock Edge	▲▲	8 miles (12.9km)	72
20	Wilderhope	▲	3 miles (4.8km)	76
21	Much Wenlock	▲	6.25 miles (10.1km)	79
22	Grinshill Cliff	▲	5.25 miles (8.4km)	82

WALK		GRADIENT	DISTANCE	PAGE
23	Merrington Green	▲	5.5 miles (8.8km)	85
24	The Witterage	▲	5 miles (8km)	88
25	Shrewsbury	Negligible	6 miles (9.7km)	91
26	Lyth Hill	▲	7.75 miles (12.5km)	96
27	Ellesmere	▲	7.25 miles (11.7km)	99
28	Whittington Castle	Negligible	6 miles (9.7km)	102
29	Frankton	▲	5.3 miles (8.5km)	105
30	Oswestry Racecourse	▲	4 miles (6.4km)	108
31	Montgomery Canal	▲	6.5 miles (10.4km)	112
32	Hope Valley	▲▲	9.5 miles (15.3km)	115
33	Stiperstones NNR	▲▲	4.5 miles (7.2km)	118
34	Stiperstones	▲▲	4.8 miles (7.8km)	121
35	Stapeley Hill	▲	3.6 miles (5.7km)	126
36	Earl's Hill	▲▲▲	4 miles (6.4km)	129
37	Bishop's Castle	▲	7 miles (11.3km)	132
38	The Long Mynd	▲▲▲	7.5 miles (12.1km)	135
39	The Stretton Hills	▲▲	6 miles (9.7km)	138
40	Caer Caradoc	▲▲▲	6.6 miles (10.6km)	142
41	Ludlow	▲▲▲	5.25 miles (8.4km)	145
42	Stokesay Castle	▲▲	6.25 miles (10.1km)	148
43	Wart Hill	▲▲	6 miles (9.7km)	151
44	Flounder's Folly	▲▲	6.5 miles (10.4km)	154
45	Craven Arms	▲▲▲	4.4 miles (7km)	157
46	Hopton Woods	▲▲	5 miles (8km)	160
47	Bury Ditches Hill Fort	▲▲	5.4 miles (8.7km)	163
48	Offa's Dyke	▲▲▲	8 miles (12.9km)	166
49	Clun Valley	▲▲▲	5.5 miles (8.8km)	170
50	Black Hill and Cwm	▲▲	5.7 miles (9.7km)	173

HOW TO USE THIS BOOK

Each walk starts with an information panel giving all the information you will need about the walk at a glance, including its relative difficulty, distance and total amount of ascent. Difficulty levels and gradients are as follows:

Difficulty of walk

● Easy

● Intermediate

● Hard

Gradient

▲ Some slopes

▲▲ Some steep slopes

▲▲▲ Several very steep slopes

Maps

Every walk has its own route map. We also suggest a relevant Ordnance Survey map to take with you, allowing you to view the area in more detail. The time suggested is the minimum for reasonably fit walkers and doesn't allow for stops.

Route map legend

– –▶– –	Walk route	▨	Built-up area
①	Route waypoint	▨	Woodland area
– – – –	Adjoining path	🚻	Toilet
●	Place of interest	🅿	Car park
△	Steep section	⊞	Picnic area
|//	Viewpoint	)(	Bridge
⁗⁗⁗	Embankment		

Start points

The start of each walk is given as a six-figure grid reference prefixed by two letters referring to a 100km square of the National Grid. More information on grid references can be found on most OS Walker's Maps.

Dogs

We have tried to give dog owners useful advice about how dog friendly each walk is. Please respect other countryside users. Keep your dog under control, especially around livestock, and obey local by-laws and other dog control notices.

Car parking

Many of the car parks suggested are public, but occasionally you may have to park on the roadside or in a lay-by. Please be considerate about where you leave your car, ensuring that you are not on private property or access roads, and that gates are not blocked and other vehicles can pass safely.

Walks locator map

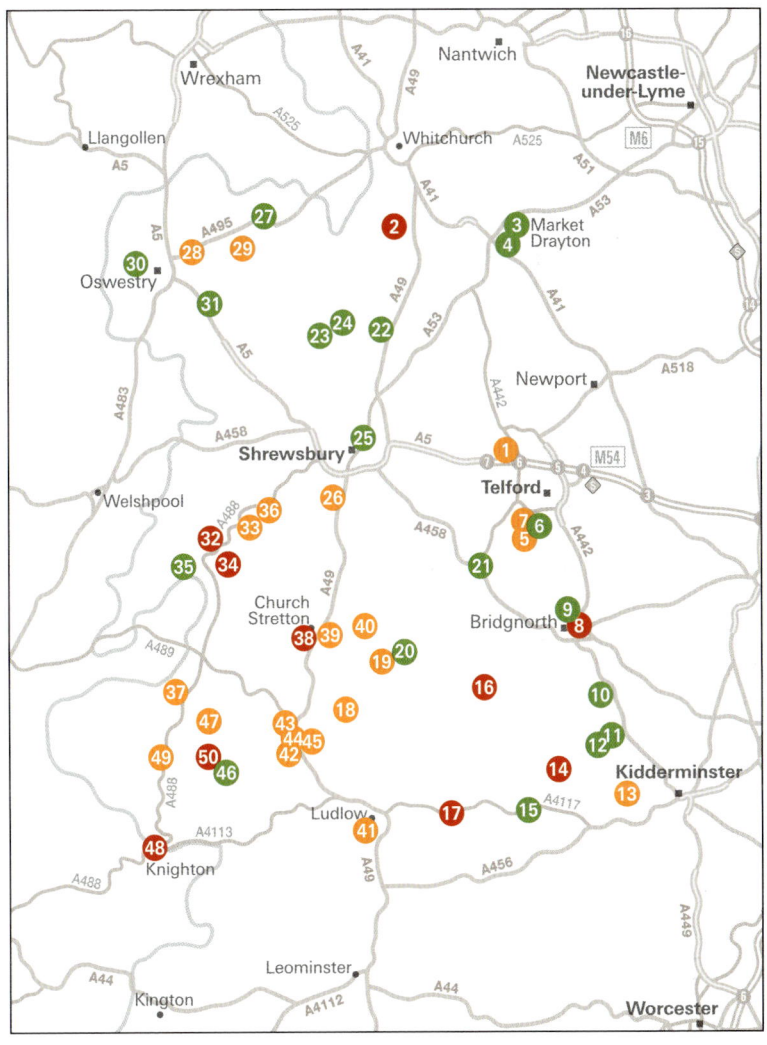

EXPLORING THE AREA

It lacks a coastline, and none of its hills quite achieves mountain status, but Shropshire has just about every other desirable feature a discerning walker could wish for. Perhaps nowhere else in England will you find a county so deeply rural and with so much variety. But don't take our word for it. Choose a clear day, then make your way to the top of The Wrekin, and look down on that 'land of lost content' so wistfully evoked by A E Housman, the author of *A Shropshire Lad*.

The Severn

Take binoculars with you and trace the course of Britain's longest river as the Severn sweeps through the county, from the Breidden Hills in the west to Wyre Forest in the southeast, effectively dividing Shropshire in two. To the north is a patchwork of dairy fields, hedgerows, copses and crops, broken at intervals by rugged sandstone ridges such as Grinshill or Nesscliffe, and dissected by a complex network of canals. Spilling over the border into neighbouring Cheshire and North Wales is the unique meres and mosses country, with serenely smooth lakes glinting silver in the early morning light, interspersed with russet-tinged expanses of alder-fringed peat bog, where only the cry of the curlew disturbs the silence.

South of the Severn lies the Shropshire Hills Area of Outstanding Natural Beauty. Where to start? There is almost too much. With Wenlock Edge perhaps, one of the most famous escarpments in the country, despite being not especially high or dramatic. It's only when you walk the Edge that you fully discover what a magical place it is – glorious woods and unexpectedly steep slopes plunging to innumerable secret valleys, meadows, streams and farmhouses, all tucked away, invisible from the outside world.

Long Mynd And The Wrekin

If the Edge superficially lacks drama, that could never be said of the Stretton Hills, rising magnificently above the little town of Church Stretton, especially Caer Caradoc, with its shockingly steep southern slopes and a prehistoric fort encircling its summit. Across the Stretton Gap lies the Long Mynd. Viewed from The Wrekin, the Mynd is a dark bulky smudge. Seen from Caer Caradoc, it's an undulating plateau cut by valleys so steep they're often almost vertical. But look at the Mynd from the south and it takes on a very different character, more like a range of round-topped hills. In reality, the Long Mynd is all of these things, and it offers endless walking possibilities, not to mention a view to equal, or even surpass, that from The Wrekin. To stand on its western tops, looking across the Onny Valley towards Wales and the setting sun, is to gaze on a scene so sublime you'll be itching to get out there. Near at hand beckons Stiperstones, its long crest jagged with rocky tors, and south of it Heath Mynd,

Stapeley, Bromlow Callow and innumerable others rolling away to the border. Further south and west, Offa's Dyke snakes over the gloriously remote rounded tops of Clun Forest, which merge imperceptibly with the Kerry Hills of Radnorshire, where that loveliest of rivers, the Teme, has its source.

And let's not forget the Clee Hills. Brown Clee dominates the Severn Valley near Bridgnorth, providing a worthy backdrop for exquisite Corve Dale. It never looks better than in early morning mist, its intricate patchwork slowly emerging as the sun breaks through. And then there's Titterstone Clee, rearing high above Ludlow. Its slopes are scarred by quarrying and blighted by radar installations, yet its massive presence and charisma remain undimmed, and the view from its southern flank is claimed to be the finest in England.

PUBLIC TRANSPORT

Over the years, bus services in Shropshire have improved dramatically everywhere except the Clun Valley. Every walk in this book was accessed easily by public transport. The county council is keen to increase the use of public transport, as are other interested parties such as the National Trust. Several leisure bus services are aimed specifically at walkers, but ordinary, everyday services will get you there. Details are available from Traveline on 0871 200 22 33, while tourist information centres and libraries have free timetable booklets.

Walk 41

WALKING IN SAFETY

All these walks are suitable for any reasonably fit person, but less experienced walkers should try the easier walks first. Route-finding is usually straightforward, but you will find that an Ordnance Survey map is a useful addition to the route maps and descriptions; recommendations can be found in the information panels.

Risks

Although each walk here has been researched with a view to minimising the risks to the walkers who follow its route, no walk in the countryside can be considered to be completely free from risk. Walking in the outdoors will always require a degree of common sense and judgement to ensure that it is as safe as possible.

- Be particularly careful on cliff paths and in upland terrain, where the consequences of a slip can be very serious.

- Remember to check tidal conditions before walking on the seashore.

- Some sections of route are by, or cross, busy roads. Take care, and remember that traffic is a danger even on minor country lanes.

- Be careful around farmyard machinery and livestock, especially if you have children with you.

- Be aware of the consequences of changes in the weather, and check the forecast before you set out. Carry spare clothing and a torch if you are walking in the winter months. Remember that the weather can change very quickly at any time of the year, and in moorland and heathland areas, mist and fog can make route-finding much harder. Don't set out in these conditions unless you are confident of your navigation skills in poor visibility.

- In summer remember to take account of the heat and sun; wear a hat and carry water.

- On walks away from centres of population you should carry a whistle and survival bag. If you do have an accident that means you require help from the emergency services, make a note of your position as accurately as possible and dial 999.

Countryside Code
Respect other people:

- Consider the local community and other people enjoying the outdoors.

- Co-operate with people at work in the countryside. For example, keep out of the way when farm animals are being gathered or moved, and follow directions from the farmer.

- Don't block gateways, driveways or other paths with your vehicle.
- Leave gates and property as you find them, and follow paths unless wider access is available, such as on open country or registered common land (known as 'open access land').
- Leave machinery and farm animals alone – don't interfere with animals, even if you think they're in distress. Try to alert the farmer instead.
- Use gates, stiles or gaps in field boundaries if you can – climbing over walls, hedges and fences can damage them and increase the risk of farm animals escaping.
- Our heritage matters to all of us – be careful not to disturb ruins and historic sites.

Protect the natural environment:
- Take your litter home. Litter and leftover food don't just spoil the beauty of the countryside; they can be dangerous to wildlife and farm animals. Dropping litter and dumping rubbish are criminal offences.
- Leave no trace of your visit, and take special care not to damage, destroy or remove features such as rocks, plants and trees.
- Keep dogs under effective control, making sure they are not a danger or nuisance to farm animals, horses, wildlife or other people.
- If cattle or horses chase you and your dog, it is safer to let your dog off the lead – don't risk getting hurt by trying to protect it. Your dog will be much safer if you let it run away from a farm animal in these circumstances, and so will you.
- Everyone knows how unpleasant dog mess is and it can cause infections, so always clean up after your dog and get rid of the mess responsibly – bag it and bin it.
- Fires can be as devastating to wildlife and habitats as they are to people and property – so be careful with naked flames and cigarettes at any time of the year.

Enjoy the outdoors:
- Plan ahead and be prepared for natural hazards, changes in weather and other events.
- Wild animals, farm animals and horses can behave unpredictably if you get too close, especially if they're with their young – so give them plenty of space.
- Follow advice and local signs.

For more information visit www.gov.uk/government/publications/the-countryside-code

ALL AROUND THE WREKIN

DISTANCE/TIME	8.5 miles (13.7km) / 3hrs
ASCENT/GRADIENT	1,585ft (483m) / ▲ ▲
PATHS	Woodland footpaths, urban streets, quiet lanes, 7 stiles
LANDSCAPE	Hills and woods on the edge of Wellington
SUGGESTED MAP	OS Explorer 242 Telford, Ironbridge & The Wrekin
START/FINISH	Grid reference: SJ651113
DOG FRIENDLINESS	Dog heaven, except on firing days
PARKING	Belmont or Swimming Pool East car parks, both on Tan Bank, off Victoria Road, Wellington
PUBLIC TOILETS	At the Station car park

Those who live in Shropshire know that The Wrekin is more than just a hill. For all true Salopians it is a sort of focal point and symbol of Shropshire, the embodiment of home, a sentiment implied in the traditional toast 'To all friends around The Wrekin'. Although it reaches only a modest 1,335ft (407m), its splendid isolation makes it seem higher. This illusion is strengthened by its shape: while basically a whaleback, it appears conical from certain angles, like a mini-mountain, giving the impression of an extinct volcano. It isn't, though it is volcanic in origin, an eroded remnant of a vast chunk of rock thrust to the surface around 700 million years ago, putting it among the oldest rocks in the world.

If that origin seems a bit mundane, you might prefer the alternative provided by local folklore, which tells of the giant Gwendol Wrekin ap Shenkin ap Mynyddmawr (or the Devil in another version) who was on his way to Shrewsbury to dam the River Severn with a shovelful of soil. He met a cobbler who guessed what he was up to, showed him the sackful of shoes he was carrying and told him he had worn them all out trying to find Shrewsbury. Frustrated, Gwendol dumped his shovelful on the spot, sparing Shrewsbury from flooding and creating The Wrekin. (It didn't work, however – Shrewsbury floods nearly every winter.)

The return leg of the walk takes you through The Ercall Nature Reserve. The Ercall (pronounced 'arkle') is a small, steep, wooded hill important for its geology as well as its woodlands and wildlife. Much of The Ercall is composed of Wrekin quartzite, a hard, white, crystalline rock around 535 million years old. There are also older volcanic rhyolites, and within these there is what geologists call an intrusion of granophyre, a fine-grained granite formed 560 million years ago. The great engineer Thomas Telford (1757-1834) used Ercall granophyre when he resurfaced the Roman Watling Street to create his Holyhead Road, on which the modern A5 is based. Stop to read the information boards in the nature reserve to learn the geology and ecology of The Ercall.

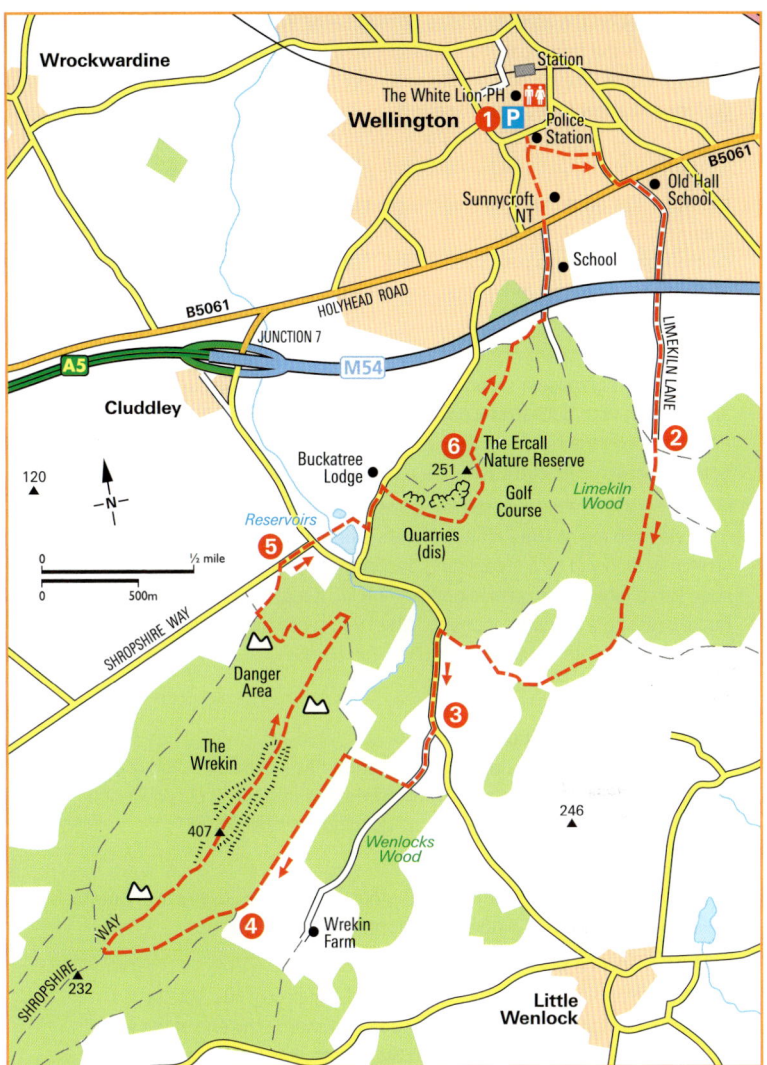

1. Walk along Tan Bank away from the town centre. Cross Victoria Road and go forward a little way, still on Tan Bank, before turning left on a path just after the police station. Walk to New Church Road and turn right. At Holyhead Road, turn left, then cross to Limekiln Lane, noticing the Old Hall School (built in 1480) on the corner. Soon the slopes of The Wrekin appear, as Limekiln Lane heads under the M54 into open country.

2. At the end of the lane, go straight on into Limekiln Wood; the path leads along the edge of the wood at first. At a junction, keep straight on, then after a few paces fork right into the heart of the wood. Ignore branching paths, sticking to the well-trodden main route. At the top, bear right. Pass some boulders in the track, descend to a junction and turn left. Go left again when you come to a road.

3. Turn right on the access road to Wrekin Farm. When you reach Wenlocks Wood, leave the farm road, turning right on a field-edge footpath which heads towards The Wrekin. A stile soon gives access to its eastern slopes. Go forward a few paces, then turn left.

4. Branch right where a signpost indicates a permissive path. Follow this round the hill to a cross path; turn right and climb a steep, eroded track up the ridge. Continue over the summit, past the telecoms station, and follow the main track down. When you glimpse a house (Wrekin Cottage) through trees on the right, look for a path descending sharply back left. Follow this down as the gradient eases, fork right then in a few paces turn right near the wood's edge.

5. Meet a lane and turn right to a T-junction. Join a footpath opposite. Skirt a reservoir and glimpse a second before meeting a lane. Turn left. As you draw almost level with Buckatree Lodge, turn right into The Ercall Nature Reserve. Pass a pool on the right and then an impressive former quarry on the left. Soon you reach a junction: ignore a path doubling back left and go forward a few paces. The main track swings left and climbs to the ridge top.

6. To visit the top of The Ercall, turn left; otherwise, go right. A fairly level stretch is followed by a steepening descent, where the path forks. Go right and soon join a lane which passes under the M54. Keep straight on to Holyhead Road. Cross to a footpath opposite. When you reach a road go straight across to another footpath, then turn left on to Tan Bank.

Where to eat and drink
Wellington's compact, bustling town centre has a good selection of cafés and pubs. The White Lion on Crown Street is a traditional pub, over 400 years old, with a kitchen serving up good home-cooked food.

What to see
Limekiln Wood is full of intriguing humps and hollows, overgrown now by ferns and ivy but still hinting at its former role as a quarry.

While you're there
Visit one of the National Trust's more unusual properties. You'll pass close by it when you cross Holyhead Road towards the end of the walk. A Victorian suburban house called Sunnycroft, it is typical of many built for prosperous professionals and businessmen, and has survived largely unaltered, its original contents still in place.

EXPLORING WHIXALL MOSS

DISTANCE/TIME	10 miles (16.1km) / 3hrs 30min
ASCENT/GRADIENT	98ft (30m)
PATHS	Some road walking (take care on blind bends on Post Office Lane), about 15 stiles (some in disrepair)
LANDSCAPE	Dairy country, canals, Whixall Moss
SUGGESTED MAP	OS Explorer 241 Shrewsbury
START/FINISH	Grid reference: SJ537337
DOG FRIENDLINESS	On lead in nature reserves and where cattle present, some electric fences
PARKING	Where bridleway meets lane by Prees Station, take care not to block access
PUBLIC TOILETS	None on route

North Shropshire is meres and mosses country. Meres are lakes or ponds, but mosses are perhaps less familiar. They are raised peat bogs, which may not sound particularly interesting. Reserve judgement until you have explored Whixall Moss, part of Fenn's, Whixall and Bettisfield Mosses National Nature Reserve (NNR). Only the best or rarest places receive NNR designation, but Whixall is also a European Special Area of Conservation and a Ramsar Site of International Wetland Importance. Since most of our mosses have been destroyed by forestry, agriculture and peat digging, it is also very rare. Commercial peat cutting ceased here in 1991 and since then work has been in hand to restore the moss, as far as this is possible.

A moss is waterlogged, stagnant and acidic. Despite this, or because of it, 1,700 insect species can be found in this habitat. However, some are so specialised they can't easily survive elsewhere, which is one reason that mosses are so important. The raft spider, for instance, is very much at home here, as is the rare white-faced darter (a damselfly). Uncommon birds of prey such as the hobby patrol the skies and the snipe finds a refuge here in winter. Characteristic plants include cotton sedge, bogmoss, cross-leaved heath, bog rosemary, cranberry and sundew – which feasts on insects. When mosses are drained for peat cutting such species are inevitably lost. There are few rights of way through the reserve but, in 2001, a partnership between English Nature, the Countryside Council for Wales and British Waterways developed three circular trails, parts of which are included in this walk, along with the adjacent Llangollen Canal. Canalside fens overflow with plants such as great hairy willowherb, water figwort and flag iris. In places carr (wet woodland) has developed, characterised by species such as alder and willow. Mallard ducks, mute swans and kingfishers haunt the canal, along with dragonflies and damselflies.

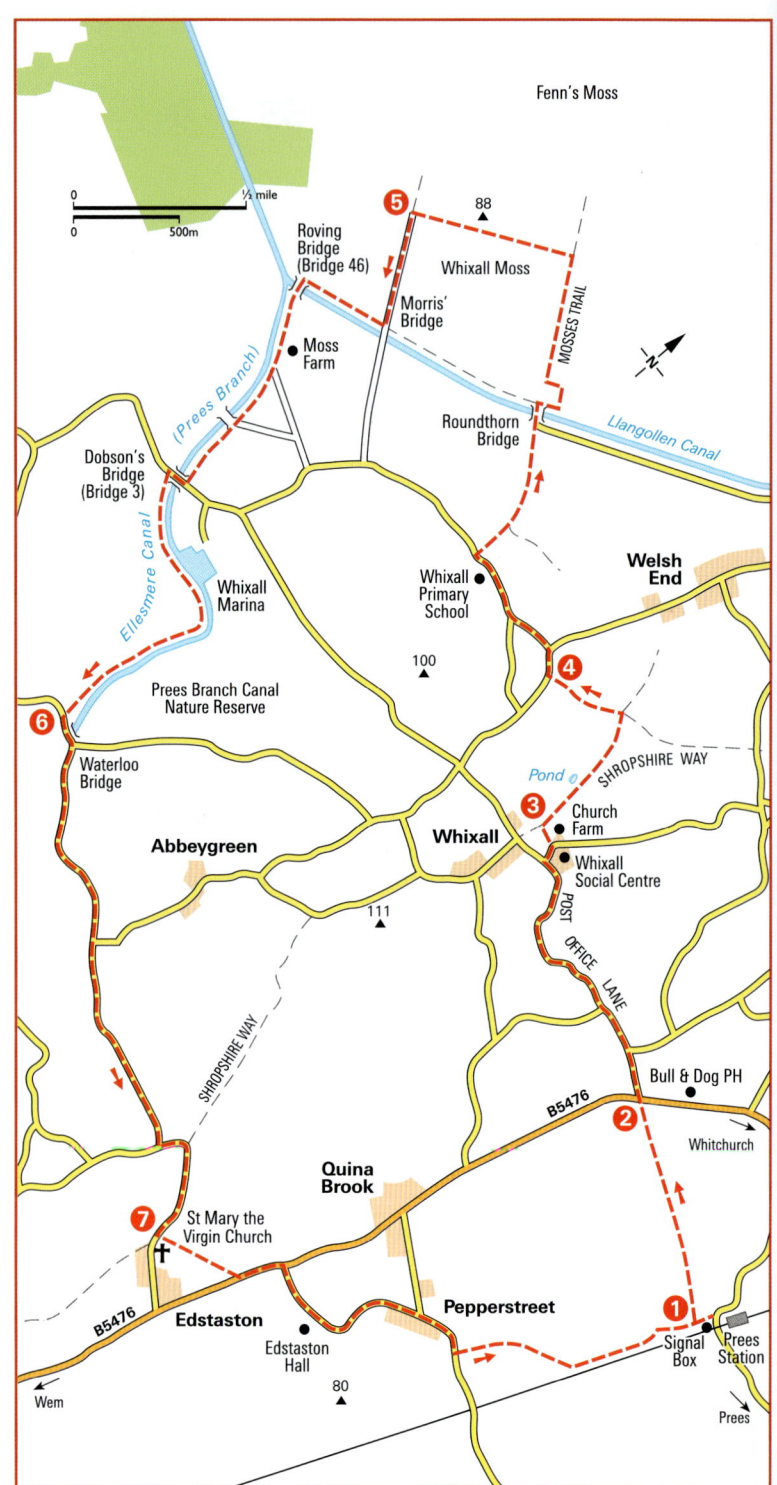

Fenn's Moss

Roving Bridge (Bridge 46)

Whixall Moss

88

Morris' Bridge

MOSSES TRAIL

(Prees Branch)

Moss Farm

Roundthorn Bridge

Llangollen Canal

Dobson's Bridge (Bridge 3)

Welsh End

Whixall Marina

Whixall Primary School

Ellesmere Canal

Prees Branch Canal Nature Reserve

100

SHROPSHIRE WAY

Pond

Waterloo Bridge

Abbeygreen

Whixall

Church Farm

Whixall Social Centre

POST OFFICE LANE

111

SHROPSHIRE WAY

Bull & Dog PH

B5476

Whitchurch

Quina Brook

St Mary the Virgin Church

Pepperstreet

B5476

Edstaston

Edstaston Hall

80

Signal Box

Prees Station

Wem

Prees

1. Join the bridleway by the signal box. After 100yds (91m) turn right through a gate (blocked stile hidden in the hedge nearby) into a field. Follow the right-hand edge to a stile. Cross to the other side of the hedge, but continue in the same direction. Keep straight on across four more fields to the B5476.

2. Walk along the road opposite (signed 'Whixall') and keep straight on at two junctions. Take care here. Turn right by Whixall Social Centre, then left on to a driveway before Church Farm.

3. At Farthing Cottage, turn right. Cross a field, passing a pond, then continue across the next field. Go slightly left across a third field to a pair of stiles and a footbridge. Don't cross these, but go through a gate, left, opening into a large field. Turn left, keeping about 100yds (91m) from its left-hand edge. On reaching a row of three large oaks, go diagonally right to a gate and then cross another field to a lane.

4. Turn right, then left at a junction and straight on at the next. Join the first path on the right after Whixall Primary School. Cross four fields to the Llangollen Canal and cross Roundthorn Bridge, then turn right to an information board telling you about the NNR. Take a leaflet from the box – it acts as a permit to enter the reserve. In 100yds (91m) turn left, following the orange-coded Mosses Trail.

5. At Point 8 on the trail, turn left to meet the canal at Morris' Bridge. Turn right on the towpath to a canal junction, then cross Bridge 46 (Roving Bridge) to join the Prees Branch. The towpath changes sides at Bridge 3 (Dobson's Bridge). Beyond Whixall Marina the canal is disused and has become a Shropshire Wildlife Trust nature reserve.

6. Pass some houses and meet a lane. Turn left, then immediately right, signposted 'Edstaston'. Keep straight on past a turning on the left, but turn left when you come to a T-junction and follow the lane into Edstaston.

Just before the church go through a gate on the left; a second gate and then a stile lead into a field. Go diagonally across this to the B5476. Turn left, then cross to a lane on the right. Follow it past Edstaston Hall and turn right at a T-junction. Turn left on a bridleway (sign decaying). In 274yds (300m) bear right to a gate and continue to the railway. Follow it north, bearing slightly left to join a clear track which leads back to Prees Station.

Where to eat and drink
There's nothing on the route, but The Bull and Dog pub (on B5476), 230yds (210m) north of the junction with Post Office Lane, near the start. There are further facilities in Prees.

What to see
In summer this is a great walk for butterflies, especially around Whixall Moss and along the canal. In June and July this includes the large heath butterfly, a protected species.

While you're there
Brown Moss (between Prees and Whitchurch) is an interesting contrast to Whixall Moss. Shropshire County Council manages it as a nature reserve and countryside recreation area. There's not much peat now, but it has a series of lovely pools, set in sandy heath and woodland. Perfect for a picnic.

SOUTH FROM MARKET DRAYTON

3

DISTANCE/TIME	5.25 miles (8.4km) / 2hrs
ASCENT/GRADIENT	165ft (50m)
PATHS	Streets, towpath, sandy track and quiet lanes
LANDSCAPE	Market town, canal and mixed farmland
SUGGESTED MAP	OS Explorer 243 Market Drayton
START/FINISH	Grid reference: SJ674344
DOG FRIENDLINESS	On lead between Point 4 and Walkmill Bridge
PARKING	Car park on Towers Lawn, next to bus station
PUBLIC TOILETS	At bus station

In 1245, at the behest of Abbot Simon of Combermere Abbey, Henry III granted Market Drayton a charter for a Wednesday market and two annual fairs. Marketing has been its main role ever since, serving a large area of rural Shropshire, Staffordshire and Cheshire. Abbot Simon wasn't just thinking of the local peasants and farmers – his monks had their own produce to sell. They cultivated vines and kept honeybees, as well as participating in dairy farming, which flourished in the fertile countryside. Food has always been the main focus for Market Drayton's traders and, even today, the town is full of small, independent shops selling a wide range of locally made produce. Every Wednesday Cheshire Street is still submerged by a flood of colourful stalls heaped high with food, along with goods from the Staffordshire Potteries. So you can buy your cake and the plate to eat it from too.

To compete in the modern world, Drayton now markets itself and the theme is still food, as it tries to entice tourists to the 'home of gingerbread'. First made here in 1817, for many years there were four gingerbread dynasties in town, each with its own secret recipe. People then enjoyed gingerbread in 'junks as big as my foot', but nowadays you can buy it fashioned into hearts, teddy bears, sheep or even footballers. Traditionally, Draytonians dunked their gingerbread in port but one of the most popular recipes also used rum. Billington's gingerbread is still made locally to a secret recipe, but Drayton also boasts plenty of other specialities, such as damson jam, damson cheese and damson gin, which possibly goes down well with a bit of rum-soaked, port-dunked gingerbread. Go into one of the bakers in town and you can choose from other local treats like butter buns, lardy cakes and oven bottoms, while pikelets and oatcakes from the Potteries are popular too. Since the 16th-century, Drayton has been famous for dairy goods. Yogurt is made in a factory on the edge of town, but farm-made yogurts are also on sale in the shops, along with excellent cheeses. It is said that the only un-pasteurised Cheshire cheese still made in England comes from Market Drayton.

Robert Clive was born near Market Drayton in 1725 and he terrorised the town as a boy. His despairing family packed him off to India where he achieved great wealth and prestige in the process of establishing British supremacy there. Despite his fame, it's his culinary contribution they celebrate in Drayton. At the Clive and Coffyne (a coffyne is a pie case) they serve an award-winning Clive of India Pie which is said to be based on a recipe given by Clive in 1768 to the bakers of Pézenas in France.

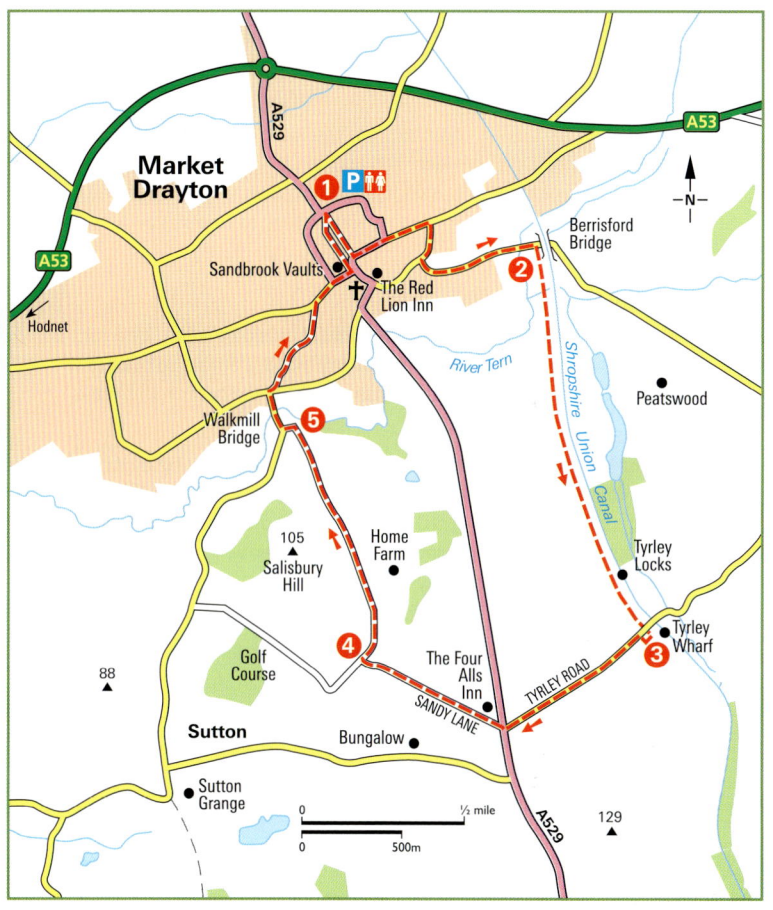

1. Walk past the bus station, cross at the zebra crossing, then turn left down Queen Street (part pedestrianised) then left on Stafford Street. Go straight on at the first junction, right at the next on to Great Hales Street and then left on Berrisford Road (use the easily missed footway on the left until forced to join the road).

2. You'll soon come to Berrisford Bridge, also known as 40 Steps Aqueduct, which carries the Shropshire Union Canal over the road. Go up the steps and turn right on the towpath. This part of the Shroppie system was originally the Birmingham and Liverpool Junction Canal, which went from Autherley to Nantwich. The engineer was Thomas Telford and the boldness of his design is apparent along this stretch, with its massive cuttings and embankments. The deep cutting on the approach to Tyrley Locks has its own microclimate, and positively drips with ferns, mosses and liverworts. The towpath marks the county boundary – this stretch of the canal is in Staffordshire.

3. Go under Bridge 60 by Tyrley Wharf then up steps to the lock gate. Turn sharp right to the lane (Tyrley Road) and turn left. This leads to the main road (A529) and a pub called The Four Alls Inn. Cross with care to Sandy Lane.

4. Sandy Lane comes to a T-junction with a track. Turn right here; it's still Sandy Lane, but this part is a private road and dogs must be kept on a lead. It heads north towards Drayton, overlooked by Salisbury Hill, where a Yorkist army under the Earl of Salisbury camped in 1459 before heavily defeating a Lancastrian force twice the size.

5. When you meet a road, turn right to cross the River Tern at Walkmill Bridge (a pack-horse bridge). Cross a wider road and go up Kilnbank Road opposite. Where it ends, turn right. After passing Sandbrook Vaults, onto Cheshire Street, carry on to join Queen Street which leads back to Towers Lawn.

Where to eat and drink

The Four Alls Inn is a popular place with lots of outside seating, ideal for families with dogs. Market Drayton has many friendly, attractive pubs for refreshment and a bite to eat. You'll pass several of the best on this walk.

What to see

With a flight of five locks and a group of gorgeous buildings, Tyrley Wharf is a place to linger. It's hard to imagine this was once a real working wharf – rough, tough, noisy, smelly and mucky. It served the Peatswood Estate and was also a change-over point for the tow horses, which were expected to do about 25 miles (40km) a day.

While you're there

Hodnet Hall Gardens at nearby Hodnet, about 5 miles (8km) southwest of Market Drayton, is worth a visit, with over 60 acres (24.3ha) of landscaped gardens around an Elizabethan-style house built in the 1870s. Enjoy the woodland walks and lovely water gardens.

WISTANSWICK'S WIDE OPEN SPACES

DISTANCE/TIME	5.5 miles (8.9km) / 2hrs 15min
ASCENT/GRADIENT	256ft (78m) / ▲
PATHS	Field paths, sometimes undefined, ancient tracks and quiet lanes, 18 stiles
LANDSCAPE	Gently rolling, open arable land and pasture
SUGGESTED MAP	OS Explorer 243 Market Drayton
START/FINISH	Grid reference: SJ676291
DOG FRIENDLINESS	Limited opportunities for dogs to run free
PARKING	Large lay-by on minor road near Wistanswick, about 500yds (457m) east of A41
PUBLIC TOILETS	None on route

There's an openness about this walk which is unusual in lowland Shropshire. Partly this is due to the large size of many of the fields the walk crosses, where old hedgerows have been grubbed out to allow cultivation on a larger scale. For instance, what is now a single field, south of the track which you cross between Points 7 and 8, is shown on maps of the late 19th century as no fewer than eight.

But it's not all 'grain prairies', and the openness is also due to the fact that the walk crosses a couple of gentle ridges. You may barely notice the gradients but you can't fail to notice the way the views open out on the rises.

There are also some more enclosed, intimate passages on the walk, never more so than on the delightful – but all too short – bridleway that takes the return leg as you turn off Sandy Lane. Sunken and tree-shaded, it has all the hallmarks of an ancient track, and it's a natural continuation of a lane to/from Market Drayton. It's tempting to wonder if it continued further south, but those Victorian maps don't show any sign of it and it looks far more likely that the footpaths further west, which you follow a little later in the walk, correspond with an older track.

The only village on the walk is Wistanswick, a small place with fewer than 50 houses. It has a small but handsome United Reformed Church, but Church of England worshippers use St Peter's at Stoke upon Tern, a couple of miles to the west.

Much of the walk crosses land historically belonging to Colehurst Manor. This is a Grade II* listed Elizabethan manor house, though the estate's history stretches back much further. It's a shame the walk doesn't go past it, but the road has become rather too busy for comfort. It had become partly derelict when acquired by the present owners but has been lovingly restored. It's not normally open to the public but is a popular wedding venue and also offers luxury accommodation.

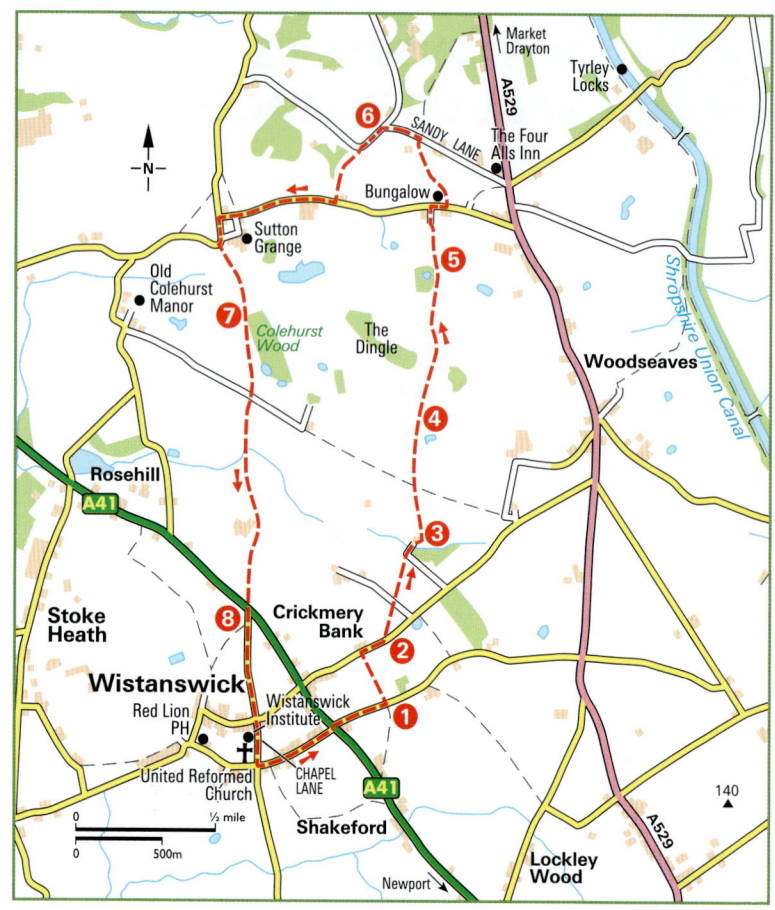

1. Go through a gate with a footpath sign at the west end of the lay-by, up a field to a hedge-corner. Continue with the hedge on your left. Cross a stile to a road and turn right, passing the houses of Crickmery Bank. After 100yds (91m) there's a footpath sign on the left, with a gap in the hedge just to its right.

2. Cross a field to a stile almost hidden in trees under a power line pole (the third from the road). Follow the fence to another stile, cross and go diagonally to the far corner of the field. Cross a stile and join a track. Bear left, then go straight ahead, passing right of a white house, to a stile.

3. Bear slightly left to another stile, and continue in the same line towards a stile between two gates left of a tall oak. Walk up the slope, heading towards the left-most trees on the skyline. Reaching the top, you'll see two gates: go through the left-hand one and along the hedge.

4. Where the hedge turns away, go straight ahead across the large field to a gate and stile. Continue ahead towards the right side of a clump of trees. (Theoretically, the right of way goes straight through, but vegetation and pools make it impassable). Keep the trees on your left, then bear right to a gate and stile.

5. Go straight ahead, pass farm buildings and join a lane. Turn right, pass a bungalow, then go left at a footpath sign. Follow the left-hand hedge then continue, following a furrow where a hedge used to be. A short green track leads to Sandy Lane. Turn left.

6. Where the lane bends right, go left on a track. At another bridleway junction, go slightly left down a beautiful sunken track. Follow this and emerge onto another lane. Turn right then left at a T-junction. As the road bends right, go straight ahead over a stile to a gate. Continue straight across a large field, aiming left of a clump of trees in front of a larger wood.

7. Cross a stile and continue alongside the wood, then straight ahead to the point where a hedge on your left meets a track. Go a few paces left then cross another field to trees in a dip, in line with farm buildings, and The Wrekin beyond. Find a stile left of the trees, then bear left to another stile. Aim left of trees to the left of the farm, to find a way-mark post. Follow the edge of the trees to a stile and continue straight ahead over several more to the A41.

8. Cross into a lane. Walk to a crossroads and straight across into Chapel Bank. Pass the Wistanswick Institute and United Reformed Church then turn left. Walk to the A41 and go straight across (signed Goldstone, Cheswardine). Walk along here to the lay-by.

Where to eat and drink

A slight deviation from the walk route brings you to The Red Lion at Wistanswick, a true village pub: the sort where the mobile library calls regularly. They're open every day from noon and the classic home-made meals look like excellent value; there's a daily choice of vegetarian quiche for example. Real ales usually include at least one from Rowton Brewery, near Telford.

What to see

The landscape is dotted with small pools, though most are easily missed as they tend to be encircled by trees. Good examples are just before Point 5 and again just before Point 7. They're not in natural hollows or along stream courses and are very likely to be dew ponds, artificially dug and lined with puddled clay, to maintain a water supply for livestock. Cattle today are often supplied with mains water at metal troughs, so many dew ponds have become neglected.

While you're there

Some way away, but one of Shropshire's biggest tourist attractions, is the Royal Air Force Museum at Cosford, which is right next to an active airfield. There are many aircraft on display in huge hangars, including the oldest surviving Spitfire. There's also the 4D Experience, 'Flying with the Red Arrows': 3D visuals plus dynamic seat movements and other special effects.

AN IRONBRIDGE CIRCUIT

DISTANCE/TIME	4.5 miles (7.2km) / 1hr 45min
ASCENT/GRADIENT	640ft (195m) / ▲ ▲
PATHS	Mostly excellent, muddy in places, lots of steps (down only), 7 stiles
LANDSCAPE	Wooded hills and mixed farmland above Severn Gorge
SUGGESTED MAP	OS Explorer 242 Telford, Ironbridge & The Wrekin
START/FINISH	Grid reference: SJ672033
DOG FRIENDLINESS	Will love woods, but keep under control in fields
PARKING	Bridge Car Park at south end of Iron Bridge
PUBLIC TOILETS	In The Square at Ironbridge

The little town of Ironbridge is built of mellow brick, its attractive buildings clinging in tiers to the north side of the gorge, overlooking the River Severn. Though it is part of a UNESCO World Heritage Site and a major tourist centre, it has not lost its charm, retaining a maze of steep, narrow streets that mingle with patches of woodland, open to the public and managed by the Severn Gorge Countryside Trust.

The Iron Bridge itself was built by Abraham Darby III, grandson of the man who started it all by smelting iron ore with coke, although the original idea and design were by the largely forgotten Shrewsbury architect Thomas Pritchard. The lack of a bridge across the Severn had become a handicap to the development of industry in the gorge. The bridge was cast in Darby's foundry at Coalbrookdale, cost around £6,000 and contains 378 tons of iron. It carried all kinds of traffic right up to 1934. To get more background, check out the exhibition in the Tollhouse at the south end of the Bridge.

Away from the bustle of the gorge it's almost a different world. After crossing gentle farmland, you come first to St Bartholomew's Church and then to Benthall Hall. The church is an interesting building and worth a visit – just check out that sundial! Next-door Benthall Hall, which was built of stone in the 16th century, presents a stunning face to the world. It's quite something inside as well, and as it's owned by the National Trust you can have a look around (best to check first as it is only open on certain days). There are plaster ceilings and lots of carved oak. Mr and Mrs Benthall still live here so it's a real home, with a warmer feel than many National Trust properties.

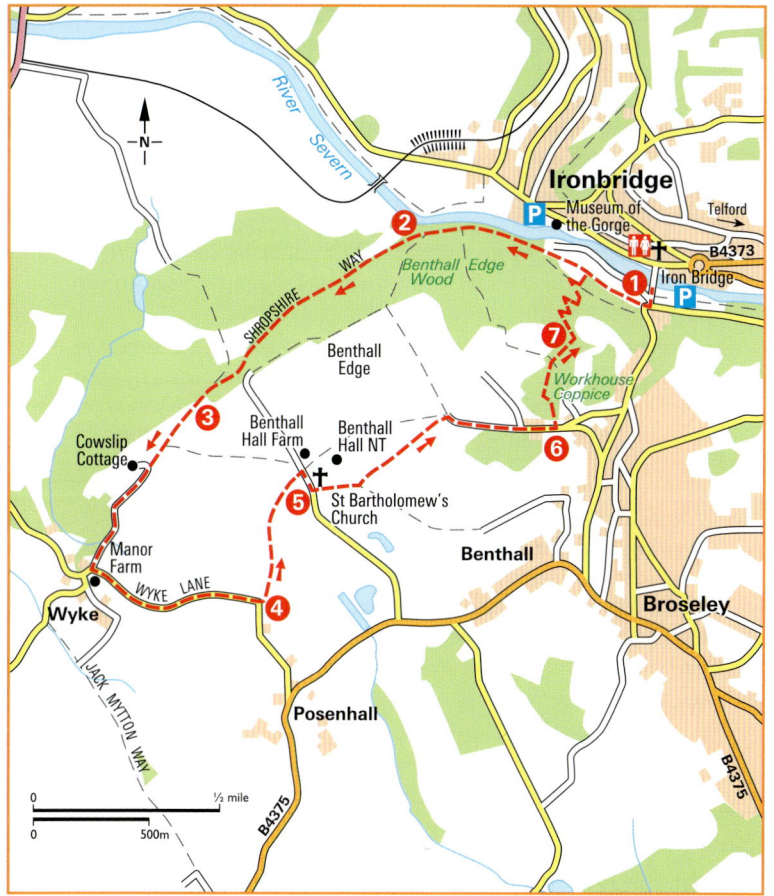

1. Without crossing into Ironbridge, and with your back to the bridge, turn right into Benthall Edge Wood, taking the higher of two tracks and soon passing under a disused railway bridge. When the track comes to an end, cross a stile on the left and turn sharp left, going uphill to arrive at a major path junction.

2. Turn right here (signed for Benthall Hall). Stay on the main path, through damp, jungly woodland, nearly always climbing steadily and keeping the same heading. Approaching the top, the path curves round a hollow. Ignore a gate and track on the left and continue, slightly downhill and then roughly level, along a narrower path just inside the edge of the wood.

3. Leave the wood at a stile and continue along the edge of a field, then bear left and down to a stile just left of Cowslip Cottage. Follow the lengthy access track to a lane. Turn left and follow the lane to a sharp right-hand bend.

4. Turn left here on a footpath between hedges, sometimes muddy in a couple of spots. Pass a pool and enter a field. Follow the hedge on the right at first then keep going, bearing slightly right to join a vague tractor track. Turn right along field-edges to meet a track by Benthall Hall Farm. Turn right, then left onto a lane to St Bartholomew's Church.

5. Backtrack down the lane a short way then turn left on an obvious bridleway across parkland, soon passing in front of Benthall Hall. Go through a gate at the far side, after which the clear path continues along two field-edges, meeting a track at the far side. Turn right and at a junction carry straight on down a lane. Approaching another junction, turn left into Workhouse Coppice (owned by the Woodland Trust).

6. The path soon forks – carry straight on. At the next junction, by a memorial marker, turn right, downhill, then left at a T-junction, and straight on at two subsequent junctions. As you approach the far side of the wood, turn right on a stony track. Before long you'll come to the first of several flights of wooden steps, opposite a bench.

7. Lots more steps, interspersed with boardwalks, make the descent easier, if rather over-civilised. Just keep going down. At the bottom cross a stile and turn right on the old railway track that you followed at the start. Very soon this goes under the old bridge again and leads out back to the Iron Bridge.

Where to eat and drink

You'll be spoiled for choice in Ironbridge. Possibilities include the Tontine Hotel opposite the bridge and the White Hart, both with outside tables, or the Coracle Micropub. If you go down and left from the Tontine, there are a few cafés: Darby's and Truffles can both be recommended; on a busy day the best choice may be whichever has a free table.

What to see

Benthall Edge Wood is a real jungly tangle of trees, shrubs and ferns. You'd never guess this was once the scene of frenetic industry, but look more closely and you'll spot the clues. The hummocky nature of the ground and the presence of deep pits point to the fact that Benthall Edge Wood was mined and quarried for coal and limestone from the 13th century onwards. In the 19th century it was almost cleared of trees, so it's heartening to look at the natural regeneration that has occurred since industry ceased.

While you're there

A good starting point for understanding Ironbridge is the Museum of the Gorge, in a Gothic warehouse built in the 1830s by the Coalbrookdale Company. The displays concentrate on the history of the gorge and include a huge scale model showing it as it was in 1796.

COALPORT'S CHINA HISTORY

DISTANCE/TIME	5 miles (8km) / 2hrs
ASCENT/GRADIENT	295ft (90m) / ▲
PATHS	Mostly excellent, though path through Lee Dingle may be muddy
LANDSCAPE	Woodland, riverbank and heritage townscape
SUGGESTED MAP	OS Explorer 242 Telford, Ironbridge & The Wrekin
START/FINISH	Grid reference: SJ677033
DOG FRIENDLINESS	No sheep or cattle so can run fairly freely
PARKING	Next to Bedlam Furnaces on Waterloo Street, between Ironbridge and Jackfield Bridge
PUBLIC TOILETS	At Ironbridge end of Waterloo Street

Coalport china is famous the world over, and rightly so, for it's exquisite stuff. The story of how it came to be made here is interesting too. Coalport, which is much smaller today than it was at its peak, was planned as a canal-river interchange and a complete new town by ironmaster William Reynolds. Between 1788 and 1796 he built warehouses, workshops, factories and cottages on formerly undeveloped land by the river. Crucially, he also constructed the Shropshire Canal to link the East Shropshire Coalfield with the River Severn. The terminus was at Coalport Wharf, between the Brewery Inn and Coalport Bridge.

The canal greatly aided the new town's development, especially after the completion of the Hay Inclined Plane in 1793. This is one of the country's major industrial monuments, the best preserved and most spectacular of its kind. It was the means by which boats were transferred from the top to the bottom of the gorge. Equivalent to 27 locks, but worked by only four men, it could pass six boats in an hour, a feat which would have taken three hours using a lock system. The boats were carried up and down the almost 1 in 4 gradient on wheeled cradles. The incline is now part of Blists Hill Museum, but you can see part of it on this walk. After the canal was superseded by a railway it silted up, became overgrown and was infilled during the 1920s. It was partially restored in 1976 and again in the 1990s. In 1795 the Coalport China Company was founded by John Rose in the large building which is now a youth hostel and café. Across the former canal is a later china works, now Coalport China Museum, showing factory life and manufacturing techniques. Even if you don't go inside the museum, the whole site, with mellow brick buildings and enormous kilns, is wonderfully evocative. China manufacture ceased here in 1926 when the company moved to the Potteries. Coalport China is now part of the Wedgwood group.

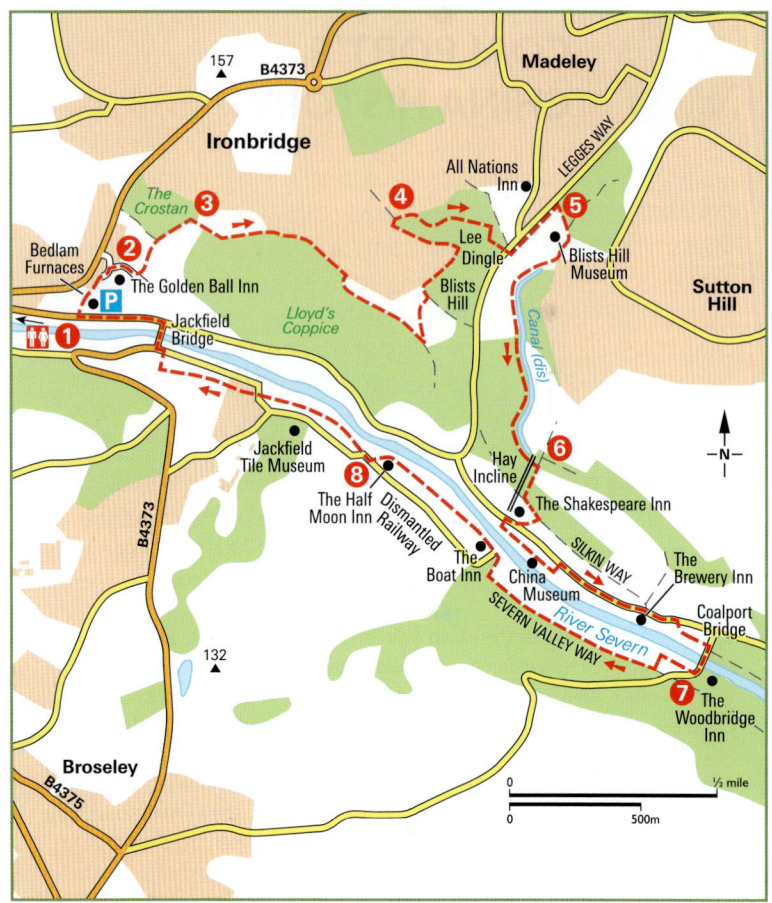

1. Climb steps left of the furnaces, go right a few paces then up more steps into parkland, then zigzag up via pergolas and steps. Turn right at the top and emerge facing The Golden Ball Inn.

2. Skirt left of the pub then keep right at a junction along Wesley Road, to pass the pub car park. Go left at another junction and through a gate into a wood called The Crostan. A stepped path climbs to a junction where two paths are indicated. Take the right-hand one, signed 'Lloyd's Coppice', climbing by the woodland edge to another waymarked junction.

3. Turn right on a level path (South Telford Way marker), which runs across two meadows into woodland, with Lloyd's Coppice clinging to the steep slope on your right. Ignore innumerable smaller paths. At a waymarked junction, signed 'Madeley', fork left. The track swings left, then a stony track goes to the right, with houses on its left.

4. After a sharp bend left and a straight section, a few steps on the right lead down past a redundant stile into Lee Dingle. The main path is normally obvious: at a clear fork keep right and descend steps, soon emerging to a road. Cross Coalport Rd to Legges Way, turn left under two bridges, then turn right at the entrance to Blists Hill Museum.

5. Go straight on then turn right just above the coach park, skirting the Blists Hill site. Keep close to the railings and soon you'll see the canal through the trees. Keep on parallel to the canal until you glimpse the top of the great Hay Incline, then descend just to its left, alongside more railings.

6. Descend to a former railway at a bridge under the incline. Turn left here then fork right at an embedded railway wheel and zigzag down to the road. Turn right and go past The Shakespeare Inn. Cross a bridge over the incline, then turn left and left again to the tow path of the Shropshire Canal. Re-cross the canal at the next footbridge and walk past the China Museum, Coalport Youth Hostel and its café. Join the road and continue in the same direction. Join the Silkin Way via The Brewery Inn car park; follow it to Coalport Bridge and cross the river.

7. Turn right on the Severn Valley Way, which passes through Preen's Eddy picnic area, then climbs away from the river to follow a former railway trackbed. Turn right at a sign for Silkin Way via Jackfield Bridge; the lane loops round left to The Boat Inn. Continue past cottages, follow a track below Maws Craft Centre and continue along another narrow track.

8. Emerge into a car park by the Half Moon. As the exit track bends left, bear right on a level track. Emerge into a street, pass Jackfield Tile Museum and carry straight on at Jackfield Sidings, passing behind the Black Swan. When a bridge crosses the path go right and down to the road. Cross Jackfield Bridge, then turn left. Pass Ye Olde Robin Hood Inn and the former Bird in Hand Pub and return to Bedlam Furnaces.

Where to eat and drink

Though early in the walk, The Golden Ball is an excellent choice, with a cosy wood-floored bar, well-kept ales and good-value food. Beer lovers won't want to miss the legendary All Nations Inn, for decades one of only a handful of brew-pubs in the UK. It's retained a traditional feel and is still a great place to find excellent beer.

What to see

Bedlam Furnaces were built in 1757 by the Madeley Wood Furnace Company and taken over by William Reynolds in 1794. They were used to smelt iron ore and are blast furnaces similar to those developed by Abraham Darby I. If a blast furnace was allowed to cool its lining would crack, so smelting was continuous, with employees working 12-hour shifts.

While you're there

Blists Hill Museum re-creates the sights, sounds and smells of a late Victorian town. The staff wear period costume and you can exchange your money at the bank for Victorian coinage to spend in the shops or pub. Watch someone mucking out a pigsty, operating a steam engine or pouring iron in a foundry, or learn about the scary side of Victorian medicine in the chemist's shop.

REVOLUTION AT COALBROOKDALE

DISTANCE/TIME	5 miles (8km) / 2hrs
ASCENT/GRADIENT	770ft (235m) / ▲ ▲
PATHS	Woodland paths, lots of steps (mostly descending), may be fallen trees at Strethill, 3 stiles
LANDSCAPE	Wooded hills of Severn Gorge
SUGGESTED MAP	OS Explorer 242 Telford, Ironbridge & The Wrekin
START/FINISH	Grid reference: SJ664037
DOG FRIENDLINESS	Excellent, but keep under strict control at Strethill (sheep)
PARKING	Dale End Park (long stay) or Museum of the Gorge (3hrs max up to 5pm)
PUBLIC TOILETS	In Museum of the Gorge car park

People have been smelting iron for many centuries, but production was originally small scale because smelting was dependent on timber which first had to be made into charcoal – a slow and laborious process. All that changed at Coalbrookdale in 1709 when Abraham Darby I perfected a method of smelting iron with coke instead of charcoal. It may sound a small thing, but it sparked a revolution that changed the world. At long last iron could be made cheaply in large quantities and it came to be increasingly used in many areas of engineering.

By 1785 the Coalbrookdale district had become the foremost industrial area in the world. It was particularly celebrated for its innovations: the first iron bridge, the first iron boat, the first iron rails and the first steam locomotive. Tourists came from far and wide to see the sights, and artists came to paint it all – furnaces lighting up the night sky was a favourite subject. Decline eventually set in due to competition from the Black Country and South Wales and the area fell into decay. Since the 1960s, the surviving industrial relics have been transformed into a fascinating collection of museums and the gorge has been designated a UNESCO World Heritage Site. Perhaps even more remarkable than the industrial heritage is the way nature has reclaimed sites of industrial despoliation and made them beautiful again. These regenerated woods and meadows are managed by the Severn Gorge Countryside Trust and are accessible to the public.

The ironmasters were paternalistic types who built decent houses for their workers and took an interest in their moral well-being. When you walk through Dale Coppice and Lincoln Hill Woods you will be using the Sabbath Walks, designed by Richard Reynolds to provide healthy Sunday recreation for his workers. The idea was that this would keep them from drinking, gambling and sexual promiscuity. A rotunda was erected at one viewpoint, but has since been demolished, though you can still enjoy the view. It's mostly woodland now, but you will see the remains of a great quarry that bit deep into Lincoln Hill. It extends so far underground that tours of its limestone caverns were popular with 19th-century day-trippers. Bands played in the illuminated caverns and thousands came on excursion trains from the Black Country and Birmingham.

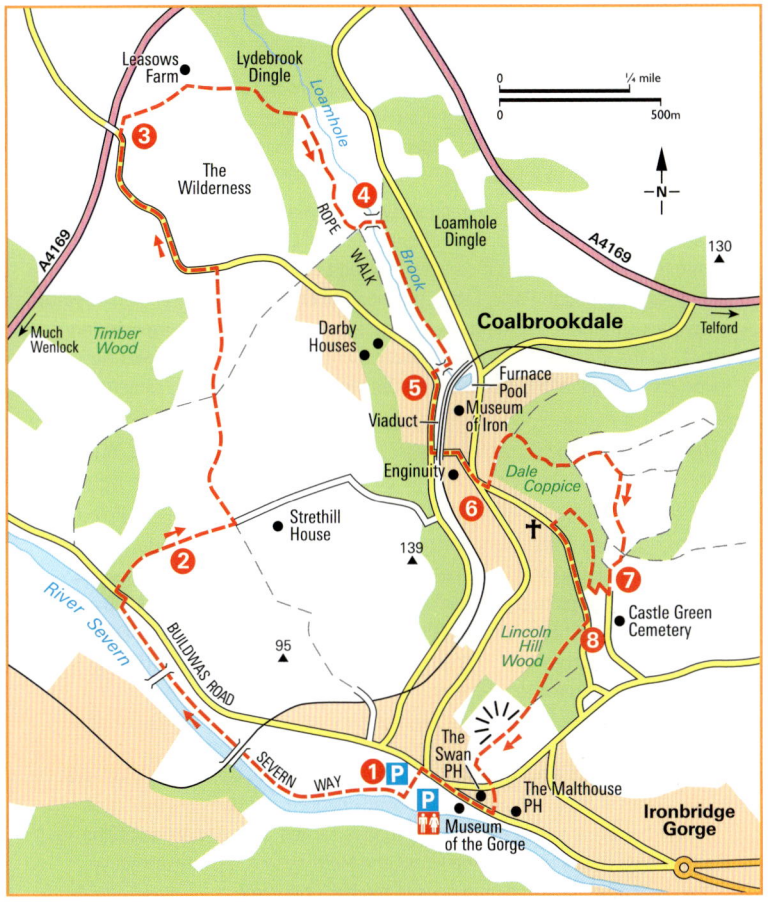

1. From either car park, walk to the river and turn right, upstream. Take care as the path is narrow and there's a big drop to the river in places. Pass under two bridges. Keep following the path until three steps lead up to Buildwas Road. Turn left for a few paces, then cross to a footpath that ascends through woodland. The path keeps close to the edge at first, then climbs obliquely to the right.

2. Cross a stile and continue in the same direction over pastureland. Pass under a pylon, then join a farm track climbing to a gate and stile. Cross, then turn right and follow the hedge to a junction. Turn left within the same field and follow three field edges, then go up a steep meadow to a lane. Turn left.

3. Leave the lane just before it bridges the A4169, turning right on a tarmac track. Just before Leasows Farm, go through an iron gate on the right, then

downfield to enter Lydebrook Dingle at a stile. A waymarked path descends through the wood, with numerous steps. Continue along a path called Rope Walk.

4. Turn left and descend Loamhole Brook Steps. Cross Loamhole Brook at a footbridge and climb 42 steps on the other side. Turn right and follow the undulating boardwalk to Upper Furnace Pool. Cross its far end on the first of two footbridges to meet the road.

5. Your onward route is to the left, but a short detour right leads to the Darby Houses, Tea Kettle Row and the Quaker Burial Ground. Resuming the walk, go down to Darby Road and turn right alongside the viaduct. Turn left under the viaduct at a junction with Coach Road. Follow the road between the Museum of Iron and Enginuity to a junction.

6. Cross into Church Road. Immediately after a disused chapel turn left then go up steps to enter Dale Coppice. Follow a sign for Church Road at a junction, then follow more steps up through the woods. At the next junction go straight ahead, signed 'Rough Park'. Leave the wood to enter grassland and go forward a few paces to meet a gritty path. Turn left, then shortly fork right, ignoring grassy paths. Bear left at another junction, then bear right at the next two to some gates. Walk along a track. Dale Coppice is on your right, a cemetery on your left.

7. Partway along the cemetery, a narrow gap accesses Dale Coppice. Turn right, then left, going downhill to a junction marked by a bench. Turn right, then left when a sign indicates Church Road, then left again up the road.

8. Turn right into Lincoln Hill Wood and follow signs to the Rotunda, presently arriving at a viewpoint where the Rotunda formerly stood. Descend a very steep flight of steps to a junction. Turn right, then left down more steps and left again, signposted to Lincoln Hill Road. Pass behind a house and along a track to a road. Cross to a footpath opposite, which descends to a drive beside the Lincoln Hill lime kilns. Turn right to return to the start.

Where to eat and drink

The Swan is open all day. Well-behaved children and dogs are welcome in the bar area, but no dogs where food is served. Almost next door (the other side of Lincoln Hill lime kilns), the Malthouse is equally attractive and welcomes children, and dogs in the bar or outside.

What to see

Upper Furnace Pool in Loamhole Dingle is the pool that powered the bellows that blew the furnace where Abraham Darby I first smelted iron with coke. The area of open water has been reduced by a profuse growth of marsh horsetail.

While you're there

The Museum of Iron brings the Darbys' achievements to life and includes the Darby Furnace where it all began. Equally fascinating are the ironmasters' homes and the workers' houses at Tea Kettle Row, near Darby Houses.

8

UP JACOB'S LADDER
TO RINDLEFORD

DISTANCE/TIME	6.5 miles (10.4km) / 2hrs 30min
ASCENT/GRADIENT	540ft (165m) / ▲ ▲
PATHS	Steep and eroded in parts (beware landslips), 1 stile
LANDSCAPE	Wooded cliffs, bracken-filled valleys and mixed farmland
SUGGESTED MAP	OS Explorer 218 Wyre Forest & Kidderminster
START/FINISH	Grid reference: SO720934
DOG FRIENDLINESS	Generally excellent, but keep on leads in The Batch
PARKING	Severn Park, off A442 on east bank of River Severn at Bridgnorth
PUBLIC TOILETS	Severn Street Car Park, also Listley Street in Bridgnorth opposite the library

The most dramatic of Shropshire towns, Bridgnorth clings to the top of a cliff. Or at least High Town does – for Bridgnorth is two towns in one, with Low Town occupying the riverside. The two are linked by a modern road, seven ancient stairways, a cartway and a funicular railway of 1892. Until recently it was Britain's only inland cliff railway and it remains the only electrically powered one, with colliery-type winding gear.

It's often said that Bridgnorth, with its clifftop setting, resembles a continental town and if you do this walk you'll get an inkling of what is meant. It's only when you climb to the viewpoints on High Rock and Pendlestone Rock that you really get to see Bridgnorth in context. The modern town sprawls in the background, but the old town is distinct from it in a way reminiscent of many European countries. The Spanish, for instance, usually preserve an old town and build a modern one next to it, while here in Britain we knock it down and build on top. This is not the case in Bridgnorth. It does look almost continental from High Rock, perched on its cliff and watched over by its twin church towers. The red sandstone one to the north belongs to St Leonard's, the original parish church. During the Civil War it was used as an ammunition store by Royalist troops. When the Roundheads scored a direct hit, the ensuing fire proved disastrous. It was skilfully rebuilt, but is now redundant. The classical-style church to the south is built of white sandstone and dedicated to St Mary Magdalene. It was constructed between 1792 and 1794 to the design of Thomas Telford, replacing the Norman chapel attached to Bridgnorth Castle, and is now the parish church.

Bridgnorth's cliffs are formed from sandstone, a soft, easily eroded, easily hewn rock. The sandstone country of south Shropshire, north Worcestershire and south Staffordshire is riddled with caves, natural and man-made, many of which were inhabited until the 1960s. This is not so grim as it sounds – caves are warm in winter and cool in summer. When equipped with electricity and piped water, they can be far more salubrious than some types of conventional housing. There are still plenty of former cave-homes in Bridgnorth, including some on Cartway.

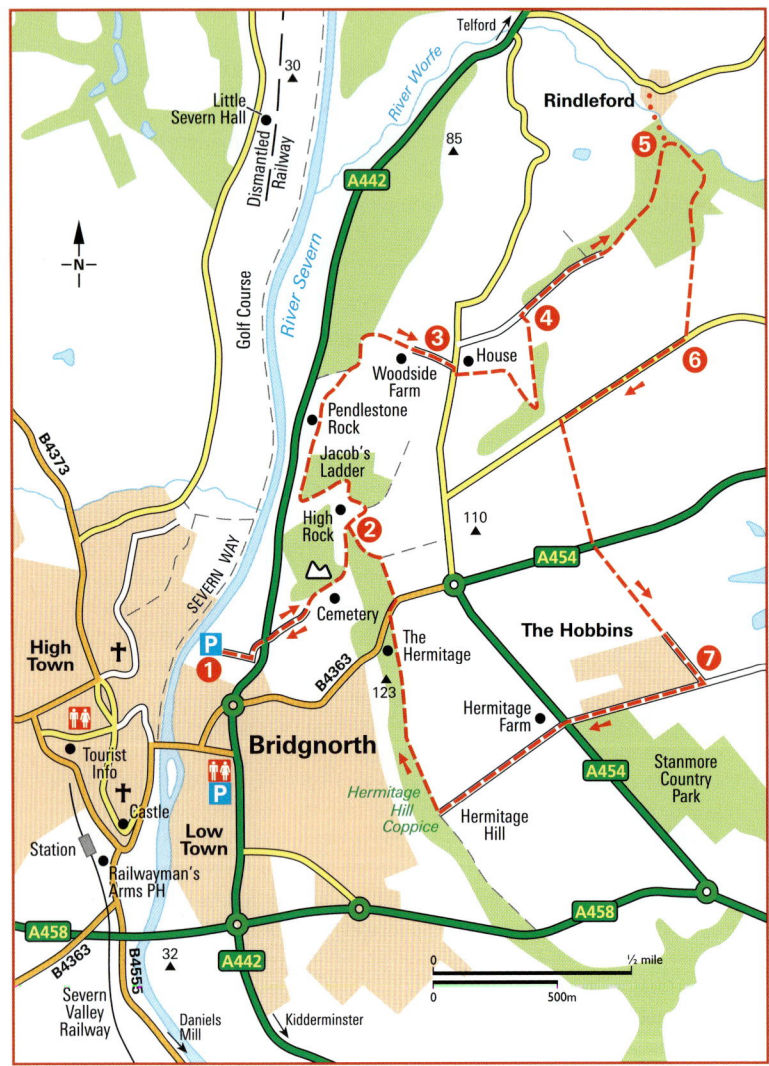

1. Follow the car park access track to the A442, turn left, then right, signposted 'cemetery'. At the cemetery take a footpath, left, climbing steeply. The gradient eases: turn right on a fenced path, then climb again through woods. At the top keep left to reach a waymarked junction.

2. Fork left, descending quite steeply before the path (known as Jacob's Ladder) levels out to contour in an undulating fashion round High Rock and then Pendlestone Rock. At a junction, keep to the higher path, which soon swings right. Leaving the trees behind, it passes Woodside Farm, then merges with the farm access track.

3. Meeting a lane, turn right for a few paces, then left at a footpath sign. Pass a house and go through a gate into a field. Proceed along the edge almost to the end, then turn right to a gate opposite. Turn left into a narrow field and descend in the bottom of a valley.

4. Meet a track by a sandstone building and turn right along a steep-sided valley. Where the main track bends right, keep straight on along a grassy path through bracken. Eventually you come to a junction with a sandy track beside the River Worfe.

5. Your onward route is to the right, but first it's worth a short detour to the left to explore the lovely hamlet of Rindleford. Resuming the walk, return to the junction and follow the sandy track, first by the river then swinging right to climb gently out of the valley.

6. Turn right when you reach a lane. After 600yds (549m) turn left at a way-marked gate and follow a footpath along a field edge. This leads to the A454 and continues on the other side, past a housing estate called The Hobbins.

7. Turn right on another road, which runs past Stanmore Country Park, to the A454. Cross to a track opposite, by Hermitage Farm. Follow the track round right at the top. As you approach metal gates, go through a gap in the hedge and continue along a narrow path, always close to the edge of the wood. Audibly nearing the B4363, look for a parallel path on the left, which descends past The Hermitage. Cross the road, go up to a lamppost and join a narrow path on the left. Follow this, with very steep slopes on the left until you meet point 2. Now, a sharp left turn takes you back down past the cemetery to the A442 and Severn Park.

Where to eat and drink

Bridgnorth is bursting with appealing pubs, restaurants, bistros and tea rooms. There is the interesting Railwayman's Arms on Bridgnorth Station, a converted waiting room packed with rail memorabilia.

What to see

The Hermitage is a series of caves gouged out of the sandstone. One local legend tells of its occupation in AD925 by a hermit called Ethelred or Ethelward, a grandson of Alfred the Great. This may not be such an unlikely tale, for Bridgnorth was founded in 912 by Alfred the Great's daughter Ethelfleda.

While you're there

Daniel's Mill is a picturesque working watermill which has been in the same family for more than 200 years. The huge waterwheel was cast at Coalbrookdale in 1854. The mill, next to the Severn Valley Railway, is fun to visit. There's a tea room and you can buy flour here (check for opening times).

BRIDGNORTH AND THE SEVERN WAY

DISTANCE/TIME	4 miles (6.4km) / 1hr 30min
ASCENT/GRADIENT	197ft (60m) / ▲ ▲
PATHS	Easy riverside paths, lanes and urban pavement, 2 stiles
LANDSCAPE	Riverbank, golf course and historic town
SUGGESTED MAP	OS Explorer 218 Wyre Forest & Kidderminster
START/FINISH	Grid reference: SO720934
DOG FRIENDLINESS	On lead at all times
PARKING	Severn Park, off A442 on east bank of River Severn in Bridgnorth
PUBLIC TOILETS	Severn Car Park, also Listley Street in Bridgnorth

Bridgnorth is a remarkable town and you could spend several days just exploring its streets; get a free town map from the tourist information centre on Listley Street (closed Thursday and Sunday) to ensure you don't miss anything. It really is a very special little place.

This short walk leaves the town to offer a better sense of its setting. For much of its length, the walk runs alongside the course of Bridgnorth Golf Club. The club is believed to have been founded in 1889, moving to its present site in 1906. Originally, the course had only nine holes and was confined between the Severn Valley Railway and the river. The closure of the line in 1962 presented an opportunity and the present 18-hole course was "played in" 10 years later. You can see the line of the railway continuing as a low embankment at Point 3 on the walk. The embankment is now used by the Mercian Way, part of the National Cycle Network.

This is the first of a couple of encounters with the course of the dismantled Severn Valley Railway. Though it survives as a steam line between Kidderminster and Bridgnorth, the northern part of the line, from Bridgnorth to Shrewsbury, has been lost. While there is occasional speculation about reopening the line from Bridgnorth to Coalport, it's clear that this would be a very difficult operation. How would the Golf Club members feel, for instance?

The second meeting with the railway's course, in the depths of Ropewalk Dingle, is much more striking. Here it first enters a deep cutting and then disappears into a dark tunnel. You can't see very far into the tunnel unless you take a powerful torch, but you can still gain a sense of the engineering effort that was required. Bored through the sandstone bedrock, the tunnel is 550yds (503m) long and runs directly under the medieval High Town. A ventilation shaft was created near the halfway mark, and still opens into a vent on High Street. The southern exit is immediately north of Bridgnorth Station.

Ropewalk Dingle was formerly gardens and an orchard belonging to Severn Cliff House, but had become very neglected. A £10,000 grant enabled

Bridgnorth District Council to clear part of the site, upgrade paths and add information boards, but most of the mature trees were left undisturbed as the area is an important roosting site for several species of bat. The name Ropewalk Dingle was selected by public vote.

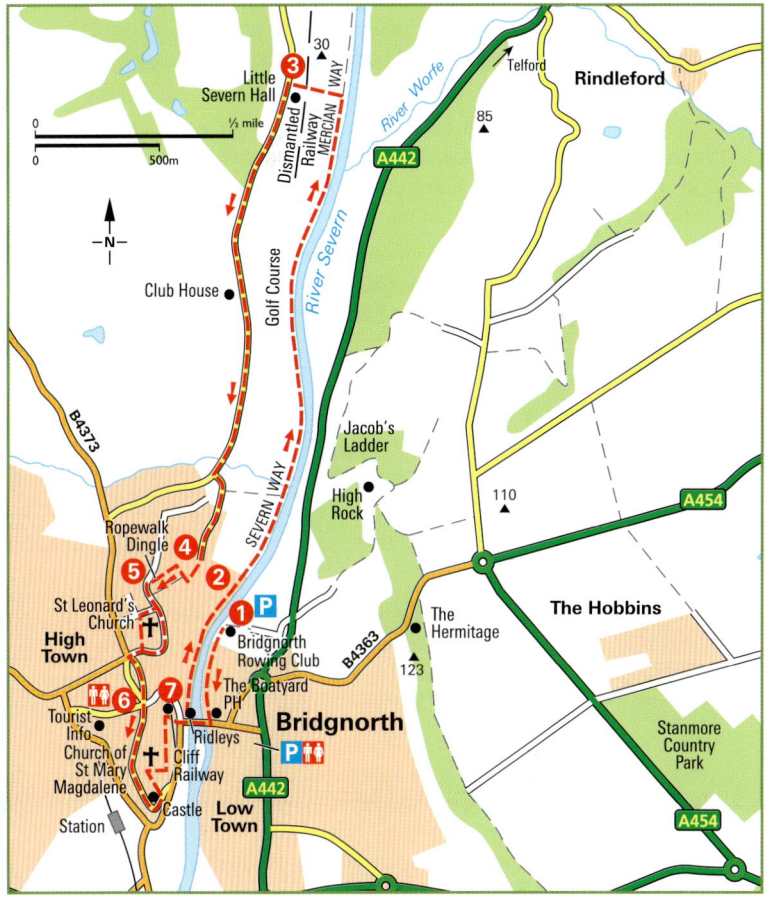

1. Walk downstream from Severn Park by the river. Pass Bridgnorth Rowing Club, then walk between The Boatyard pub and its beer garden to the bridge. Cross the river and turn right on Cartway, then return to the riverside. Use an elevated walkway on the left while you can. You'll pass the ruins of a medieval Franciscan friary.

2. After passing the last house, the path continues along the edge of playing fields. Cross a footbridge and continue along the edge of a golf course, crossing another footbridge along the way. Cross a stile at the far end of the golf course and turn left along a field-edge, then cross an embankment at a small car park.

3. Go straight on along a stony track that passes to the right of Little Severn Hall to meet a lane. Turn left and follow the lane towards Bridgnorth. At the

edge of town, turn left along Bramble Ridge. At the end, go forward into Ropewalk Dingle.

4. The most direct route goes up the path on the right, but it's worth going forward along the lower edge of the green. Don't go down a ramp on the left but continue on the level way, into a cutting and so to the mouth of a tunnel. Double-back a few paces then climb steep steps. At a junction (with more steps above) turn right along a roughly level path to find a signboard near the top of the Dingle.

5. Continue up the main path to meet a street and turn left. When it bends right, keep straight on along Mold Court to St Leonard's Church. Go either way round the church, then down Church Street, opposite the church door to the High Street. Turn left and walk past the town hall to the end of the High Street.

6. Continue, almost straight ahead, on West Castle Street. Where it starts to descend, fork left. Go through a grand gateway into the Castle gardens. Walk round the tottering castle ruins (a U-shaped route), leave the gardens and turn right to pass the imposing front of the Church of St Mary Magdalene. Descend steps and turn left on Cliff Walk.

7. Pass the upper terminus of the cliff railway. A little further on, turn sharp right down a narrow lane with many steps to emerge past the lower terminus onto Underhill Street. Cross the bridge and walk upstream to return to Severn Park.

Where to eat and drink

Bridgnorth is full of places for refreshment. Ridleys on the River, beside the bridge, has a café vibe but also serves hand-pumped ale. There's a good range of light meals and including breakfast and snacks. There's a secluded courtyard too.

What to see

The sandstone bluff to which High Town clings has its counterpart in High Rock and Pendlestone Rock; this walk gives frontal views of the cliffs across the river, which are completely draped in wire netting these days to shelter the road below from rockfall. You may feel this makes them look like some form of modern art.

While you're there

If you don't fancy walking down the steep steps near the end of the walk, you could take a ride down on the Cliff Railway instead. Originally driven by a water-balance system, it's now electrically powered. The Winding House Tea Rooms has windows onto the Engine Room and winding gear.

HAMPTON LOADE AND DUDMASTON HALL

DISTANCE/TIME	5 miles (8km) / 2hrs
ASCENT/GRADIENT	328ft (100m) / ▲
PATHS	Easy to follow and easy to use
LANDSCAPE	Woods, parkland and farmland in and above Severn Valley
SUGGESTED MAP	OS Explorer 218 Wyre Forest & Kidderminster
START/FINISH	Grid reference: SO747865
DOG FRIENDLINESS	On lead near livestock, can run free on green lanes and woods – consult any National Trust notices posted
PARKING	National Trust car park by River Severn in Hampton Loade
PUBLIC TOILETS	None on route

Hampton Loade is a tiny place famous for its former cable ferry which closed in 2016. The station is beautifully kept and full of character. Great wicker baskets of damsons used to be loaded on to the trains here and transported to Manchester to be made into dyes for the cotton trade. There is a new footbridge 4 miles south linking Alveley and Highley near the Severn Valley Visitor Centre or a 12 mile drive from Bewdley.

The Severn Valley Railway, later part of the Great Western Railway, provided a link between Shrewsbury and the industrial areas of the West Midlands, with coal from Highley being an important cargo. The line closed in 1963, but became one of the first lines in the UK to be reopened by enthusiasts, with the first services running in 1970. It now operates over 16 miles (26km) between Bridgnorth and Kidderminster. Trains run daily throughout the summer months and other school holidays, and at weekends for most of the rest of the year. The majority are steam-hauled.

Dudmaston is one of the National Trust's nicest properties. The estate has been in the same family for 850 years and the 17th-century hall retains the atmosphere of a family home, having been occupied by Sir George and Lady Labouchère until the 1990s, though they gave it to the National Trust in 1978. It contains an outstanding collection of contemporary art and a wealth of exquisite botanical art from earlier centuries. The extensive gardens and grounds are gorgeous and offer a variety of walks.

The Hall and grounds are normally fully open in the afternoon, from April to September, though nearly always closed on Fridays and Saturdays. Even outside these times, however, rights of way through the estate allow you to appreciate much of its beauty, as you can on this walk.

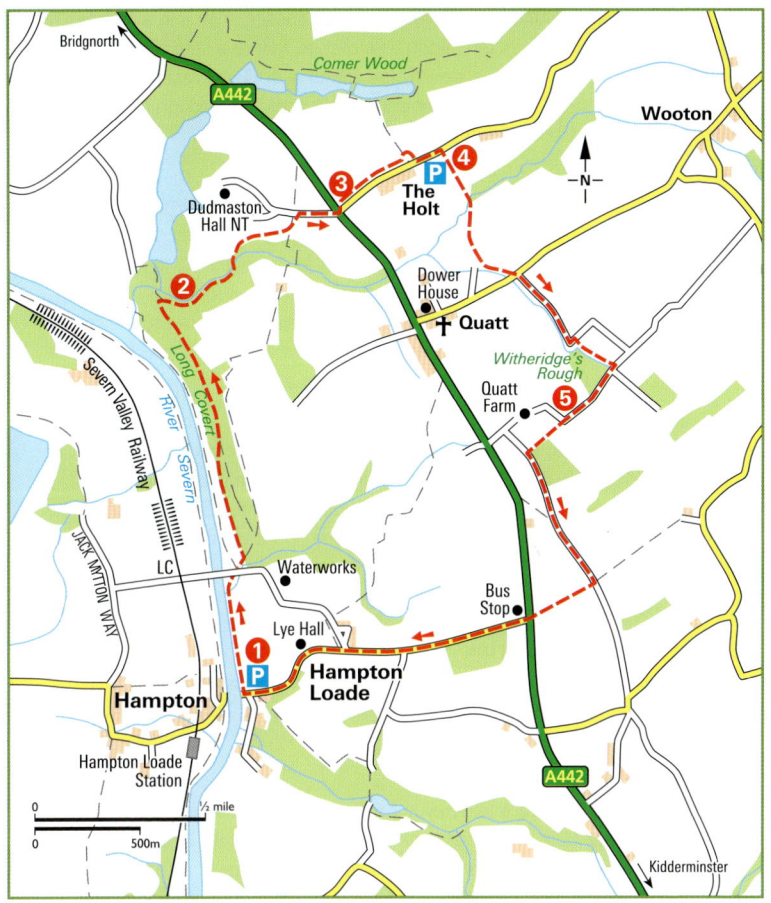

1. Start from the end of the car park and walk upriver. Cross a small brook as you approach a waterworks, then bear right, under a larger bridge, heading away from the river to gates where you enter woodland. The path climbs to a fork, where you go left to walk the length of Long Covert. Ignore a path descending back left. After about 0.75 miles (1.2km) the path arrives at a triangular clearing with a signboard. Turn right on another path which follows the rim of a dingle. Swing by a bench, descending towards a brook.

2. Ignore a wooden footbridge and continue on the same side a little further until you can cross the brook at stepping stones. Climb out of the dingle to a gate into the pasture/parkland surrounding Dudmaston Hall. Follow a track to the right, which gives brief glimpses of the Hall. Go through a small gate then immediately right through another gate, joining Dudmaston's access road. If you intend to visit Dudmaston Hall, this is as good a time as any; to continue with the walk, follow the access road past the car parks to the A442.

3. On arriving at the A442, cross over to a lane opposite, then join a clearly marked footpath just to its left, along a field-edge. Ignore a stile on the right, loop round trees surrounding a barn, and continue until you rejoin the road at a hedge-gap opposite a small National Trust car park. Go through the car park to a gateway in the bottom left corner.

4. Turn right on a field-edge bridleway. Descend into a valley, then climb out of it again and continue to a footpath junction in a field corner. Turn left, still on the bridleway, and follow the field-edge to a lane. The bridleway continues opposite, by a field-edge. In the corner turn left for a few paces, then go through a gap and along the edge of the next field, with woodland (Witheridge's Rough) on your right. At the end of the wood, close to the corner, join a track and turn right. Soon there are excellent views of Wenlock Edge, The Wrekin and the Clee Hills.

5. Leave the track when it turns right to Quatt Farm and go straight on through a field gate. At the far end of the field, go through another gate and turn left on a stony track, with woodland on your left and a hedge on your right. As the hedge comes to an end, a sudden view is revealed of the Clee Hills. Turn right down a field-edge to the A442. Cross to the lane opposite, next to a wooden bus shelter, and go down to Hampton Loade.

Where to eat and drink
You might enjoy the Stables, the National Trust's tea rooms at Dudmaston, though opening hours are limited. There's also The Squirrel on the A442 towards Alverley.

What to see
Dudmaston is one place where you can see the survival of almost all the traditional attributes of a south Shropshire estate: the hall, landscaped gardens and parkland, woodland, farmland and a village of estate cottages (Quatt). The National Trust works with the community and gives priority to local people when letting cottages. It also promotes local facilities and places restrictions on its tenant farmers so that they have to take environmental concerns into account – retaining sheep pasture, for instance, instead of converting every field to crops.

While you're there
A short detour from the walk will take you into Quatt, a model estate village designed by London architect John Birch in 1870. The timber-framed bus shelter is a more recent addition, but reaches the same high standard. The 18th-century Dower House is a handsome building and the brick church opposite, rebuilt in 1763, contains many fine tombs of the Wolryche family, who lived at Dudmaston.

ALVELEY AND THE SEVERN VALLEY

DISTANCE/TIME	5 miles (8km) / 2hrs 30min
ASCENT/GRADIENT	425ft (130m) / ▲
PATHS	Riverside paths, green lanes, can be uneven and slippery in places and shallow streams in winter, 5 stiles
LANDSCAPE	Meadows, woods and gentle slopes
SUGGESTED MAP	OS Explorer 218 Wyre Forest & Kidderminster
START/FINISH	Grid reference: SO753840
DOG FRIENDLINESS	On lead near Hampton Loade (tame ducks), visitor centre and cattle by river
PARKING	Visitor centre at Severn Valley Country Park, Alveley
PUBLIC TOILETS	At visitor centre (10am–4pm)

The Severn Valley Country Park straddles the river, linking the former coal-mining communities of Alveley and Highley. Alveley Colliery Bridge, a footbridge known locally as Miners' Bridge, provides the physical linkage, enabling walkers to cross from one side to another. Both Alveley and Highley have a long history of mineral extraction. Quarrying was important in the beginning, especially at Alveley, but coal mining began in the Middle Ages at Highley. It was 1935 before a shaft was sunk at Alveley, but not very long after that the mine became uneconomic. It closed in 1969, leaving high unemployment and a ruined landscape. Natural regeneration began at once, with pioneer species such as silver birch recolonising the fertile soils. Meanwhile, an industrial estate was built to provide jobs for some of the miners, while others found work in Bridgnorth or Kidderminster.

Once the industrial estate was established, a landscape reclamation scheme was launched in 1988, to give a helping hand to the natural process. The transformation of the post-industrial landscape has been so successful that it's hard to believe that the woods, meadows, ponds and wetlands of the country park have replaced a scene of spoil heaps and dereliction. The site has cultural significance too, and every year a Miners' Memories Day is held at the visitor centre when ex-miners meet up to share their memories. Well dressing and tree dressing have recently been introduced to the park in an attempt to re-establish traditional rural customs which can foster a sense of involvement with both landscape and community.

There are waymarked trails within the country park, but it also acts as a gateway to other footpaths in the Severn Valley. Towpaths run along both banks of the river, but Alveley is also at the heart of a superb network of green lanes, many of them deeply sunken after generations of use. Some use stream beds, which occupy dingles carved out by tributaries of the Severn. Though they're often dry underfoot in summer, all are tree-hung, fern-filled refuges for wildlife. The Severn is no Amazon, yet there are places where you could almost believe yourself to be on the fringe of some great rainforest as you follow centuries-old footpaths threading their mossy way through high-banked dingles extravagantly clothed in layers of fern. Holly, ash and wild cherry meet overhead, casting a soft green shade in which wild flowers such as wood sorrel and wood anemone flourish in spring.

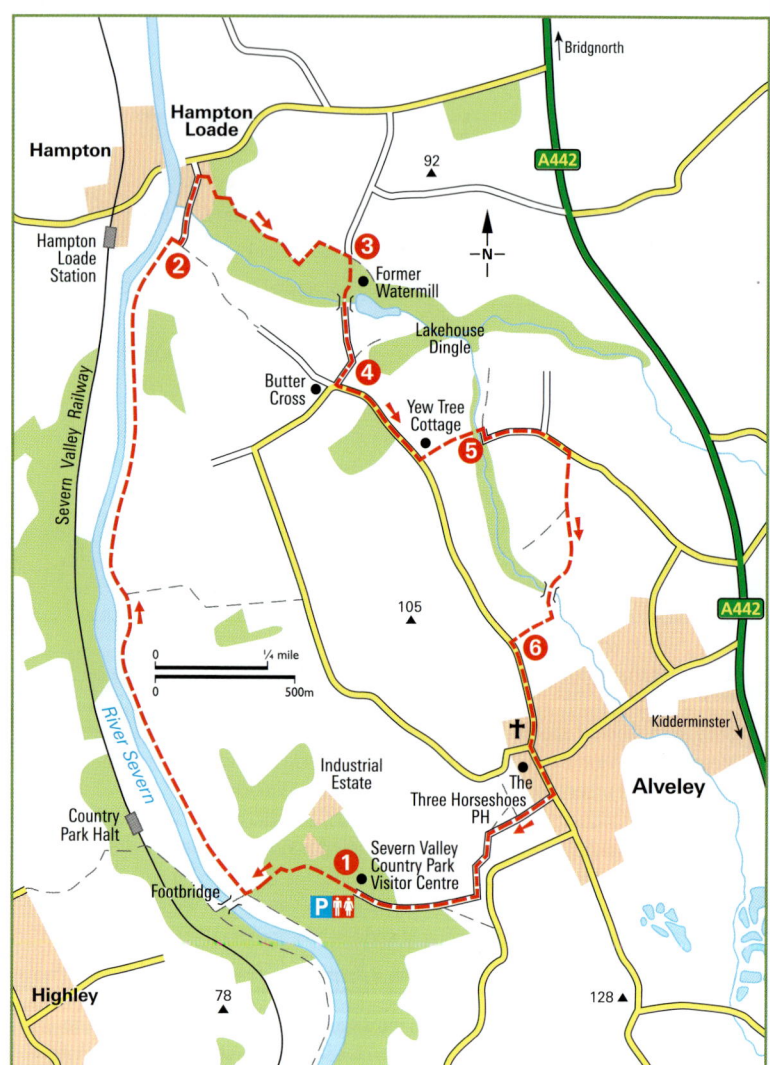

1. Walk down to the river from the country park visitor centre, using whichever route you prefer, the easiest probably being to follow National Cycle Route 45 directly to a new footbridge which replaces Miners' Bridge (1937). Don't cross the bridge, but descend steps to the riverbank and walk upstream for nearly 2 miles (3.2km).

2. Follow a short track to a car park. Turn left to Hampton Loade. Turn right immediately before the former pub, and go past a house called the Haywain. Cross the garden to enter a wood just left of a stable. Continue into a field, follow the right edge and then cross to a gate in the top left corner. Turn right and cross another gate under power lines in the next corner. Proceed to a track and turn right.

3. After a few paces, look for waymarkers and a path on the right. Descend through woodland to Lakehouse Dingle. Cross a footbridge near a former watermill. Keep following a pebbly track, then turn right on a concrete track, to meet a lane on a bend.

4. Turn left, staying on the lane until you've passed Yewtree Cottage and its more modern neighbour. Turn left after the second house, on an obvious field-edge track. At the bottom of the field look for a waymarked gap in the hedge, where the way descends through trees to a dingle.

5. Climb to meet a lane and turn right. After 100yds (91m), join a track on the right. When it bends right, keep straight on instead, along a tree-lined green lane. Before long it becomes narrower and descends to a brook. Sadly this lovely track now bears witness to the havoc wrought by irresponsible 4x4 users, and though access is now barred by boulders at the far end it is still used (or abused) by motorbikes. If you'd rather not risk meeting one, continue along the lane from Yew Tree Cottage into Alveley.

6. Turn left when you meet a lane and walk into Alveley. Pass the church, turn left and walk past the pub, shop and bus stop; 100yds (91m) further on, look for a narrow footpath on the right, between a stone wall and beech hedge. Follow this and it soon swings left and leads into the country park. Turn right and descend to the car park.

Where to eat and drink

The visitor centre tea shop is open Wednesday to Sunday and holiday Mondays. Alveley village's well-stocked shop is next to The Three Horseshoes, which claims to be Shropshire's oldest pub (1406).

What to see

When you reach Point 4 on this walk you will have arrived at an ancient crossroads that is marked by the enigmatic Butter Cross. Nobody knows what it signifies or even how old it is.

While you're there

The Severn Valley Railway operates a full steam-hauled service from May to the end of September and a reduced service the rest of the year. The stations are beautifully kept - the nearest to Alveley reached by a footbridge (which replaced the Miners' bridge built in 1937) is the Country Park Halt which was opened recently to allow easy access to the country park by train.

12

SEVERN VALE SCULPTURE TRAIL

DISTANCE/TIME	5.5 miles (8km) / 2hrs 30min
ASCENT/GRADIENT	490ft (149m) / ▲
PATHS	Woodland, pasture and riverside towpath, many stiles
LANDSCAPE	Two wooded valleys and ridge between
SUGGESTED MAP	OS Explorer 218 Wyre Forest & Kidderminster
START/FINISH	Grid reference: SO745830
DOG FRIENDLINESS	On lead along east side of Borle Brook, in pastureland near Whitehouse Farm and in Highley churchyard
PARKING	Severn Valley Country Park, Station Road, Highley
PUBLIC TOILETS	At car park

The first thing to say about this walk is yes, it is a weird shape! That's purely because of the appalling state of some of the other local footpaths, but don't let that put you off. The paths on this route are fine and it's an excellent walk in beautiful countryside.

You don't expect to find mining towns in Shropshire, but Highley is one, albeit in miniature. An ex-mining town, to be precise, but if that conjures up a depressing image, Highley confounds expectation again. Its terraces of well-built, well-preserved and obviously well-loved Victorian houses are trim, attractive and harmonious, their period features mostly intact and their gable walls and window sills all painted bright red in an idiosyncratic touch which may sound disastrous, but actually works perfectly. The Victorian (or possibly Victorian-style) street signs are charming, too.

Quarrying was important here long before mining. Although coal mining began in the Middle Ages, large-scale operations commenced only in 1878, peaking in the 1930s. Most of the coal dug at Highley went down a tramway to Highley Station on the Severn Valley Railway (SVR). The tramway is now a footpath, which you'll follow on this walk. Tramways and railways were built to link other mines to the SVR. Billingsley Colliery Railway ran along the west bank of Borle Brook, joining the SVR at Brooksmouth. A tramway ran along the east bank and both are now footpaths, also used in this walk. The mines closed in 1969 and the former industrial areas on both sides of the river have been transformed into a country park. Highley has also gone in for some public artwork, including a sculpture trail, known as the Seam Pavement Trail, by West Midlands artist Saranjit Birdi. This is a series of seven bronze plaques depicting Highley's past. The imaginative designs incorporate miners' nicknames gleaned from archive information and consultation with locals. The names, including such gems as Dick the Devil, Flaming Heck and Joyful Clappers, were passed down through the generations, forming what Saranjit calls a seam through time. The plaques are terrific, with possibly the most striking being Trail Boss, Name Poem and Plough and Lady. The last depicts Lady Godiva (of Coventry fame), who owned Highley Manor in the 11th century. Saranjit Birdi is also responsible for the sculpture A Song of Steam Trains at Highley Station.

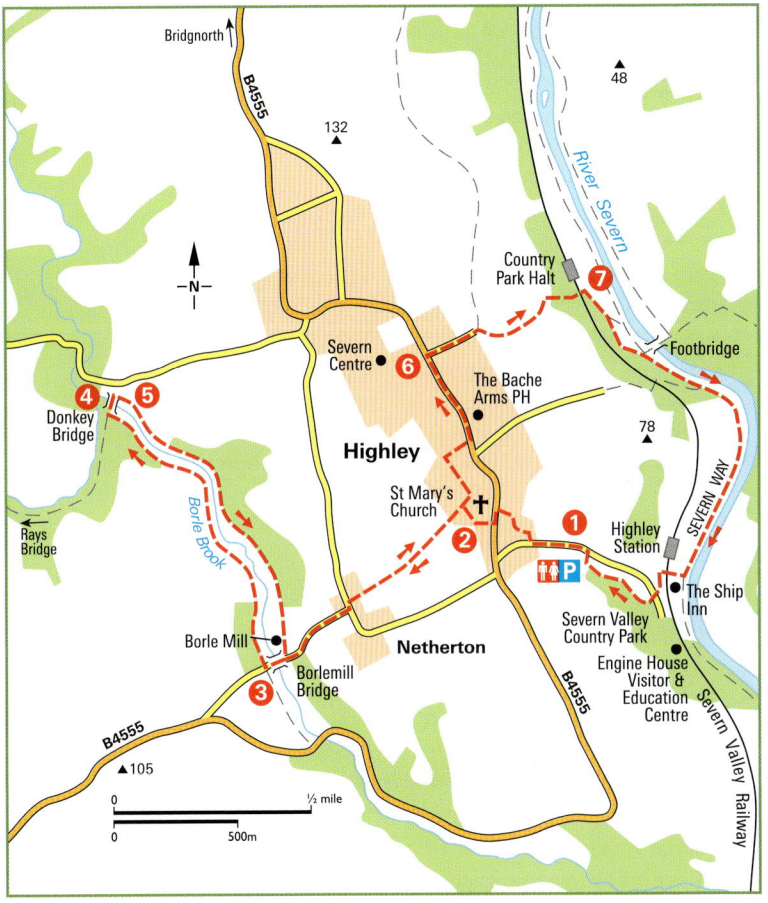

1. Turn left up Station Road. When you're almost at the top, turn right at a sign for the Seam Pavement Trail. Follow a footpath (Smoke Alley) to the main road. Turn left, then cross into St Mary's churchyard.

2. Go through the churchyard, leaving it by the side of timber framed Church House. Follow a stony track, pass to the left of Springfield and go left on a public footpath which runs along field-edges to a lane. Walk steeply down another lane almost opposite.

3. Cross Borlemill Bridge and turn right on a public footpath. It's hidden among conifers, but it's opposite an easily seen path on the other side. After passing a house, continue along field-edges and then through the woodland which borders Borle Brook.

4. The path arrives at Donkey Bridge (an 18th-century packhorse bridge), which you will need to cross. Before you do so, however, it's worth going a few paces to the left to see an old railway bridge. (If you're keen to trace the Billingsley Colliery Railway as far as you can, you should turn left on a bridleway which goes to Rays Bridge, but you'll have to return the same way, owing to the impassability of other footpaths).

5. Cross Donkey Bridge and go up slightly to a sign-board and picnic tables, then turn right on a well-worn, level path. Follow this, with waymarks appearing wherever they might be needed. Turn left when you come to the lane and retrace your steps to Highley. Pass to the left of the church and left again on Church Street. Follow it to High Street (again watching for the pavement trail plaques) and turn left.

6. Opposite the Severn Centre, turn right on Vicarage Lane, which will take you past four 400-year-old pollarded beeches, known locally as the Seven Sisters (some say there were once seven trees, others say it's Severn Sisters), to a junction where you fork right over a cattle grid. The track descends to four gates. Go through the one on the right and continue down.

7. Cross the railway by Country Park Halt and turn right on a good track. At a junction with a surfaced track, turn left to a new footbridge on the site of the former 1937 Miners' Bridge. Don't cross but descend to the riverbank and continue downstream. When you reach The Ship Inn, built for bargemen and opened in 1770, turn right to Highley Station. Cross the line, then turn left until you come to a path climbing through woods. This is the former tramway and it goes directly up taking you back to the car park.

Where to eat and drink

There is masses of choice in Highley village. The Bache Arms, on High Street, welcomes dogs, provided they are on a lead, and well-behaved children. There's a nice new café in the Severn Centre, open every day, (but check opening times.) At The Ship Inn at Stanley, near Highley Station and the River Severn, there are tables outside by the river, while you will find seasonal buffet facilities at the station.

What to see

There are two other sculptures in Highley. Miners' Tribute by Lee Brewster includes a colliery winding wheel and stands on the former colliery site near the car park, while David Howorth's clock sculpture, incorporating a statue of a miner, is on High Street. Pick up a sculpture trail leaflet at Highley Station – and why not arrive by train? It's much more fun.

While you're there

The Engine House Visitor & Education Centre, part of the Severn Valley Railway is worth a visit. You can enjoy themed exhibitions of unique railway vehicles, there is also a café plus a gift shop.

13

A WYRE FOREST CIRCUIT

DISTANCE/TIME	5 miles (8km) / 2hrs 30min
ASCENT/GRADIENT	575ft (175m) / ▲
PATHS	Woodland and field paths, popular with horses and bikes
LANDSCAPE	Mostly broadleaved woodland, with some conifers
SUGGESTED MAP	OS Explorer 218 Wyre Forest & Kidderminster
START/FINISH	Grid reference: SO743784
DOG FRIENDLINESS	On lead in Longdon Orchard and on path to Kingswood
PARKING	Forestry Commission car park at Earnwood Copse, on south side of B4194, west of Buttonoak
PUBLIC TOILETS	None on route

Wyre Forest is shared between Shropshire and Worcestershire, with Dowles Brook forming the county boundary. It was once a royal hunting forest, but the placename Kingswood is the only obvious reminder of that today. In the days of the Norman kings, the forest stretched from Worcester to Bridgnorth. It's considerably smaller today, and partially afforested with alien conifers, but it remains one of the largest and finest semi-natural woodlands in the country.

Despite the conifers, there is still lots of broadleaved woodland, including species such as beech, silver birch, rowan, holly and hazel. But English oak is overwhelmingly dominant. There are two types of English oak – common (also known as pedunculate) and sessile (sometimes called durmast). Common oak usually dominates in the Midlands, but not in Wyre Forest, where the sessile oak is king. The underlying coal measures mean that much of the forest soil is acidic, the preferred habitat of the sessile oak.

English oak supports more wildlife than any other British tree, including an impressive 284 insect species. For centuries local people were also dependent on oak, which provided timber for houses, ships, pit props, fencing and other uses. Small timber was used by broom makers and basket weavers, and also served as firewood. Oak twigs were bound together in bundles and used to make tracks suitable for horse-drawn carts, while oak bark, rich in tannin, was used for curing leather. The forest is dotted with hamlets, such as Buttonoak, which grew out of woodland clearings known as assarts, where squatters settled illegally to make a living as basket weavers, broom makers or charcoal burners. Walk here in autumn and you will see squirrels and jays everywhere, busily burying acorns. Some will be retrieved in due course, but those forgotten will germinate in spring to launch a new generation of oak trees. Unless, that is, the saplings are eaten by deer. Fallow deer are very common in Wyre. Go quietly, with your dog on a lead, and you should see some.

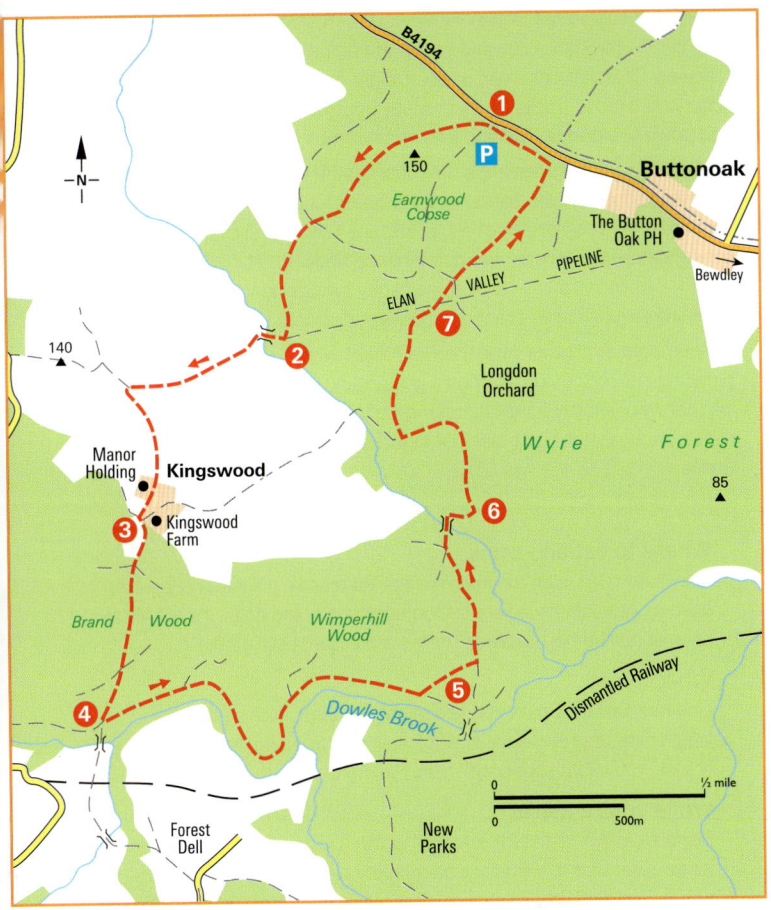

1. Walk through a gate on to a forest road and immediately turn right on a footpath ('WBRA' waymarker) into Earnwood Copse. Keep straight on at all junctions, eventually joining a sunken path not far from the edge of the forest. Fork left to pass under an over-hanging yew tree and continue downhill.

2. The path meets what looks like a firebreak but is actually the route of the Elan Valley pipeline, bringing Welsh water to Birmingham. Turn right and cross a footbridge in the trees to the right of the pipeline. Walk up a bank into arable fields and then head uphill, keeping just left of the hedge. At the end of the second field, turn left and go through a hedge gap, soon recrossing the hedge at a waymarked gate. A stile in a field-corner leads to a dark leafy tunnel, then a clear track, which passes a restored and extended cottage.

3. Soon you reach a T-junction at the edge of the forest. Go a few paces left then swing right on a path past a barrier. Keep straight on at all junctions, descending steadily through Brand Wood.

4. At the bottom, just above Dowles Brook, swing left on the main track. Follow this for 1.25 miles (2km), with Wimperhill Wood on your left.

5. Turn left on another bridleway, which crosses a narrow marshy area, then climbs through scrub and young woodland. It's waymarked and easily followed. Cross a forest road, keep straight on, then turn right at the next waymarked cross-tracks (post inconspicuous on the left) before swinging left and down to a bridge. The bridleway now climbs along the rim of a valley.

6. Reaching a more open area, turn sharp left (still on the bridleway). Here birch and other natives are regenerating fast following clear felling of the conifers that grew here. You're approaching Longdon Orchard now, a conservation area where your dog must be under strict control. At a T-junction go left, into conifers; the track immediately swings right again. Follow it to a waymarked junction where the bridleway goes right.

7. Keep right at another fork, then turn right when you meet the Elan Valley pipe-line again. Soon turn left on a good track, National Cycle Network Route 45, then very shortly follow it, forking right. Follow it to the edge of the forest near Buttonoak, then turn left just before the road to return to Earnwood Copse.

Where to eat and drink
The Button Oak is on the main road at Buttonoak. It's a friendly place, used to welcoming walkers, including children and dogs. It's not always open at lunchtime, however. There's a pleasant beer garden.

What to see
Linger at Dowles Brook and you might see birds such as dippers, kingfishers or grey wagtails, all of which occur along the brook. With a bit of luck, you might spot crayfish and young trout in the brook itself.

While you're there
Bewdley, in Worcestershire, is well worth a visit. Once a busy Severn port, it now caters for tourists instead of boat builders and bow-hauliers (men who pulled the boats upstream). Bewdley's waterfront is said to be the finest in the Midlands, with its fine 17th- and 18th-century architecture.

HUNTING FOR HOBBITS AT BAGGINSWOOD

DISTANCE/TIME	6.3 miles (10.1km) / 2hrs 30min
ASCENT/GRADIENT	755ft (230m) / ▲ ▲
PATHS	Field-edges with no clear paths, farm and forest tracks, 23 stiles
LANDSCAPE	Rolling farmland, woodland and forest
SUGGESTED MAP	OS Explorer 218 Wyre Forest & Kidderminster
START/FINISH	Grid reference: SO699800
DOG FRIENDLINESS	On lead except in woods at the end
PARKING	Lay-by by track entrance beside Birchen Park Forest
PUBLIC TOILETS	None on route

Pack a sense of adventure for this walk, as much of it is little-trodden, with paths that are virtually non-existent. Navigation is actually pretty straightforward as the route largely follows field-edges and stiles and waymarks are all in place, but they can virtually disappear behind the lush vegetation of the field-corners in high summer. It's actually good environmental practice by the farmers to leave broad margins clear of commercial crops, so let's not grumble. And let's not exaggerate either; this is not the Darien Gap and you won't need a machete – though shorts-wearers will need to watch out for nettles! It's precisely that feeling of being (quite literally) off the beaten track that gives this walk its charm.

'Going on was not altogether easy. They had packs to carry, and the bushes and brambles were reluctant to let them through.' J R R Tolkien, *The Fellowship of the Ring*.

Many places have cashed in on the worldwide success of J R R Tolkien's books, notably *The Hobbit* and *The Lord of the Rings*. More recently, Peter Jackson's epic films have brought Tolkien's imagined world of Middle Earth to a vast new audience – and because they were filmed in New Zealand, many people imagine that Tolkien, too, was a New Zealander. In fact, though born in South Africa, he grew up in the West Midlands, and never visited New Zealand. Most of the inspiration for Middle Earth lies in the stark contrast between the industrial blight of the Black Country and the idyllic countryside just a stone's throw away. It's Worcestershire, not Shropshire, which is the main inspiration for the hobbits' homeland, The Shire, but Tolkien was fascinated by placenames, and it's hard to imagine that the name Bagginswood did not attract his attention and inspire the names of his heroes, Bilbo and Frodo Baggins. To be honest, there's not much to see at Bagginswood, and it's highly unlikely that its Tolkien connections go any further than suggesting a name. On the other hand, it's exactly the sort of landscape that Tolkien cherished.

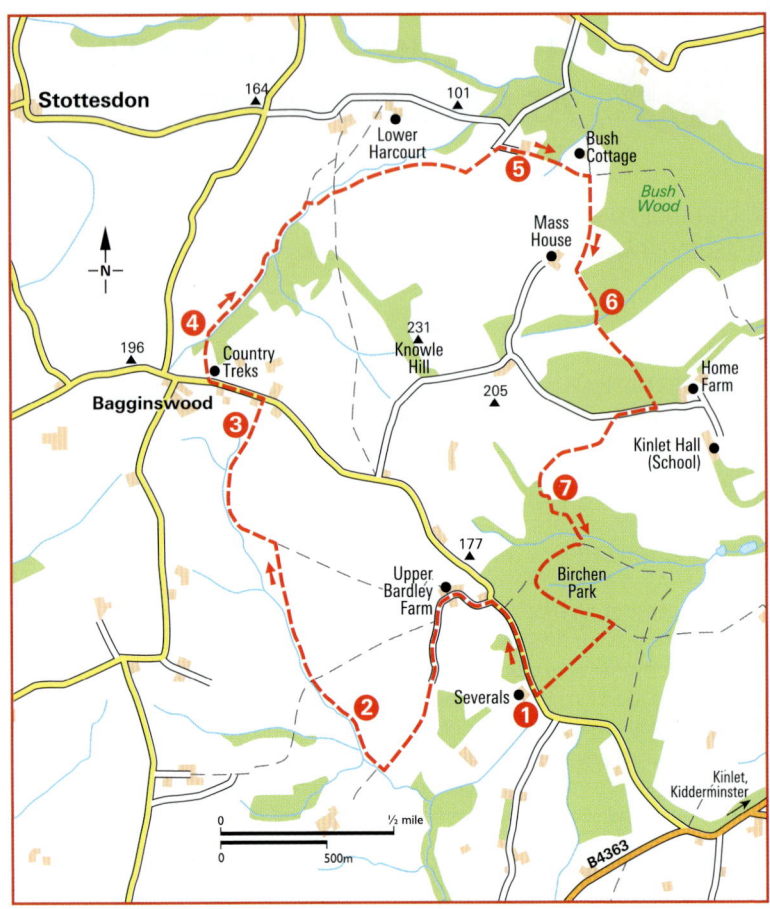

1. Turn right along the road for 500yds (457m) then turn left on the track to Upper Bradley Farm. Go through the farmyard and, after the last building, go right a few paces to find a clear track between hedges. Follow this then continue down the left edge of a large field. At the bottom go right skirting trees, ignore a track leading to a ford and continue along the bottom edge of the field. In the corner find a footbridge hidden in the foliage.

2. Continue in similar vein along the lower edges of several fields, with the stream hidden in the trees just to the left. One plank bridge has a very wobbly handrail, but the bridge itself is solid. In the sixth field, the right of way is shown ascending the slope before slanting back to the far end, but if there are growing crops the farmer would surely prefer you to stick to the unplanted margin.

3. At the end the path is signed through a junk-filled yard, but you can avoid this by using a second stile a few paces to the right. Emerge to the road and turn left for 150yds (137m) to a footpath sign and stile on the right. Cross a yard (Country Treks) to a second stile and descend ahead through horse paddocks to a small gate at the bottom.

4. Follow field-edges, with a stream in the trees on the right. After four fields, way-marks lead down to the right. Ford the stream (it's usually about 2 inches deep) and go up to a stile, then go left, downstream. Pass a gate and two stiles then bear right up a field to a gate under a tree. (This field has a stream, sometimes dry, down the middle). Through the gate, turn left along the hedge to a track and go right.

5. Follow the track past a cottage; ignore a track down to another (Bush Cottage). Shortly there's a stile, with bridleway waymarks, on the right. Go straight up the field to a gate. Ignore the track in the next field and go straight over the crest and down to a double stile at the corner of a wood. Follow the edge of the wood through a dip then continue ahead to another gate. Turn left then ignore the track and find a little path along the wood-edge and then into it.

6. Descend to a stream, then go half-left to a waymark post in a cleared area. Go straight up the slope then bear left as the gradient eases, to a waymarked gateway. Turn right on the track to a stile. Cross this or use the gap on the right and follow the right edge of the field. Go through a gate then descend left in a dip, with scattered trees on your right.

7. A waymarked gate leads into woodland. Descend the track to a four-way junction and go half-right (bridleway). Climb past a cleared area then take a waymarked path on the left. Follow this to a clear track and turn right, straight up to the parking place.

Where to eat and drink

The nearest watering hole is the Eagle and Serpent at Kinlet, a cosy village pub with several small rooms and a pleasant beer garden. Two well-kept guest ales are normally on tap and the menu offers a selection of pub classics. There is the Kabin Café also at Kinlet offering breakfast, snacks and sandwiches.

What to see

On part of this walk, you'll notice Geopark Way waymarks. The Geopark Way is a 109-mile (175km) route from Bridgnorth to Gloucester, taking in several ranges of hills and exploring 700 million years of earth's history. For most, the highlight will be the traverse of the Malvern Hills, on the borders of Herefordshire and Worcestershire. On this walk, there's little exposed rock to be seen but beneath your feet are the Pennine Coal Measures and it's only a short distance to Highley, where coal was mined commercially.

While you're there

Just over the border in Worcestershire, near Kidderminster, is the West Midlands Safari Park. 'Safari Park' may conjure up an image of driving through parkland past big cats and other exotic fauna, but there's a good deal more on offer, with many areas accessible on foot, such as 'Walking with Lemurs'. There's also a small amusement park if some of the younger ones need a change of pace.

AROUND CLEOBURY MORTIMER

DISTANCE/TIME	4.8 miles (7.7km) / 2hrs
ASCENT/GRADIENT	558ft (170m) / ▲
PATHS	Mostly field paths across pasture, many stiles
LANDSCAPE	Pastoral country with secluded valleys and panoramic views
SUGGESTED MAP	OS Explorer 203 Ludlow or OS Explorer 218 Wyre Forest & Kidderminster
START/FINISH	Grid reference: SO672757
DOG FRIENDLINESS	On leads
PARKING	Town centre Childe Road (East) and Childe Road (West) car parks, Cleobury Mortimer
PUBLIC TOILETS	At Childe Road West car park

It's hard to say whether Cleobury Mortimer is a town or a village. Once the stronghold of Norman baron Ralph Mortimer, who built a castle here and soon established control over much of the border country, it has a significant entry in the Domesday Book. The Mortimers went on to rule the Marches for centuries, but their centre of power soon moved to Wigmore, then to Ludlow, and Ralph's castle at Cleobury was eventually destroyed by Henry II in 1155.

As you leave it behind, do stop occasionally to glance back at the view of Cleobury, set against the backdrop of the Clee Hills and dominated by the octagonal spire of St Mary's Church, which has a marked twist in it. This is due to the warping of the timbers and has admitted Cleobury to the membership of an exclusive club – the slightly bizarre-sounding European Twisted Spires Association. The only other British member is Chesterfield, in Derbyshire.

Just across from the Church (you'll see it as you reach the end of the walk) is The Wells, a spring-fed pool which was the town's main water supply for many centuries. It's said that waggoners would drive their wagons through the pool in the hope that the water would swell the wood, causing the spokes to fit more tightly into the wheels. Inevitably in more modern times doubts were raised about the quality of the water, especially as it lay directly below the church graveyard, and the pool is now purely ornamental.

Cleobury is quickly left behind and after a bit of climbing a superb panorama of fields, woods and hedges presents itself, with all of Worcestershire spread out in front of you, rising to the Malvern Hills. As you go forward, Herefordshire comes into view on your right, with the Black Mountains marking the Welsh border.

After more short descents, climbs, and two crossings of the River Rea, another track gives a good view over to the square, red-brick Mawley Hall. You'll pass much closer to the Hall later on, but barely see it, so get a good look while you can.

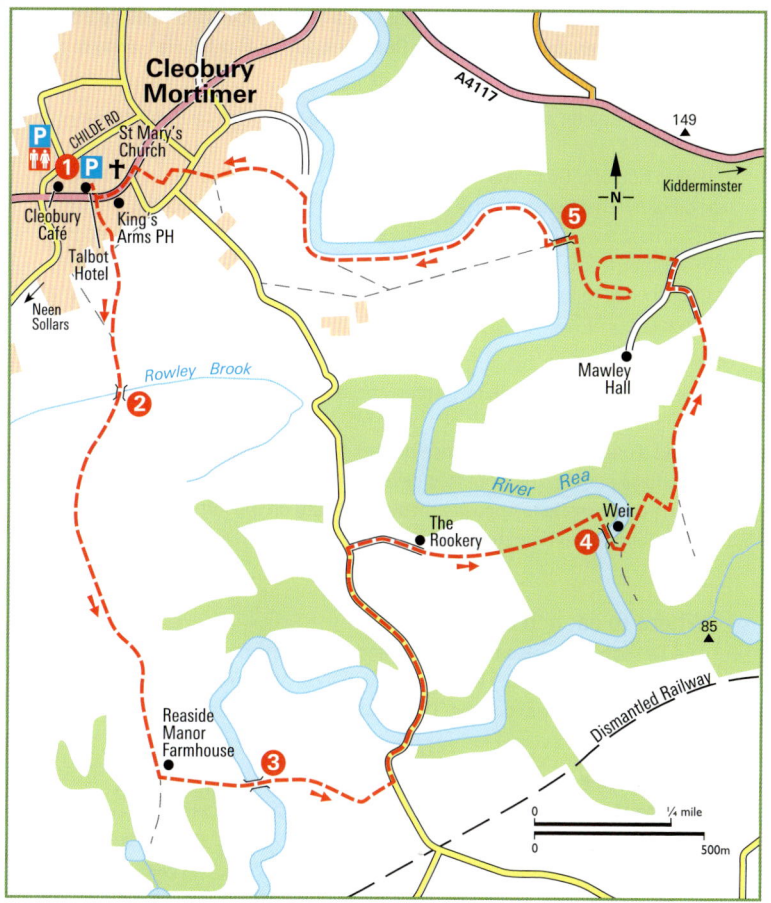

1. Walk through the alleyway under the Talbot Hotel to the main street. Go down Eagle Lane opposite. When the lane bends right, cross a gate into a field. Go up right to a gate, then go diagonally to the top right corner of the next field. Cut rightwards across the corner of another, then go diagonally across the next to meet the far hedge, in line with a solitary oak. Follow the right-hand hedge down to Rowley Brook and turn right to cross a bridge.

2. Climb diagonally, passing another solitary oak. Cross a stile in the hedge, squeeze past another and go straight on by the left-hand hedge, along a level field. Go through a gate and down the next field to meet a track; turn left then swing right towards Reaside Manor Farm. Pass between the farmhouse and its outbuildings, cross a stile and bear left past an oak tree (complete with treehouse). Descend the slope, continue to a footbridge and cross the River Rea.

3. Climb to the far right corner of the next field, which funnels into a short a track. Follow this over a slight rise then turn left into a leafy tunnel. Follow this to meet a lane. Turn left along the narrow, high-banked lane for nearly

0.5 miles (800m), until you can turn right on a stony track, which leads past The Rookery, then down to the River Rea. Look out for Mawley Hall away to the left here.

4. Cross the Rea on a footbridge to the right of a weir. This peaceful spot by the weir was once the site of a charcoal furnace, built in the 16th century for smelting iron ore. Go forward to cross a stone bridge then turn left on a grassy track. Follow this twisting track uphill and then go diagonally across a small field to meet a wider track which takes you past Mawley Hall. At a T-junction with another track, turn right past paddocks, then left at a footpath sign. The path descends to loop round a walled garden, then doubles back right towards the river.

5. Crossing the Rea again, turn right and follow the river. When you reach a lane, you can take this back to Cleobury or, better, look for a grassy bridleway on the left, climbing to the left of a brick-fronted house, then on through grass-land and along a leafy tunnel. Once houses take over at Mortimer Hill, start looking for a path on the right that descends beside Mortimer Cottage. Continue down the lane opposite then take a path on the left beside a stream. Reach Church Street and turn left, back to the Talbot passageway.

Where to eat and drink
The Talbot Hotel welcomes children and dogs in the bar or the beer garden. The King's Arms has comfy sofas, local ales, and sandwiches made the way they should be. The Cleobury Café is probably the best of the cafés in town.

What to see
Reaside Manor Farmhouse is an outstanding early 17th-century sandstone building, with gables, a marvellous porch and star-shaped brick chimney stacks. The late 16th and early 17th centuries were periods of great prosperity when yeoman farmers all over the country built themselves fine houses like this.

While you're there
Neen Sollars, a village on a ridge between the River Rea and Mill Brook, lies south of Cleobury. There are lovely walks, substantial traces of the dismantled Bewdley-to-Tenbury railway (including a viaduct) and a 14th-century church with an exceptional monument to explorer Humphrey Conyngesby, who was born in 1567. Described as 'a perfect scoller...and a greate traveyler', he disappeared without trace in 1610. The monument was erected in 1624, by which time his family had obviously given up hope of his return.

BROWN CLEE

DISTANCE/TIME	7 miles (11.3km) / 3hrs 30min
ASCENT/GRADIENT	1,460ft (445m) / ▲ ▲ ▲
PATHS	Generally good, but can be very boggy in places, 3 stiles
LANDSCAPE	Hill, moorland, pasture and plantation
SUGGESTED MAP	OS Explorer 217 The Long Mynd & Wenlock Edge
START/FINISH	Grid reference: SO607873
DOG FRIENDLINESS	Excellent, but under strict control near sheep
PARKING	Verges by Brown Clee Picnic Area, on unclassified road west of Cleobury North
PUBLIC TOILETS	None on route

Choose a clear day for this walk, because the stunning view from Abdon Burf, the higher of Brown Clee's twin summits, extends from the Cotswolds to Cadair Idris. At 1,770ft, the shire's highest hill, overtopping its sibling, Titterstone Clee, by 23ft (7m), and Stiperstones by just 13ft (4m). Brown Clee may be high, but it's not wild, though it appears so in places. It is a perfect illustration of just how intensive rural land use can be. There's hardly anything this hill hasn't been used for at one time or another in its long history.

Nobody knows when people started making use of the Clee Hills, but forts were built on Brown Clee in the Iron Age. Those on Abdon Burf and Clee Burf have been destroyed by quarrying. A third, Nordy Bank, still stands on Clee Liberty. Iron Age people hunted on the hills, and the tradition continued for centuries, with the Clees part of a royal forest for a time.

Brown Clee Hill must have been used for stock grazing since the hill forts were built, or even before that. More recently, in the Middle Ages, all of the hillside above the encircling roads was common land, divided between several parishes, while an outer ring of parishes also had grazing rights. Stock from the outer parishes was driven to and from Brown Clee on tracks known as outracks or strakerways, most of which are now footpaths or bridleways. Many are deeply sunken through long use, and commoners' sheep and ponies still graze Clee Liberty.

Mineral extraction also has a long history in the Clee Hills. Brown Clee is riddled with shafts and is said to be the highest ex-coalfield in Britain. Ironstone was dug from the coal measures from the Middle Ages onwards and fed a number of forges around the hill. More recently, a type of volcanic rock called dolerite (also locally known as dhustone) was exploited, mostly for road building, and the ruins of a stone-crushing plant still disfigure Abdon Burf. Wagons then transported the stone down a steep incline to the railway at Ditton Priors. Quarrying ceased in 1936 and the incline is now a footpath (though not a right of way), used in this walk to gain access to the hill. You can still see parts of the actual tramway in places.

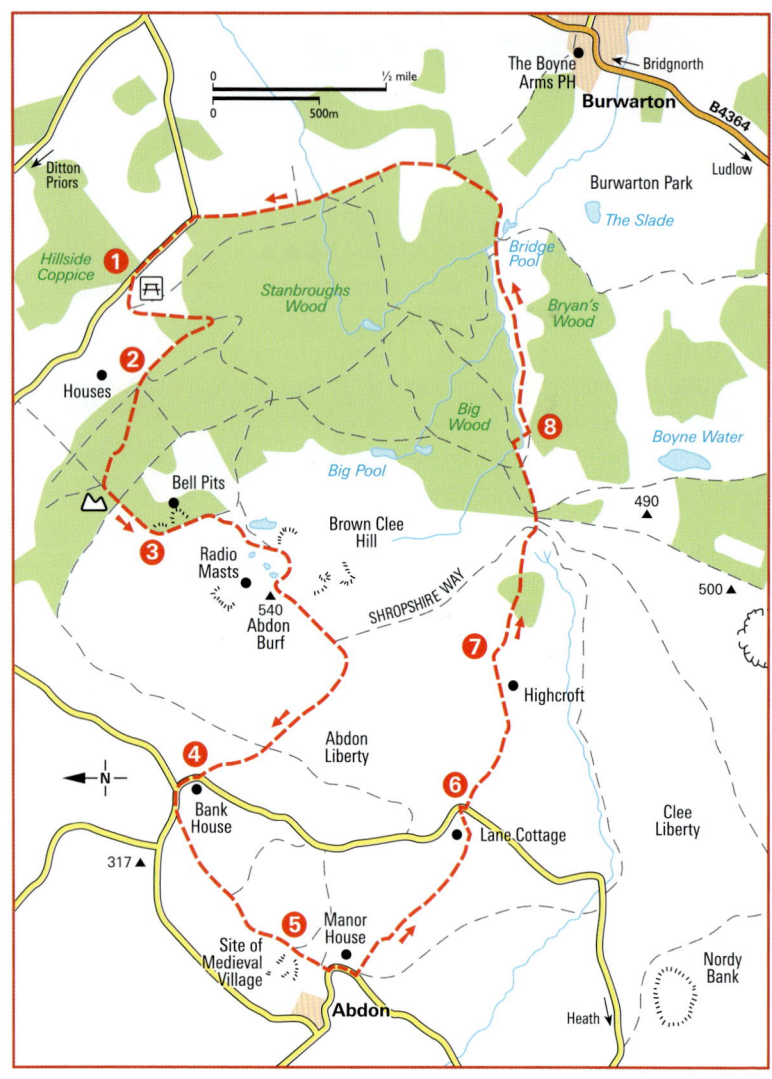

1. By the north end of the picnic field, at a 'Forest Trail' sign', a footpath climbs to the right then swings back left. Follow it into woodland, with conifers on the left. Soon go right on a level forest track which runs along the woodland edge, soon with a field on the right.

2. There are two houses just below the field. As you draw level with the second one, there's a turning circle on the left, where a path rises diagonally through a plantation. Follow this to a steep straight track (the former tramway). Turn left, soon crossing a cattle grid into heathland.

3. Continue less steeply, past conspicuous mounds of quarry spoil. The track turns sharp left. It's easy now to Abdon Burf, with its ugly masts and awesome views. From the summit, a rough path descends southwest (use the view indicator to confirm the direction). Follow it down to a line of posts. Go through

these and keep descending by a fence. The path swings right, becoming a hollow way.

4. Meeting a lane, turn right, then left at a junction and soon left again at a gate. The waymark points diagonally right, but go straight ahead along the left-hand edges of several meadows, and maintain the same direction as the path merges with the sunken remains of an old green lane.

5. As you approach Abdon, a gate gives access to a garden. Go straight through, with signs directing you past the house and down the drive to a lane. Turn left, go past farm buildings and continue to a collection of barns. There's a stony track opposite – walk a few paces along it to a bridleway on the left. Follow it uphill. Where it appears to come to a dead end, enter the field on the right and continue until a stile gives access to a board-walk in the garden of Lane Cottage.

6. Meet a lane and go a few paces right to a stile on the left. Climb steep pasture towards a fence/ hedge on the skyline. Cross it at a stile, continue to the far corner of the next field, then turn left on a track. At Highcroft, the track continues as a hollow way.

7. Go through a gate into pasture and follow the right-hand fence to the top corner. Pass through a gate and continue to a line of beeches on the summit ridge. Go forward through the beeches, then straight on down a track, through woodland, plantation and bracken to a junction. Turn sharp right.

8. The track crosses a stream. Fork left on a narrow path descending near the stream. When you meet a concrete track, turn left. After 600yds (549m) you'll come to a junction. Branch right here if you want the pub or bus stop at Burwarton. If not, keep left and then straight ahead to return to the picnic site.

Where to eat and drink
The name of the characterful Boyne Arms at Burwarton derives from the family that owns much of Brown Clee Hill. Many walkers stop here for a drink and home-cooking. Note that it is closed on Mondays and Tuesdays.

What to see
Just after the cattle grid crossed in Point 2, there is a profusion of mounds, with corresponding depressions. These are the remains of bell pits, an early form of mining which involved digging a short shaft and working the seam from the foot of it as far as was safe.

While you're there
Visit the hamlet of Heath, west of Brown Clee. The renowned Heath Chapel stands alone in a field and is the purest example of Norman church architecture in Shropshire.

17

BEDLAM ON CLEE HILL

DISTANCE/TIME	8.25 miles (13.3km) / 3hrs 30min
ASCENT/GRADIENT	1,330ft (405m) / ▲ ▲ ▲
PATHS	Good but rough, uneven and/or boggy in places
LANDSCAPE	Moors and upland pasture with industrial remains
SUGGESTED MAP	OS Explorer 203 Ludlow
START/FINISH	Grid reference: SO595753
DOG FRIENDLINESS	Good, but keep under close control near sheep and cattle
PARKING	Car park/picnic site/viewpoint on eastern edge of Cleehill
PUBLIC TOILETS	On A4117, 100yds (91m) west of car park

Locals say the view from Clee Hill is the finest in England and it's hard to disagree. After all, where else can you see from the Brecon Beacons to the Peak District, from Snowdonia to the Cotswolds? It's stunning. But before getting too carried away with the view, we need to sort out some names, which can be confusing in these parts. For instance, it's Cleehill village, but Clee Hill. However, strictly, Clee Hill is just the area that is currently being quarried, northeast of the village. The top is Titterstone Clee Hill. Not everybody calls it that – to many who live in sight of it, in Shropshire and neighbouring counties, it's just Clee Hill or The Clee.

And then there's Bedlam. The original Bedlam was the Hospital of St Mary of Bethlehem, a lunatic asylum (as they were called) in London. Few people know that Bedlam is also a Victorian quarrying settlement on Clee Hill. On old maps it's called by that name, and at Bitterley a road sign indicates Bedlam. Bedlam is also marked on the excellent map displayed at Cleehill picnic site. Unfold your modern OS map, however, and you'll look in vain for it. It may be apocryphal, but the story goes that Bedlam's residents don't like its name because of its associations, and would prefer to rename it Titterstone Village. Still, it's reassuring to note that somebody in Bedlam has a sense of humour, as you will see when you pass Hullabaloo House.

There are other intriguing names on and around Clee Hill: Sodom, for example, but perhaps it's best not to inquire too closely into that. Random, Crumpsbrook, Hopton Wafers, Cramer Gutter, Rugpits, Titrail, Lubberland, Angelbank, Applecake Hill, Cadbury, Pastycraft, Hackenchop, Hilluppencott, Hemm and Hoopits all have their own charm. Many names relate to wildlife, such as Kitesnest, Hawkwood, Magpie Hill, Brown Owls, Lapwing, Foxwood and even Wormsacre. Others relate to the industrial heritage of the area. The bridleway you join at Cleeton St Mary, for instance, is marked on old maps as Limers' Lane, though it's often referred to as the Random bridleway nowadays, because it passes Random.

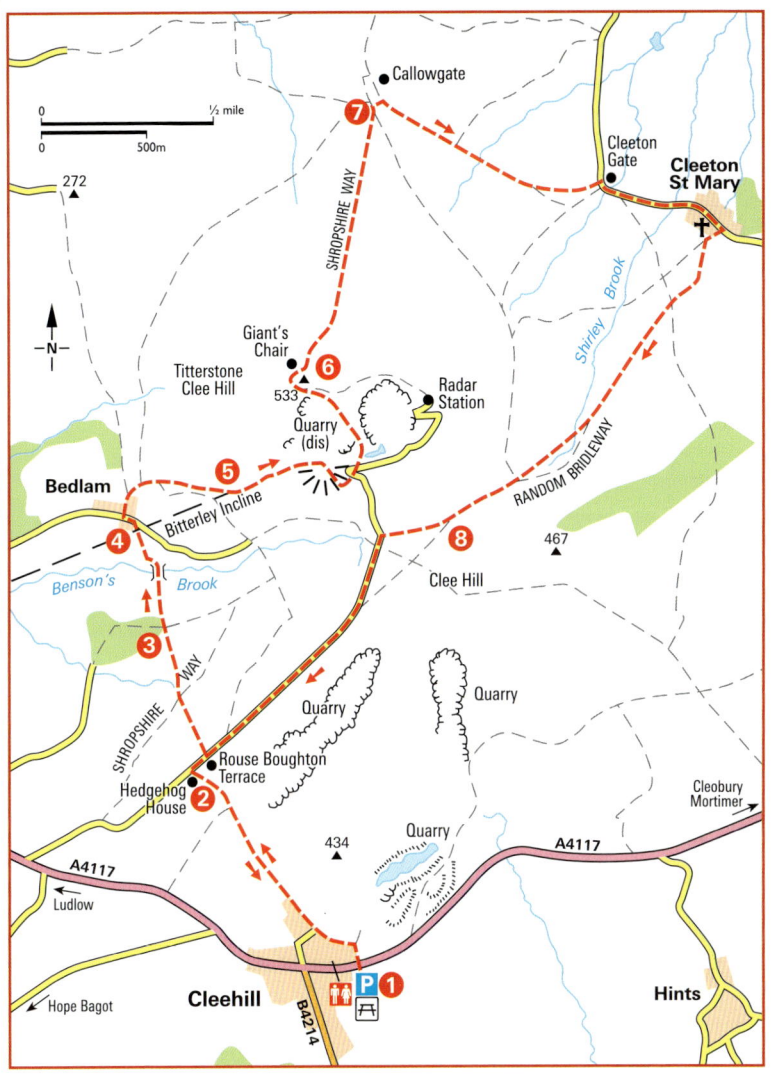

1. Walk up the lane opposite the picnic area. After 100yds (91m), turn left and follow a broad track. Its middle section is classed as Open Access Land: follow it past mining ruins.

2. Turn right at Hedgehog House onto the road that leads to the radar station. Walk to the end of Rouse Boughton Terrace and turn left, then go through a small gate on the right before a cattle grid. Follow the top edge of a thistly field. Continue along the edge of the next field and through a gate in the corner to meet the Shropshire Way, which goes to the right. Ignore it and go straight on, skirting a stream and gorse thickets and crossing a gate in a wire fence before returning to the left-hand hedgeline.

3. A green track develops, swinging right and down to cross Benson's Brook at a bridge. Follow the track up again, passing the abutments of a former tramway bridge (called Titterstone Incline on OS maps), before arriving at Bedlam.

4. Turn left into the hamlet, then fork right. Pass Hullabaloo House and climb a track to a cattle grid. Follow the track up to a farm then bear left up a smooth green track.

5. When you come to Bitterley Incline again, climb on to the embankment, joining the Shropshire Way. Follow it uphill. When you reach ruined quarry buildings, go right on a level path. Pass the last building, fork left and climb slightly. Go straight on, crossing the access road twice at a bend, then bear left up a steeper track. Skirt a large quarry to reach the radar station and trig point.

6. Some 100yds (91m) north of the trig pillar are the remains of an ancient cairn, the Giant's Chair. From this bear right, above steep scree slopes, then swing left on a clearer path and continue across bracken moorland to the red roofed farm of Callowgate.

7. Before reaching Callowgate, turn right where the bracken runs out. Follow sheep tracks to the edge of the moor and turn right again. Joining a lane at Cleeton Gate, turn right and walk to the village of Cleeton St Mary. Turn right, looping round the church and along a row of almshouses, then left on the Random bridleway, which runs along the moorland edge. Follow vague paths parallel to the fence, except where you need to cut a corner – it's obvious (and usually wet!) when you come to it.

8. When the fence makes a very sharp left turn, keep straight on to meet the radar station access road. Turn left to Rouse Boughton Terrace then retrace your steps to the start.

Where to eat and drink

There are shops, a tea room/bakery and a chippy in Cleehill, and a café nearby.

What to see

This is a great place to see buzzards or kestrels – watch the latter for a while and you'll understand why it is also called the windhover. You're also increasingly likely to see a raven or two. This member of the crow family suffered a sharp decline in numbers but is now making something of a comeback.

While you're there

Visit Hope Bagot, a lovely village tucked away on the southern slopes of Clee Hill and approached along deeply sunken lanes. There are some fine Georgian houses, particularly Hope Court and the Old Vicarage, and a 16th-century timber-framed cottage. The small church is Norman, with a possible Saxon arch over the entrance to the vestry. A great yew tree in the churchyard is believed to be more than 1,600 years old.

18

DIDDLEBURY AND WENLOCK EDGE

DISTANCE/TIME	6.25 miles (10.1km) / 3hrs
ASCENT/GRADIENT	689ft (210m) / ▲
PATHS	Mostly good but ford on Dunstan's Lane can be deep after rain, many stiles
LANDSCAPE	Wooded ridge of Wenlock Edge, patchwork of Corve Dale
SUGGESTED MAP	OS Explorer 217 The Long Mynd & Wenlock Edge
START/FINISH	Grid reference: SO479875
DOG FRIENDLINESS	On lead near livestock
PARKING	Car park for Harton Hollow Nature Reserve on east side of unclassified road between Middlehope and Westhope
PUBLIC TOILETS	None on route

Wenlock Edge needs a book to itself, so all you will get here is the merest glimpse, but it should whet your appetite for more. This great tree-clad escarpment is one of Shropshire's most famous landscape features, partly because it plays a role in A E Housman's collection of poems entitled *A Shropshire Lad*, some of which were set to music by the composer Vaughan Williams. It is best seen from the west, appearing as an unbroken escarpment running from the Severn Gorge to Craven Arms. From the east it is more elusive, rising almost imperceptibly. Within a basic ridge structure, it seems to form a series of waves or steps and consists for part of its length of two parallel edges, divided by Hope Dale.

Wenlock Edge is composed of Silurian limestone formed about 420 million years ago. Developing as a barrier reef in a tropical sea on the edge of a continental shelf, it was built up from the accumulation of sediments and the skeletons of marine creatures such as corals, brachiopods and crinoids. Earth movements and erosion then sculpted it into the escarpment.

Most of it is wooded, and much of this is ancient woodland, growing on steep slopes where there has been continuous tree cover since the end of the last ice age. The dominant species is ash, which has a special affinity with limestone, but many other types are present. Beneath the trees are lime-loving shrubs such as spurge laurel, spindle and dogwood. The ground flora is rich and varied, especially along the rides and in newly coppiced areas, where flowers respond to the increased light by growing more profusely and attracting many butterflies.

In the past, the Edge was always seen as a valuable resource to be exploited. Timber provided building materials, tools and charcoal for iron smelting. Limestone was used for building, for making lime, for iron smelting and, more recently, as an aggregate. This latter use still continues and there are unsightly quarries between Presthope and Much Wenlock, where you can walk the ridge and look down on the unedifying spectacle of monstrous machines digging up Shropshire so that heavy lorries can carry it away. There's nothing like that on this walk, where the quarries you pass are small ones, long since abandoned and now transformed by nature into mossy, fern-filled caverns of green.

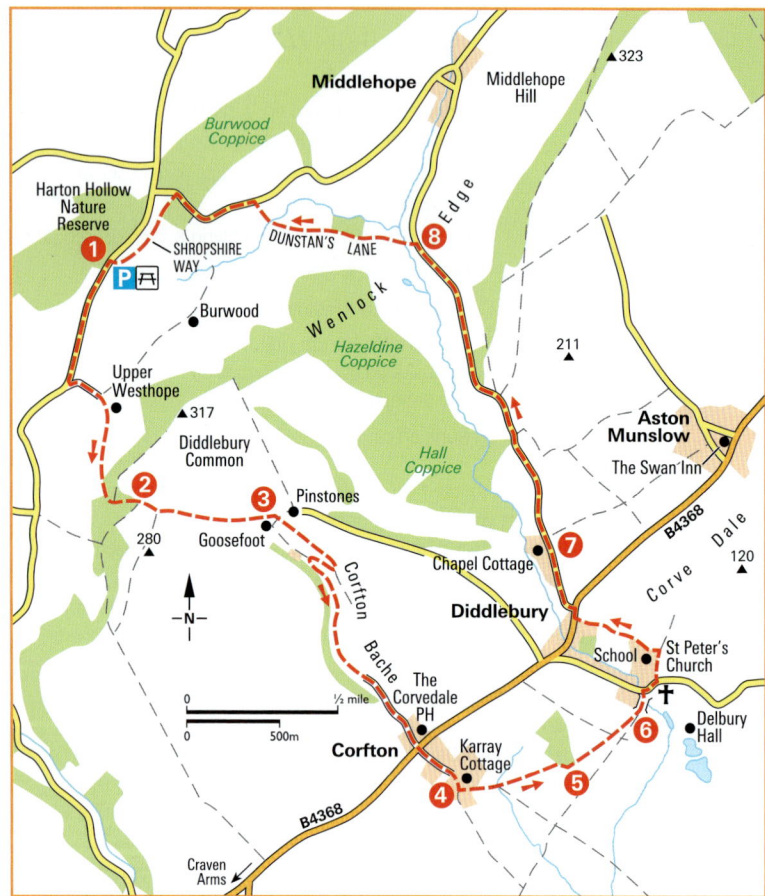

1. Turn left out of the car park along the lane. When you come to a junction, turn sharp left again, signposted 'Middlehope'. Keep straight on at the next, signed 'Upper Westhope Farm'. Where the track bends left to the farm, go slightly right to a gate and join a grassy bridleway that soon enters woodland. Keep straight on at two cross paths.

2. The bridleway emerges into pasture; keep straight on along to the corner. Go through a gate and turn right on a field-edge path, which soon becomes a wide track.

3. After passing a cottage, and with a group of barns ahead, look for blue arrows that direct you sharp right through a gate. Turn immediately left and walk above Corfton Bache, a deep valley. Pass above a group of houses then zigzag down a green track. Continue down the valley to the B4368 at Corfton and cross to a lane opposite.

4. The lane forks at Karray Cottage. Go through two iron kissing gates then bear left across a field to a prominent stile at the far side. Cross a farm track and walk to the far right corner of an arable field.

5. Go through a gap, then a little way along the left-hand edge of another field until a gate gives access to parkland. Head in the direction indicated by the waymarker. St Peter's Church at Diddlebury soon comes into view, providing an infallible guide.

6. Cross two stiles (one very rickety) at the far side of the park and go straight on down. Cross a track to find a footbridge and a path into Diddlebury. Turn right at the road, then left by the church. Join a footpath starting to the right of the village hall, then skirt around the school, to a gate and a stile immediately right of the buildings. Cross fields to the B4368. Cross to the lane almost opposite, and keep right after a few paces.

7. Climb steadily up the narrow, sunken lane. At the top, by the entrance to Aston Top, keep left, still on the lane. Descend to the valley bottom.

8. Turn left on a stony track, Dunstan's Lane, soon reaching a ford. When the main track bends right, follow waymarks straight ahead up a narrow hedged track to a lane and turn left. Keep straight on at a Y-junction. Turn left on a footpath with a Shropshire Way sign. The sometimes muddy path leads through the woods back to the car park.

Where to eat and drink

The Corvedale is a family run pub, first licensed in 1613 and has recently been renovated. The pub has a welcoming atmosphere with live music on some nights and their pizzas are reccommended.

What to see

St Peter's Church at Diddlebury has a Saxon nave, its north wall constructed of herringbone masonry, which was the style favoured by the Saxons. The north doorway is typically Saxon, and there is a Saxon window. The tower also seems to be partly Saxon, though even the experts are unsure. Do go inside – very few churches of this kind survive in England.

While you're there

Shropshire Wildlife Trust has 37 reserves altogether and welcomes the public to almost all of them. Why not visit The Cut Visitor Centre and Shop on Abbey Foregate in Shrewsbury? The centre itself is a nature reserve, with many birds breeding in the garden, which is a re-creation of a medieval physic garden. The Trust inherited this when it took up residence in 2001 and intends to save the most interesting plants while also making it a true wildlife garden.

19

WENLOCK EDGE, LITTLE LONDON AND RUSHBURY

DISTANCE/TIME	8 miles (12.9km) / 3hrs 30min
ASCENT/GRADIENT	1,302ftft (397mm) / ▲ ▲
PATHS	Generally good, one or two undefined field paths, many stiles
LANDSCAPE	Wooded escarpment, sheltered dale and broader valley
SUGGESTED MAP	OS Explorer 217 The Long Mynd & Wenlock Edge
START/FINISH	Grid reference: SO521908
DOG FRIENDLINESS	Some woodland stretches suitable for dogs to run free
PARKING	Large lay-by near big bend in road at Roman Bank
PUBLIC TOILETS	None on route

The two-tiered structure of Wenlock Edge is clear on several of these walks, perhaps never more so than on this one. The 'leading', or northwestern, edge – which we might call the true Wenlock Edge – is relatively low here: both the descent, on the way to Rushbury, and the climb back up, after re-crossing the old railway, are quite short. But then the 'secondary' edge – sometimes called View Edge – rears up, and the route climbs almost to the summit of Middlehope Hill, its second highest point. (The highest is Callow Hill, the site of Flounder's Folly).

On the gentler southeastern slope, you'll find Little London. There's both a house of that name and a separate Little London Farm, through which the walk passes. The name is actually a fairly common one for farms in the Marches and Wales because cattle drovers had a habit of naming overnight stopping places after their final destination.

Rushbury, which you pass through early in the walk, is a small village, but it's the centre of an extensive parish. There's some evidence of Roman occupation in the area, coins and other artefacts having been found near the church in the 19th century. Roman stone may also have been used in the building of St Peter's Church. There is firmer evidence of Norman occupation, including the remains of a motte, which you pass as you reach the village. The church has some herringbone masonry (probably Saxon) as well as much that is Norman. There are also some fine half-timbered houses, notably Church Farm, which is well seen from the road through the village.

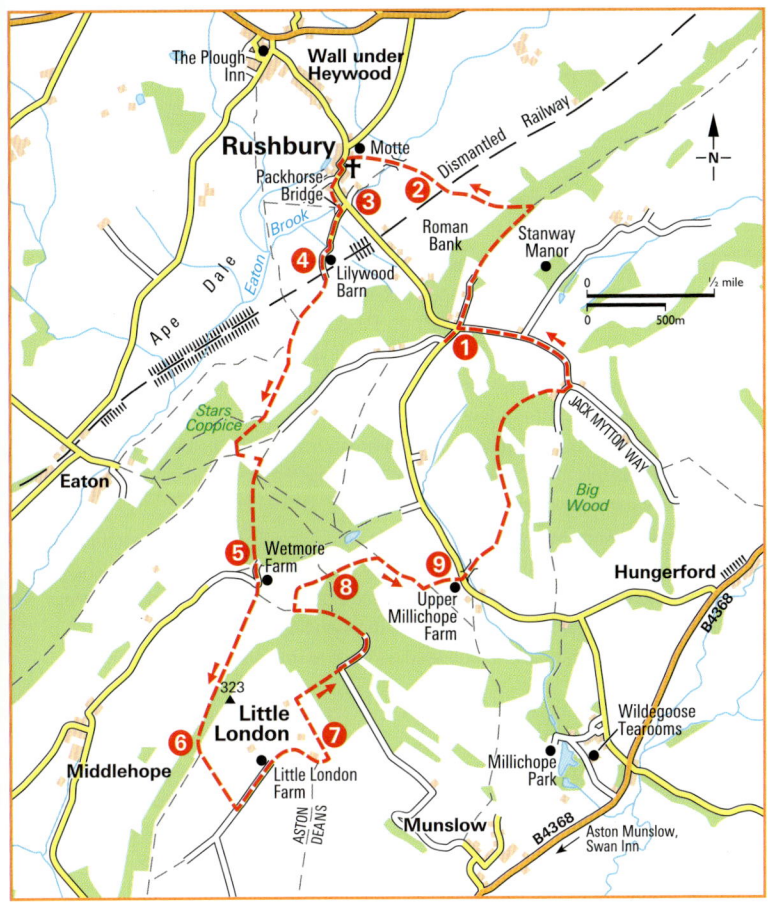

1. Walk to the bend in the road, go right then immediately left on a stony track. Walk into National Trust woodland at Roman Bank, then descend and turn left at a footpath sign. The path slants down the steep face of Wenlock Edge. Emerge into a field, follow the right-hand hedge briefly, then continue ahead past a tree to a gap in the hedge partway down. Bear left to a stile in a hedge, then cross the old railway.

2. Cross the next field to a hedge corner. Continue with the hedge on the right, cross a bridge and follow the right-hand field edge. Pass a house, cross a stile and pass the remains of the motte on your left before meeting a lane. Turn left, walk through Rushbury, then descend.

3. Just before a brook turn right on a track beside a new house. Take a green path alongside the brook, cross the packhorse bridge and follow a short track to a lane. Turn right. After Lilywood Barn the lane becomes a track.

4. Cross a bridge, enter a field and follow its right edge. In the third field cross the hedge at a waymark and resume on the other side. Continue to a gate and stile. A track climbs through a plantation to a gate. Climb to the left edge of another plantation, go through a gate and take the main track, ignoring branches left and right.

5. Leaving the wood, continue straight ahead, crossing another bridleway. Skirt Wetmore Farm, then bear slightly right past a dead tree to a bridle gate. Continue through the next field then climb steadily through woods. At the top the track bends left.

6. Go straight down, ignoring a track on the right, to meet a tarmac track. Go left, pass the derelict sheds of Little London Farm, then in 200yds (183m) bear right at a way-marked gate. Follow a hedged path, turn left at a T-junction, and find a stile on the left just after emerging from trees.

7. Go straight up until almost level with a house on the left. Turn right to a stile. Go straight ahead on a forest track, ignoring side turnings but following the track as it curves left and descends. Pass a field on the right then cross a stile and descend the field, trending right to find ruins by a large yew.

8. Go right in front of these, through a gap, past a blocked stile and through a gate into woodland. After a few paces turn left on a grassy track. Go straight over a cross-tracks, then turn right on a green track along field-edges. Follow these, curving left to pass left of Upper Millichope Farm. In the field corner follow waymarks alongside a stream to a lane.

9. Cross to a footbridge and go up the left field-edge. Continue up, switching sides at a gap and going through a narrow wood. Near the top, at a large oak, turn left across the slope to gates at the far side. Go straight ahead on a forest track, ignoring all side-tracks. Continue through fields to houses, turn left on a track and left again to join a lane leading back to Roman Bank.

Where to eat and drink

On the south side of Wenlock Edge there's the historic Swan Inn at Aston Munslow, an attractive timber-framed building with a good reputation for its home-cooked food. The Wildegoose Tearooms at Lower Millichope opens during the summer season serving light lunches and afternoon teas.

What to see

The lovely old packhorse bridge over Eaton Brook, Rushbury is a Grade II listed structure, and probably the only surviving bridge of its type in the county. Its date is uncertain, but the style is medieval. It was restored in 2002. Packhorse bridges are built with low parapets or none at all to allow easy passage to horses or mules carrying heavily laden panniers.

While you're there

Millichope Park at Munslow built in the 1830s and completed in 1840s is very much a family home, however the picturesque, landscaped garden is open to the public on various times of the year, (check for details).

ELIZABETHAN WILDERHOPE

DISTANCE/TIME	3 miles (4.8km) / 1hr 15min
ASCENT/GRADIENT	410ft (125m) / ▲
PATHS	Mostly excellent, need to ford shallow brook, many stiles
LANDSCAPE	Ridges and valleys at Hope Dale and Wenlock Edge
SUGGESTED MAP	OS Explorer 217 The Long Mynd & Wenlock Edge
START/FINISH	Grid reference: SO545928
DOG FRIENDLINESS	On lead in spring when ground-nesting birds have young, and near sheep
PARKING	National Trust car park at Wilderhope Manor
PUBLIC TOILETS	None on route

Wilderhope Manor belongs to the National Trust, but is leased to the Youth Hostels Association. It stands in Hope Dale between the twin ridges of Wenlock Edge and it's the best of several very fine houses in the area. It was built, around 1585, of the local limestone and has changed little in appearance since.

With its gables and its projecting, conical-roofed, semi-circular stair turret, it's an imposing sight. Lovely as it is, its setting is lovelier still. The Wilderhope Estate, which also belongs to the National Trust, is a glorious green jumble of wooded valleys, flower-rich meadows, ancient woodland and centuries-old hedgerows. The Trust has been acquiring sections of the Edge since 1982 and now cares for a fair-sized chunk of it. Management is aimed at maintaining its character and its wildlife interest while improving access for walkers. It's encouraging to see what a difference a little sympathetic management can make as the Trust removes conifers to allow native trees to regenerate and pursues environment-friendly farming methods, which allow wild flora and fauna to flourish.

The dominant species at Longville Coppice are ash and hazel, but there are others too, including small-leaved lime. This native lime is a far more attractive species than the hybrid lime planted in parks and gardens. Pollen records show it was one of the commonest trees of the original wildwood, but it is nationally scarce today (though locally common in places), and nobody really knows why. It may be because it grows mostly on well-drained, easily worked soils – the sort which would have been first cleared of trees by the earliest farmers. But this argument could apply to other species that have not become scarce. Lime foliage is also readily eaten by grazing animals.

Wenlock Edge is a classic example of what geographers call an escarpment. Its shape reflects the tilt of the underlying rock strata – in this case it's Much Wenlock limestone. You can hardly fail to notice as you follow this walk that the southeastern slope, on which Wilderhope Manor stands, is quite gentle, while the northwestern face, which you traverse as you walk through Longville Coppice, is much steeper. The gentler slope, roughly following the bedding of the limestone, is known as the dip slope while the steep edge, eroded across the strata, is the scarp slope. The pattern is repeated here in the secondary escarpment of View Edge, which you climb later in the walk. The rocks date from the Silurian period, around 430 million years ago. Geologists refer to this specific part of the greater Silurian as the Wenlock period.

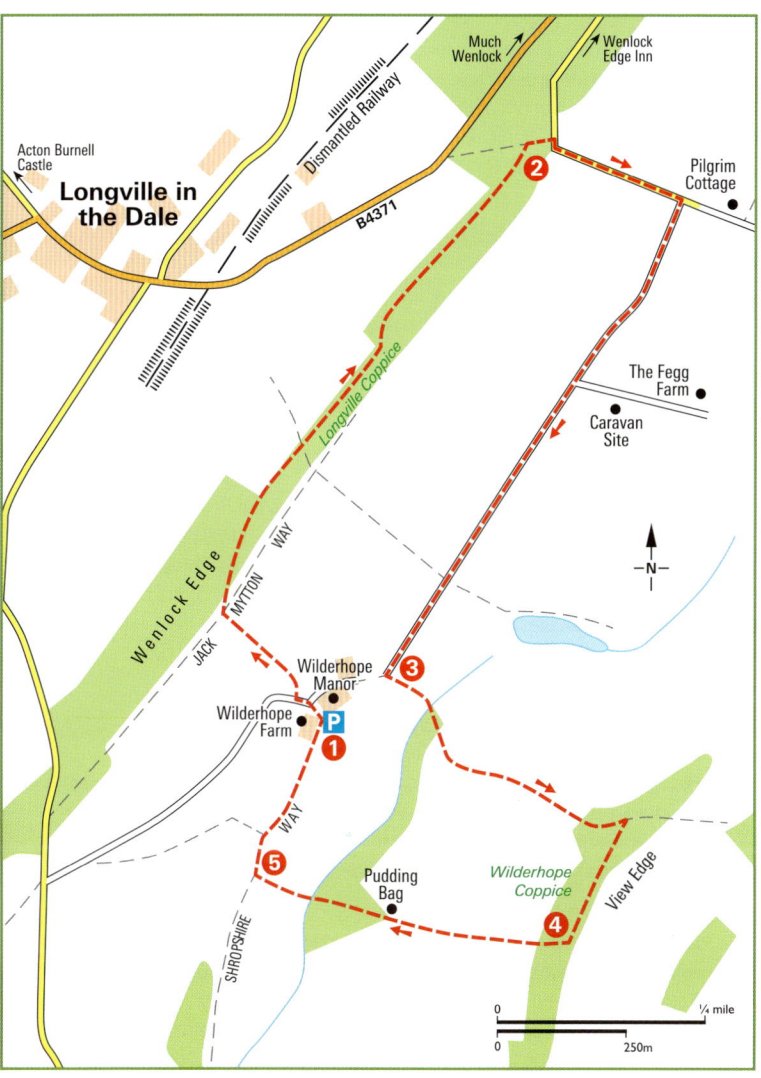

1. Go through a gate next to an old pump at the top of the car park. Go up a field to the top corner, then follow a hedge uphill to the crest of Wenlock Edge. Turn right at the top along the outer edge of Longville Coppice for about 50yds (46m). Turn left over a stile (National Trust signs for Longville Coppice Walk) and go down a stony path (slippery when wet). This soon bears right and

climbs gently. Ignore a crossing path and continue along this undulating track, carved across the steep scarp slope.

2. Go past a barrier at the far end of the coppice on to a sunken track, Pilgrims Lane. Climb this steeply to a junction and turn right on a lane. At the end of the tarmac, shortly before you reach Pilgrim Cottage, turn right on an obvious stony track. Pass the entrance to The Fegg Farm and a small caravan site. Ignore a stile on the left, where a path runs down towards a lake, and continue along the track with the tall chimneys of Wilderhope Manor appearing ahead.

3. As you approach the manor, fork left, then immediately turn left to go downhill on a wide green track. Ford a shallow brook and follow the path through trees, then uphill across two fields towards the top of View Edge (the eastern ridge of Wenlock Edge, not to be confused with the other View Edge near Craven Arms). Go through a gate into Wilderhope Coppice and turn right, still climbing, on a path that leads past beech trees.

4. After about 300yds (274m) fork right by a waymark post. Descend, then bear right down steps to leave the coppice at a stile. Walk down two fields to a meadow at the bottom, which is known as Pudding Bag. Go a few paces right to find a track which crosses the brook. Follow the track uphill to a junction.

5. Turn right on another track, joining the Shropshire Way. Walk past Wilderhope Farm to return to the car park by the manor.

Where to eat and drink

There is nowhere en route, but the Wenlock Arms Inn is not far away. It's a friendly pub/restaurant situated right on the apex of Wenlock Edge with views west down into Apedale and to the south towards Corvedale. Newly refurbished, this is a welcoming rural pub serving home cooked classic dishes and local ales.

What to see

The fields below Wilderhope Coppice are marked with a ridge-and-furrow pattern created by medieval ploughing. From the 9th century or so the open field system was developed, with the land divided into strips. Ploughing methods, using teams of oxen, shifted the soil to form a series of ridges, resulting in the pattern still visible today in many places. Where the open fields were later enclosed to form sheepwalks, the pattern survived. Modern ploughing, however, destroys it.

While you're there

Acton Burnell Castle (English Heritage) is now just a shell, but it's well worth a look. It was built in the 13th-century by Robert Burnell, Bishop of Bath and Wells and Lord Chancellor to Edward I. Close by are two stone gable-ends which are all that remain of a barn believed to have been the meeting place of the first English parliament at which the Commons were fully represented (1283). It met in Shrewsbury but then transferred to Acton Burnell. St Mary's Church, also built by Robert Burnell, is widely considered to be Shropshire's finest 13th-century building.

PILGRIMAGE TO MUCH WENLOCK

DISTANCE/TIME	6.25 miles (10.1km) / 2hr 30mins
ASCENT/GRADIENT	426ft (130m) / ▲
PATHS	Field paths, couple of boggy patches, many stiles
LANDSCAPE	Peaceful, pastoral country between Wenlock Edge and Severn Gorge
SUGGESTED MAP	OS Explorers 217 The Long Mynd & Wenlock Edge
START/FINISH	Grid reference: SO623998
DOG FRIENDLINESS	Keep under close control for much of walk
PARKING	Car park off St Mary's Lane in Much Wenlock
PUBLIC TOILETS	At car park and on Queen Street opposite main bus stop

Much Wenlock has been a market town for at least 700 years. It is a delightful little place, with charming old houses and a real working farm just off the High Street. There's something to see round every corner, so do take the time to explore fully. The town museum is a model of its kind and in the adjoining tourist information centre you can pick up an excellent leaflet that guides you round the main sights.

The town's crowning glory is St Milburga's Priory, now an English Heritage property. Much Wenlock originally developed because of the presence of a religious house, and the name Wenlock may come from the Celtic gwynloc, meaning white monastery. The Cluniac priory is in ruins today, but it was once a prosperous and powerful religious centre. It was built in the 12th and 13th centuries, but the first religious house on this site was an abbey founded around AD 680 by Merewalh, the son of King Penda of Mercia. He placed his daughter Milburga in charge in 682. Under her guidance the foundation flourished, and she was credited with miraculous works.

Milburga's abbey was destroyed around 874, possibly by a Danish raiding party, but in the 11th-century Earl Leofric and Countess Godiva of Mercia built a religious house on the same site, which was succeeded by a Cluniac priory founded by Roger de Montgomery after the Norman Conquest. Many of the existing buildings are almost entirely Early English in style and represent a rebuilding by Prior Humbert in the 13th century. Only a little Norman work survives from Earl Roger's time, but what does remain is superb, especially the decorative arcading in the chapter house and the carvings in the lavatorium (washroom). The entire scene is dominated by the towering gable of the priory church. Such grand ruins testify to the prosperity of the priory, which flourished until the Dissolution in 1540. It once drew wealth from a variety of interests, including a toll bridge on the Severn, mines, iron works, forestry and vast agricultural holdings.

Holy Trinity Church on Wilmore Street is also connected with the priory. It was founded around 680 as a place of worship for the nuns of Wenlock Abbey and was enlarged between 800 and 1050. The present nave was built around 1150 by the Cluniac monks of what had become St Milburga's Priory. Abbess Milburga was originally buried in Holy Trinity, but in 1101 her bones were transferred to the Priory and over the years many pilgrims came to worship at her shrine. A well bearing her name can still be found on Barrow Street, and people used to believe its water could cure eye diseases.

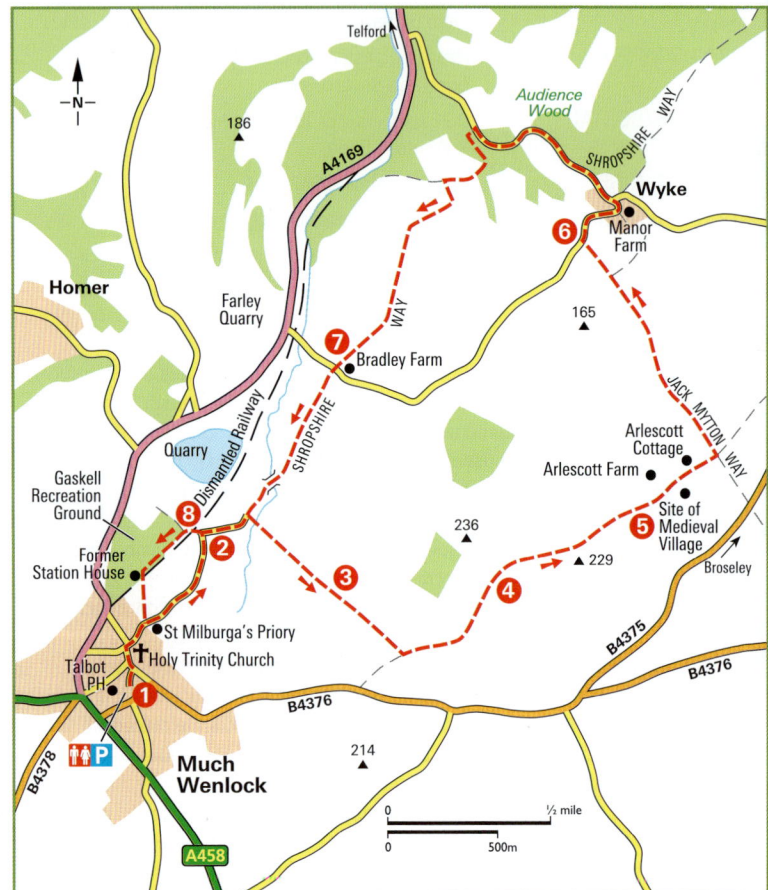

1. Go down Burgage Way, left on Mutton Shut and left again on The George Shut to High Street. Turn right to Barrow Street, then left along Wilmore Street. Pass the church, then turn first right on Bull Ring. Continue past the priory and along the lane.

2. Descend past a sewage works. At the bottom take a footpath on the right, cross a brook and follow the left-hand hedge. Where it bends left keep straight on to a stile in the far corner.

3. Follow the right edge of the next field then go along the far end to a gate through the hedge. Turn left, pass two big oaks, then follow an old field

boundary to the far corner and a stile. A path climbs through young woodland.

4. Emerge into a field. Follow the left edge, then a short hedged path. Follow a track beside a holly hedge. When it bends right keep straight on to Arlescott Farm.

5. Right of the farm, two gates lead into pasture. Turn left, towards Arlescott Cottage, and climb just right of it. Go through a gate on the left and follow Jack Mytton Way markers: watch for one pointing down left to a gap in a lower hedge. Turn right and continue to a lane.

6. Turn right, then left by Manor Farm in Wyke. Turn left again on a lane descending into a wooded valley. Turn left (Shropshire Way marker) on a stony track. Just below a house, bear left on a green track. In the first field, look for a waymark and go left to an isolated oak then turn right to a kissing gate. In the next field turn left. Cross another gate. When the rooftops of Bradley Farm and the Cavalier Centre appear, bear right towards them.

7. Go through two gates and follow the access track to a lane. Cross into a green track. Follow a field-edge then a well-trodden path diagonally across pasture. Cross a footbridge, skirt houses at Downsmill and soon meet the lane from Much Wenlock.

8. Go past the sewage works then keep straight on to join a dismantled railway. Turn left. After 300yds (274m) climb steps on the left to a fenced path, which passes the former station. Emerge near the priory, turn right and return to the start.

Where to eat and drink

You'll be spoiled for choice in Much Wenlock. Possibilities on High Street include The Talbot and the George and Dragon, both deservedly popular. The Talbot, which has been offering refreshments since 1361, has a lovely flower-filled courtyard. On the tea-shop front, there are several to choose from including the Barrow Street café which has a courtyard garden and allows dogs, or the Smoothie Café near the car park.

What to see

As you approach Arlescott Cottage you'll notice that the ground is marked by earthworks. These reveal the site of a deserted medieval village. Beyond the cottage, having joined the Jack Mytton Way, you'll see a ridge-and-furrow pattern, the result of medieval ploughing techniques. Beyond the ridge-and-furrow is a series of pronounced terraces. These are cultivation terraces, or strip lynchets, also the legacy of medieval (or possibly Celtic) farmers.

While you're there

Despite its industrial past, Broseley, 4 miles (6.4km) northeast of Much Wenlock, is another charming small town. For around 350 years it specialised in making clay pipes, which were known as Broseley Churchwardens. The wonderfully preserved Broseley Pipeworks is now a museum, (part of the Ironbridge collection of museums) and it looks much as it did the day the last pipe-maker laid down his tools in 1957.

CLIVE AND THE GRINSHILL CLIFF

DISTANCE/TIME	5.25 miles (8.4km) / 2hrs
ASCENT/GRADIENT	540ft (165m) / ▲
PATHS	Rocky, woodland and field paths, mostly well used, 2 stiles
LANDSCAPE	Sandstone outcrop, old quarries and gentle farmland
SUGGESTED MAP	OS Explorer 241 Shrewsbury
START/FINISH	Grid reference: SJ525237
DOG FRIENDLINESS	Corbet Wood is the best place for dogs to run free
PARKING	Car park in Corbet Wood, next to Grinshill Quarry
PUBLIC TOILETS	None on route

The north Shropshire plain is broken at intervals by battered ridges of red sandstone rising dramatically above the sea of green lapping at their feet. Highest and finest of them all is Grinshill Hill, a craggy lump of rock held in the grip of gnarled Scots pines and graceful silver birches existing on the thinnest of soils. It's an exciting, almost Tolkienesque sort of place, with spectacular abandoned quarries and deeply sunken hollow ways.

On its slopes stand Clive and Grinshill, both built of Grinshill stone, which has been quarried since Roman times. The stone was used for some of the grandest Victorian building projects, including several railway stations, of which Shrewsbury is a superb example. It is still quarried today, but the modern workings don't impinge on this walk. Clive is a particularly attractive village, with pretty cottages clustered below All Saints' Church. This is a Victorian rebuild but is more than redeemed by the power of its setting in a steeply sloping churchyard, overflowing with daffodils in March and offering fine views. The tall spire is a landmark for miles around.

William Wycherley, the Restoration dramatist and satirist, entertained the court of Charles II with his plays. His most famous work is *The Country Wife* (1675). Wycherley was born at Clive Hall (it's on the main street) in 1640. By all accounts, he was a dissolute rogue who chased young girls and shared one of Charles II's mistresses, Barbara Villiers, the Duchess of Cleveland. He also married the Countess of Drogheda for her money and must have been gratified when she died a year later, leaving everything to him. But it didn't do him much good because the will was contested, and the ensuing lawsuit bankrupted him. He was thrown into a debtors' prison which he endured for seven years until rescued by James II, who paid off his debts and gave him a pension. Wycherley married a young girl in 1716 when he was 75 but died 11 days later. His bones lie somewhere in the churchyard at Clive.

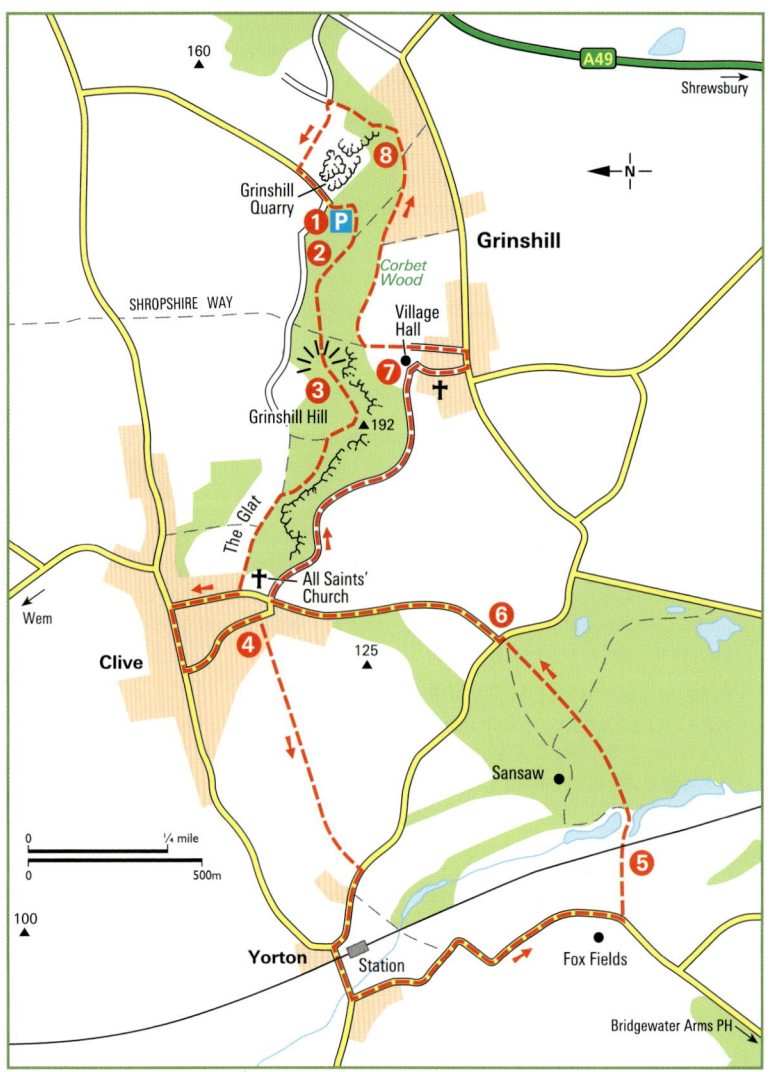

1. On the east side of the car park a bridleway starts near a stone building. Join this and shortly fork right to pass below the car park. Go straight on at a junction, passing an old sycamore tree with an amazing, exposed root system, then past a massive cliff-like slab of exposed rock.

2. When you reach a junction by another slab, keep to the bridleway, which descends left-ward. Watch out for an old wall which rises on the right, at right angles to the bridleway. Climb steeply just left of this wall and continue in the same direction, crossing the Shropshire Way, and up to a viewpoint.

3. Turn your back on the view and go uphill to join a wide path. Follow this to the left and keep left at a fork. Continue along the rising ridge to the summit. After enjoying the view, turn your back on it again and take the leftmost path. Keep left at a fork. The path joins a walled track (The Glat), which leads to All

Saints' Church at Clive. You could just turn left here, but to see more of Clive, and perhaps patronise the village shop, turn right instead, then soon left on the main street and left again on Back Lane.

4. Turn right on a track (signed 'Uplands'), which begins as gravel, then becomes a green lane. Continue along field-edges and cross a small pasture to a road. Turn right past Yorton Station, then left under the railway and left again. Soon after passing a house called Fox Fields, join a footpath on the left and cross a field and then the railway.

5. Meet a track. Turn right for a few paces, then left between two pools to enter parkland. Follow the left-hand boundary, passing Sansaw and going through an iron kissing gate next to a wooden field gate. Sansaw's garden wall now turns left – don't follow it but keep straight on to another wooden field gate. Cross a driveway and continue across more parkland to a road.

6. Turn left, then immediately right, towards Clive. Turn right opposite Back Lane on a walled bridleway, which passes below the churchyard and contours round Grinshill Hill to the Jubilee Oak and village hall at Grinshill.

7. Turn right along a track, passing the church to meet the main street. Turn left, then left again on Gooseberry Lane. Pass the village hall again (the other side this time) and rejoin the sunken bridleway. Ignore branching paths, staying on the bridleway, which rises to meet a walled grassy track. Follow this past houses.

8. As the track forks, go left and at once up steps to cross a stone step stile. Walk up through trees, soon bearing right and climbing steeply until you come to a fence and 'Keep Out' sign. Turn right along the fence, then turn left on a track, and left again at the road, past Grinshill Quarry to the car park.

Where to eat and drink

The Bridgewater Arms pub located in Harmer Hill, 4km away, is an ideal place to sample tasty pub food, local cask ales and classic cocktails; there is something for everyone here.

What to see

A variety of birds inhabits Corbet Wood, including the tiny goldcrest, Britain's smallest species (the firecrest is the same size but extremely rare). The goldcrest is plump and short tailed, olive-green above and buff below, with a distinctive black and yellow crown. Listen for a shrill, insistent zee-zee-zee call.

While you're there

Visit Moreton Corbet Castle (English Heritage). The keep of a Norman castle (c1200) stands beside the ruins of a magnificent house built around 1579 for Sir Andrew Corbet. Cromwell's troops besieged and slighted the two in 1644. They spared the church, which stands close by, completing a splendid group.

MERRINGTON GREEN AND WEBSCOTT RIDGE

DISTANCE/TIME	5.5 miles (8.8km) / 2hrs 15min
ASCENT/GRADIENT	344ft (105m) / ▲
PATHS	Field paths and bridleway, can be muddy, many stiles
LANDSCAPE	Farmland, medieval common, sandstone ridge with reclaimed quarries, panoramic views
SUGGESTED MAP	OS Explorer 241 Shrewsbury
START/FINISH	Grid reference: SJ465208
DOG FRIENDLINESS	Under control at Myddle, Merrington and Webscott
PARKING	Car park at Merrington Green Nature Reserve
PUBLIC TOILETS	None on route

The main highlights of this walk are the former quarries at Webscott and the nature reserve managed by Shropshire Wildlife Trust at Merrington Green. It's a story of contrast. Webscott is a relatively new landscape created by nature taking over a post-industrial site. Since quarrying ceased, the holes so crudely gouged out of the sandstone have been colonised by mosses, ferns and trees. The effect is delightful. Merrington Green, on the other hand, is a very old landscape which can be maintained only by human management, otherwise nature will turn it into just another woodland.

Of course, it would have been woodland originally, but in the Middle Ages it was cleared. At that time, nearly every village would have had a similar patch of land where commoners could graze stock, collect firewood and dig marl or turf. Such a system results in a range of habitats, which is often of ecological value. Merrington Green is still a registered common, but the commoners no longer exercise their rights, which means scrub is encroaching. It is controlled by hand as far as possible, but the reintroduction of grazing would be a better way.

One of the most valuable aspects of the green is the presence of three pools which have formed in old marl pits. An incredible 17 species of dragonfly and damselfly have been recorded here, making this easily Shropshire Wildlife Trust's top dragonfly location. The easternmost pool is fringed by marsh horsetail, a descendant of the giant horsetails of the primeval swamps, where the first dragonflies evolved over 300 million years ago. The largest species of dragonfly ever known is preserved in the fossil record from this time – it had a wingspan the size of a sparrowhawk's. Modern dragonflies are much smaller and a miniature miracle of design. If you get to see a resting dragonfly it's worth studying it in detail to appreciate the lethal beauty of these precision-built killing machines. Typically, an adult dragonfly will live only a few weeks, but in that time it will consume large numbers of insects, caught on the wing. Its aerial acrobatics can be spectacular and its wings beat 30 times a second, allowing a dazzling range of manoeuvres. The adult stage is preceded by two or three years spent under water as a nymph, in which form the insect is also a consummate predator. When a nymph is ready to metamorphose, it climbs out of the water onto a suitable plant. The ugly larval skin splits and a jewel-coloured adult emerges, crumpled at first, until it dries off and its wings inflate.

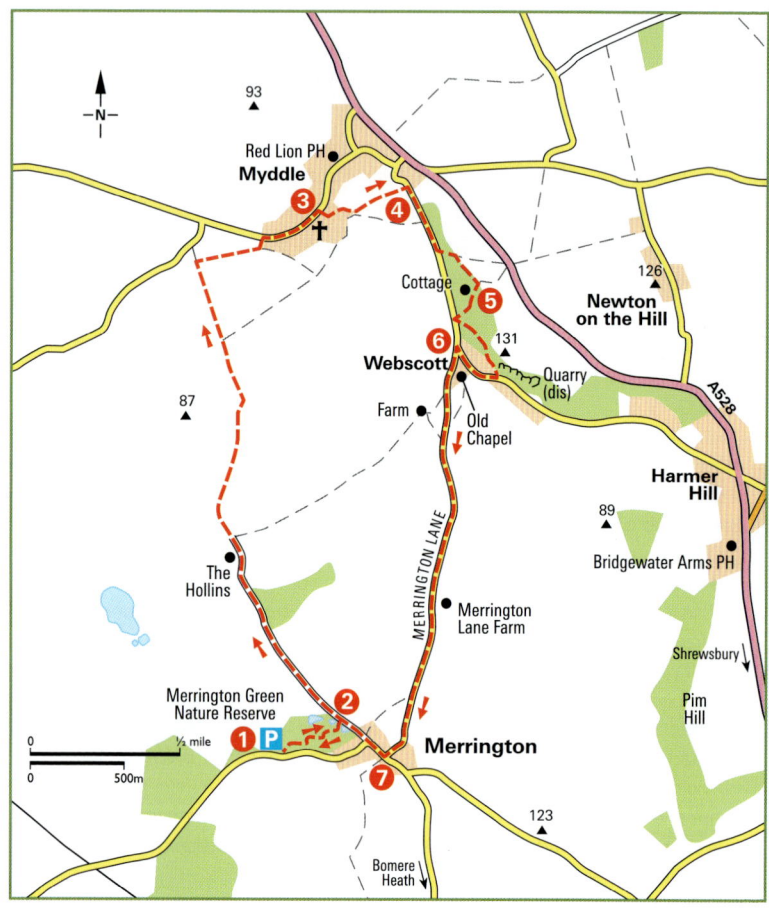

1. Take the right-hand path from the car park. Keep to the clearest path and go left at a fork, through tall bracken in summer. The path becomes clearer in woodland. Pass a pool, keeping it to your left. In the open again, turn left, back into the trees. Pass another pool (notice the difference in water levels) and continue to meet a clear track.

2. Turn left on the tree-bordered track, which runs for nearly 2 miles (3.2km). As you approach a road, look for a gate set back on the right (at a bend). Turn right and go straight across towards a white house. Meet the road on the edge of Myddle. Turn right into the village.

3. After passing the church, turn right on a walled lane, then go through a gate on the left. Pass left of farm buildings, crossing two stiles. Go straight ahead through a field to a footbridge then up to a stile and lane.

4. Turn right for 400yds (366m), then join a footpath on the left, up a wooded slope. At the top a well-trodden path turns right by the woodland edge. In theory, the right of way goes diagonally across a field to the road, but this can be impassable.

5. Either double-back from the road or simply follow everyone else along the wood's edge to a corner. Go through a gate and descend through the trees, then through a garden (dogs on lead) and past a cottage towards the lane. Just before you reach it, join another path on the left, back up the slope. Around 40yds (37m) before a stile at the top, turn right, then left, descending through a former quarry. At the bottom fork left, continue to the lane and turn right.

6. At the next junction turn left (signed 'Bomere Heath') continue along the lane for 1.1miles (1.8km). In theory there's a footpath about 100yds (91m) before the next junction that cuts off the corner, but stiles are currently overgrown, if so carry on along the lane. However, keep an eye open in case of improvements.

7. Eventually turn right at a T-junction at Merrington. When the road bends left, go straight on along a track (the same one you used earlier) until you join a path that crosses the nature reserve to the car park.

Where to eat and drink
The Red Lion at Myddle is an historic public house dating back to the 17th century. It has reopened after a two year renovation project and serves food daily and has a selection of real ales from local breweries.

What to see
As you start down the lane near Point 6, notice the former Primitive Methodist Chapel on your left. It's tiny (only two window bays) and looks as if it has been used as a garage in the not too distant past.

While you're there
In 1403, Henry IV defeated the Yorkists at the Battle of Shrewsbury. The site is simply called Battlefield, and there's a church there named after St Mary Magdalene, just to the north of Shrewsbury off the A49. It was built on the King's orders after the battle, and eight chaplains were installed to pray for the dead. It's very atmospheric, even when the church itself is closed.

ALONG THE WITTERAGE FROM MYDDLE

DISTANCE/TIME	5 miles (8km) / 2hrs
ASCENT/GRADIENT	289ft (88m) / ▲
PATHS	Clear field paths, quiet lanes and byway, many stiles
LANDSCAPE	Rolling farmland, gently elevated above surrounding plain
SUGGESTED MAP	OS Explorer 241 Shrewsbury
START/FINISH	Grid reference: SJ504238
DOG FRIENDLINESS	Mostly arable land and enclosed tracks, but livestock may be met anywhere
PARKING	Scattered small lay-bys either side of railway near Yorton Station
PUBLIC TOILETS	None on route

For much of the course of this walk you'll be guided by 'Gough Walk' waymarks. The Gough Walks are a series of six walks created by local people to commemorate Richard Gough (1635–1723), a yeoman farmer who lived at Newton Farm, Newton on the Hill. In the years 1700–1702 he wrote two books, *Antiquities and Memories of the Parish of Myddle*, and *Observations concerning the seats in Myddle Church and the families to which they belong*. Sometimes bound together as *The History of Myddle*, these provide one of the most complete accounts of rural life in England at the dawn of the 18th century. Although they are not currently in print, a Folio Society edition was produced in the 1980s, and digital versions can be found online.

The tiny hamlet of Newton on the Hill clearly has a strong sense of identity and history. An unusual and impressive token of this is the slate plaque on the wall by the postbox, listing the householders here in AD 2000. As this shows, there were then eight households. Another house has been added more recently – almost a population explosion!

Something you'll often notice on this walk, especially at weekends, is a steady traffic of light aircraft passing overhead. These are going to or coming from Sleap Airfield (pronounced 'Slape'), whose nearest runway extends to about 0.75 miles (1.2km) north of Witterage Green. The airfield was constructed during World War II and used mainly for training bomber crews, and later to train glider crews preparing to drop paratroopers in the D-Day landings and at Arnhem. It is still used as a relief field for nearby RAF Shawbury, and today it is also home to the very active Shropshire Aero Club.

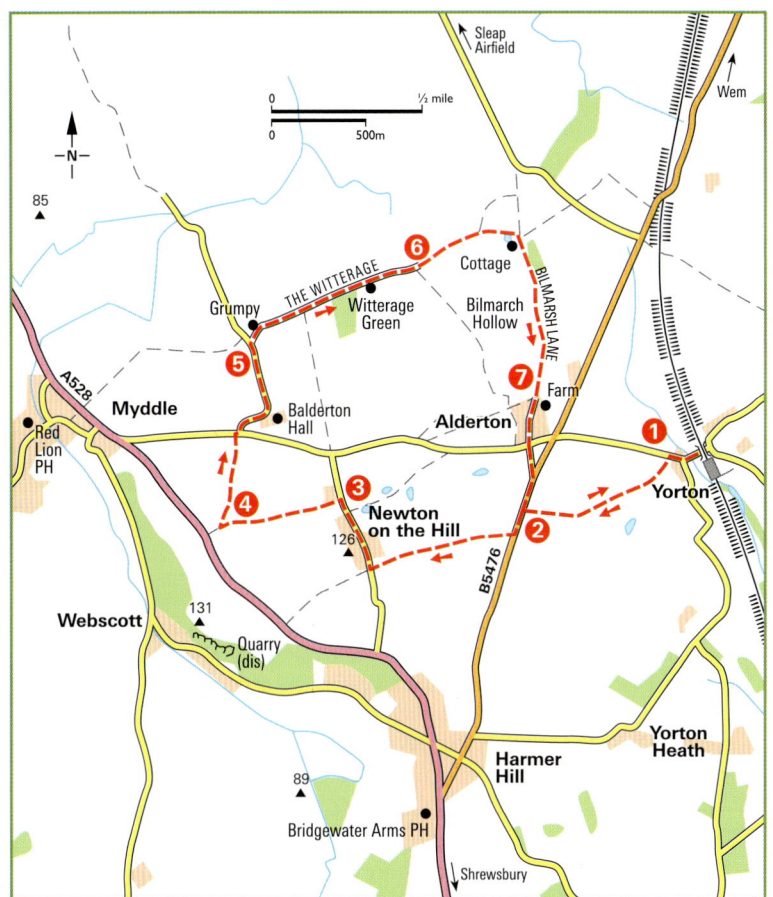

1. Walk past the triangular green in Yorton, then turn left up a track alongside No. 1. Continue with a fence on your left and a hedge on your right. At the crest of the rise the fence ends. Cross a stile under an ash tree to enter the field on the right and follow its left edge to the B5476.

2. Turn left for 150yds (137m) to a stile on the right. Follow the footpath across a field to a footbridge. Follow the right edge of the next field then skirt left round trees enclosing a pond (barely visible in summer). Go through a gateway by a disused drinking-trough to join a track between hedges. Emerge to a lane. Turn right and walk through Newton on the Hill.

3. Immediately before the last two houses on the left, turn left over a stile with a Gough Walk waymark. Go half-left to another stile then follow a line of trees down the right edge of the field. Cross a stile into a large field and follow its right-hand edge. Pass a clump of pine trees to a gate in the corner.

4. Go forward to two trees by a pond then turn right to a stile on the skyline, which has good views of the plains to the Welsh hills. Go straight down the next field to a stile. Meet a road and go right a few paces then left on a lane signed 'Houlston'.

5. After about 600yds (549m), as the lane bends gently to the left, a stony bridleway (The Witterage) forks right. The house in the fork is Grumpy. Follow the bridleway, which soon bends to the right. After passing a cottage at Witterage Green it becomes sandy and then enters a leafy tunnel, where it can be muddy.

6. As the track ends, a gate leads into a field. A notice refers to concessionary rights of way; in fact, an existing footpath has been upgraded to bridleway status. All you need to do is keep on in much the same direction, following the right-hand boundary through two fields. Go through a gate in the corner of the second field, pass a cottage, then turn right along a lovely old track, Bilmarsh Lane.

7. Pass a farm on the left and continue to a road in the hamlet of Alderton. The shortest route back to Yorton station now is to turn left then go straight over a crossroads on the B5476. However, to minimise road-walking, go straight ahead instead, with Broughton Cottages on your left. When you meet the B5476, continue for about 150yds (137m), then turn left, over a stile crossed on the outward route, and retrace your steps down the fields.

Where to eat and drink

There are pubs at Myddle and at Harmer Hill, but a more unusual choice would be the Sleap Airfield café in the World War II control tower building at Sleap Airfield. It's open daily, and serves snacks and hot meals, and its balcony gives a great view of comings and goings on the airfield. The full English breakfast will start your day off well.

What to see

Bilmarsh Lane is so level and so deeply incised into the land that it feels almost like an old railway cutting, but it's actually an ancient track and a fine example of a 'hollow way'; there are few better places to get a sense of what the term really means. It's sometimes shortened to 'holloway' and may be origin of the name Holloway for a district of London. True hollow ways are not deliberately excavated but eroded over time by the passage of carts and livestock.

While you're there

Sleap Airfield is also home to the museum of the Wartime Aircraft Recovery Group. The accelerated training process for aircrew during the dark days of World War II inevitably led to mishaps, often fatal, and Sleap saw several such crashes. It's therefore a fitting base for this volunteer group, which investigates crash sites, to be a memorial to pilots that gave their lives operating in the Shropshire area during World War II. The displays include a number of aero engines, and a reconstruction of an airfield Flight Office. The museum is open at weekends from May to October. (Since the museum is run entirely by volunteers it would be advisable to phone the airfield when planning a visit to avoid disappointment).

SHREWSBURY AND THE RIVER SEVERN

DISTANCE/TIME	6 miles (9.7km) / 2hrs
ASCENT/GRADIENT	110ft (33m)
PATHS	Streets and riverside path, impassable in floods
LANDSCAPE	Riverside meadows on edge of town
SUGGESTED MAP	OS Explorer 241 Shrewsbury
START/FINISH	Grid reference: SJ498123
DOG FRIENDLINESS	Lots of local dogs by river, some pavement pounding
PARKING	Abbey Foregate car park opposite Shrewsbury Abbey
PUBLIC TOILETS	At town end of Abbey Foregate

Poet A E Housman wrote that Shrewsbury was 'islanded in Severn stream', and there has never been a better description. The Saxon town was built within the natural moat provided by a tight loop of the Severn, completely encircled except for a small gap, making a perfect defensive site. Even the gap was guarded by a ridge, on which a castle was later built. As it moves away from the town, the Severn continues its crazy meandering and the walk described here is contained within a series of loops to the east of the historic town centre.

You can hardly miss Shrewsbury Abbey, but the Abbey Church that survives today was once part of a much larger complex, with a full range of monastic buildings. Following the dissolution of the monasteries (1536–40) by Henry VIII, the church survived as a parish church, and some of the other buildings continued in use until 1827, when Thomas Telford drove his Holyhead road through the site, proving that the vandalism of road builders is nothing new. The Abbey Church of St Peter and St Paul was founded in 1083 by Roger de Montgomery on the site of an earlier Saxon church, just outside the town walls. The most striking part of the present building is the great west tower, built in the 14th century during the reign of Edward III. Shrewsbury Abbey is the setting for the popular Cadfael novels by Ellis Peters (the pen name of the late Edith Pargeter).

There are buildings from all periods along Abbey Foregate, but Georgian is the dominant style, with an abundance of beautiful brick town houses. Shrewsbury saw extraordinary growth in the second half of the 18th century and it was then that Abbey Foregate was developed as a desirable residential suburb.

Lord Hill's Column is a sky-high tower of Grinshill stone erected in 1816 to honour the military achievements of Viscount Hill, who fought with Wellington at Waterloo. It is said to be the tallest Doric column in the world.

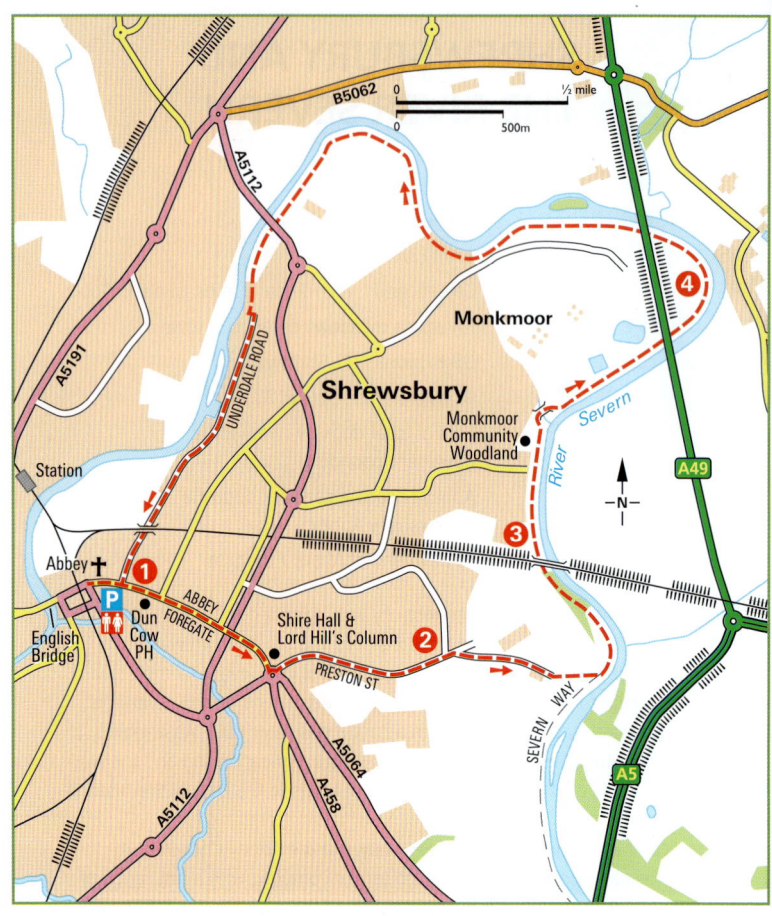

1. Walk along Abbey Foregate away from town. Go as far as the Shire Hall (all too obviously a product of the 1960s) and Lord Hill's Column. Turn left by Lord Hill, past the Crown Courts on Preston Street.

2. When the road bends left into Portland Crescent, keep straight on along a tarmac track, then take the right fork. When the track ends, the right of way remains well-defined, going straight down a field to the River Severn. Turn left on the Severn Way. After walking through a small wood, you'll soon pass under an impressive railway bridge, cast at Coalbrookdale Foundry in 1848, the year Shrewsbury acquired its first train service.

3. The path climbs to the edge of a housing estate and then runs along the edge of Monkmoor Community Woodland, where grassland has been planted with native trees. At the far side of this, a tributary stream blocks the way forward. Follow the obvious main path as it curves left, until you can cross the stream at a footbridge. Turn right to return to the river and continue towards the A49 bridge.

4. Pass under two road bridges, both carrying the A49. Soon you'll pass the suburb of Monkmoor, where Wilfred Owen lived as a boy. Pass under a third road bridge and continue on along the riverbank until the footpath turns left and emerges into a street. Turn right here and it will soon lead you back to the Abbey, through an interesting old quarter of town.

Where to eat and drink

Shrewsbury seems to have more enticing places to eat than almost any other town of its size. Even on the edge of town at Abbey Foregate there is an excellent choice. Pubs include the Dun Cow and the Crown Inn (near the Abbey). There are at least two Indian restaurants, and the Peach Tree café, bar (near the Abbey) is open from 8am for food. The choice is even wider in the town centre.

What to see

Beneath the trees behind the Abbey, you'll find a simple, moving granite memorial to the poet Wilfred Owen. Owen was born in Oswestry in 1893, the son of a railway worker, but the family moved to Monkmoor in 1907. They used to enjoy riverside walks most weekends, and on one occasion Wilfred noticed his brother's boots were covered in buttercup petals. He described them as 'blessed with gold'. Tragically, Owen was killed the week before the armistice in 1918. The memorial bears a line from one of his greatest poems, 'Strange Meeting': 'I am the enemy you killed, my friend.'

While you're there

Shrewsbury is packed with historic buildings and repays a lengthy exploration. One that's sometimes missed off the 'architecture trails' is the railway station. Opened in 1848, it was built in Tudor style to reflect the original Shrewsbury School building which overlooks it. There's wonderful attention to detail, notably in the large number of carved stone heads around the windows, not only on the façade but on the platform side too. They're worth a closer look for their very human character and expressions.

PANORAMIC VIEWS FROM LYTH HILL

DISTANCE/TIME	7.75 miles (12.5km) / 3hrs
ASCENT/GRADIENT	500ft (152m) / ▲
PATHS	Cross-field paths, mostly well-maintained, about 25 stiles
LANDSCAPE	Rolling farmland and views from Lyth Hill's grassy top
SUGGESTED MAP	OS Explorer 241 Shrewsbury
START/FINISH	Grid reference: SJ473069
DOG FRIENDLINESS	Must be on lead near livestock, also at Exfords Green
PARKING	Car park in country park at top of Lyth Hill (signposted)
PUBLIC TOILETS	None on route

Lyth Hill, which is included within a small country park, is of modest height, attaining only 557ft (169m). It's mainly grassland, with areas of scrub and woodland which support a variety of birds such as great spotted woodpecker, wood warbler and tree pipit. The country park is popular with local people, especially dog walkers, as it's within walking distance of Shrewsbury suburbs such as Bayston Hill and Meole Brace, and it's a good place for picnics or kite-flying. Most of all though, it's ideal for simply sitting back and enjoying the superb view, which is extraordinary, all the more so for coming as something of a surprise. It includes the Clee Hills, Wenlock Edge, The Wrekin, the Stretton Hills, Long Mynd and Stiperstones.

This view inspired Mary Webb, or Mary Gladys Meredith as she was born in 1881 at Leighton, a small village south of Shrewsbury. In 1902 she moved with her family to Meole Brace, where she lived until her marriage to Henry Webb in 1912. Mary was a great walker and during the years spent at Meole Brace it was Lyth Hill that was her favourite destination. She was enchanted not only by the view, but also by the small wood called Spring Coppice. In 1917, after the publication of her first novel, the Webbs bought a plot of land on the hill and Spring Cottage was built for them. This was Mary's home, apart from a short spell in London, until her untimely death in 1927. The cottage is still there today, but much altered and extended.

Mary wrote several novels at Spring Cottage, but she achieved very little fame in her lifetime. It was only after her death that posthumous praise from the prime minister, Stanley Baldwin, sparked off public interest and acclaim. Her best novels are considered to be *The Golden Arrow*, *Precious Bane* and *Gone to Earth* – the last two were made into a films and shot in Shropshire.

The interest in Mary's work waned and her novels are not fashionable today. Indeed, they're all too easy to make fun of and Stella Gibbons's classic Cold Comfort Farm was actually a parody of one of Mary's books (The House in Dormer Forest). But they are worth reading if you love Shropshire. Each is richly imbued with a strong sense of the local landscape.

Few writers have been so much in tune with their surroundings, or so able to convey its atmosphere. Mary adored Shropshire and it shows in her books. It's easy to see why she felt so passionate about it as you gaze out at the view from Lyth Hill, which she knew so well.

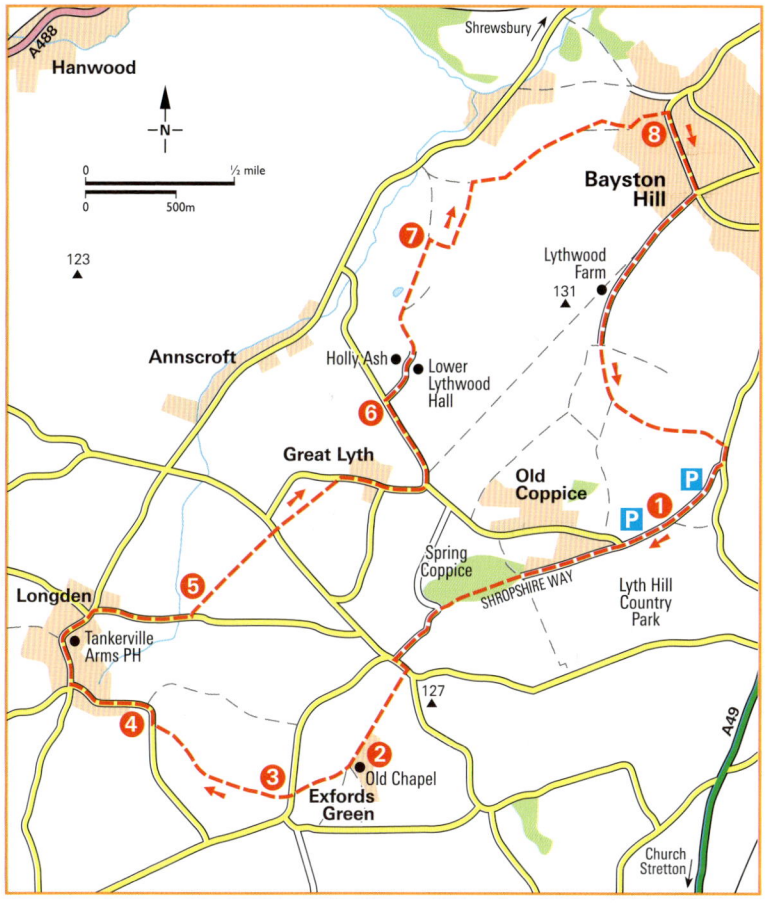

1. Head southwest on the Shropshire Way. Ignore a path branching right into Spring Coppice. The Way descends to a track. Follow this to a road, where you turn left, then first right, on a track to Exfords Green.

2. Fork right then follow a hedged path past a house and former chapel. Leave the Shropshire Way, going diagonally across a field to a stile near the far corner. Descend slightly and go through a copse to reach a lane.

3. Cross to a path almost opposite, following the left-hand edge of a field until a stile gives access to another. Head diagonally across to a stile and footbridge close to the far right corner. Continue across another field, past two oak trees. A worn path goes obliquely right across the next two fields to meet a lane.

4. Turn right, then right again at the main road. Pass through Longden. Go right again on School Lane; this descends slightly. Cross a brook, then cross a stile on the left and diagonally right across a field corner to a stile.

5. A yellow arrow directs you diagonally across the next field to a stile under an oak tree. Cross another field to reach a road. The path continues opposite, crossing two further fields until it meets a lane at Great Lyth. Turn right, keeping straight on at a junction, then turn left at the next.

6. Turn right on the access track to Lower Lythwood Hall and Holly Ash. At the end, turn left on a lush green lane. At its end turn right over a stile and cross a field. Pass left of three oak trees and keep to the right of a pond to reach a gate at the far side. Follow the edge of the next field past a gate and continue to another in the corner. Continue along a track for a few paces to a small gate on the right.

7. Walk up the right edge of the field and turn left along the top. Follow a worn path across a field to a hedge corner with a blocked gate. Continue along the hedge to a kissing gate, then along field-edges to enter a path behind houses.

8. Meeting a street, turn immediately right on a fenced path, then straight ahead on a street. Keep straight on at a crossroads and at the end turn right then first left (Bredden Way). At the top turn right then left by a postbox through trees to a lane. Turn right to Lythwood Farm. Go straight through then fork left and follow the track across fields. Cross the last field aiming left of a small reservoir. Emerge to a lane and turn right, back to Lyth Hill.

Where to eat and drink

The Tankerville Arms at Longden has hand-pulled traditional ales, which you can enjoy indoors or in the walled beer garden. A useful village shop and post office stands close by, for stocking up on chocolate and crisps. The Three Fishes, on the A49 in Bayston Hill, is a friendly pub serving good ale and food.

What to see

Take a look at the craggy rocks near the viewpoint, at the top of the hill, near the car park. At first glance they look a little like concrete, but a closer inspection reveals that they are actually formed from conglomerate, which is composed of rounded pebbles embedded in a sandy matrix. This is a Precambrian sedimentary rock dating from around 650 million years ago.

While you're there

If you'd like to know more about Mary Webb, you might enjoy the excellent museum at the visitor information centre (closed on Mondays) in Much Wenlock. Naturally, the focus is on Wenlock itself, but there is also lots about the Shropshire novelist, including a fascinating display of photographs of the filming of *Gone to Earth* in 1950. Kids needn't despair at the idea of a museum – there's plenty for them too.

ELLESMERE – MERES, MOSSES AND MORAINES

DISTANCE/TIME	7.25 miles (11.7km) / 3hrs
ASCENT/GRADIENT	180ft (55m) / ▲
PATHS	Field paths and canal towpath
LANDSCAPE	Pastoral hills with glacial hollows containing small lakes. Torch may be useful for Ellesmere Tunnel
SUGGESTED MAP	OS Explorer 241 Shrewsbury
START/FINISH	Grid reference: SJ407344
DOG FRIENDLINESS	Can run free on towpath, but under tight control elsewhere
PARKING	Castlefields car park opposite The Mere
PUBLIC TOILETS	Cross Street Car Park in the centre of Ellesmere

Ellesmere is a delightful little Shropshire town. It's well worth devoting some time to exploring it. But Ellesmere's biggest asset must be The Mere, the largest of all the meres that grace north Shropshire and south Cheshire. It attracts water birds and is important for winter migrants such as wigeon, pochard, goosander and teal. It also has a large heronry occupied by breeding birds in spring and early summer.

On this walk you will explore about half of The Mere's shoreline and follow the towpath of the Llangollen Canal past Cole Mere and Blake Mere. Cole Mere is included within a country park and there is access from the towpath at Yell Bridge (No. 54). To explore Cole Mere, walk all the way round it. Blake Mere is particularly lovely; it's separated from the towpath only by a narrow strip of woodland, but there is no other access to it.

Mere is an Anglo-Saxon word for a lake. Unlike a normal lake, however, these meres have no stream flowing in or out of them. So how were they formed? What follows here is a simplified version. During the last ice age, the landscape was scoured by glaciers and when they retreated between 10,000 to 12,000 years ago, they left clay-lined hollows which retained melting ice, forming some of the meres. Others filled up later because they lay below the level of the water table. Water levels are maintained by natural drainage (groundwater percolation) from the surrounding countryside.

The landscape is composed of gentle hills that, with the meres, form a pleasing scene. It consists of glacial drift, a mixture of clays, sands and gravels originally scoured from rocks by the glaciers and then deposited in banks and mounds known as moraines as the glaciers retreated. In places, you can identify the origins of the glacial drift. Blue-black pebbles are slates from Snowdonia or Cumbria, and pale, speckled stones are granites from Cumbria or Scotland, while pink pebbles are from the local sandstone. These glacial meres are unique in this country and rare in global terms.

North Shropshire is also renowned for its mosses, which were created by the glaciers too, but they are filled with peat rather than water. The wonderful moss at Whixall is well known, but there are several small mosses around Ellesmere too, though none with public access. The meres and mosses together form a wetland complex which, ecologically, is of national if not international significance.

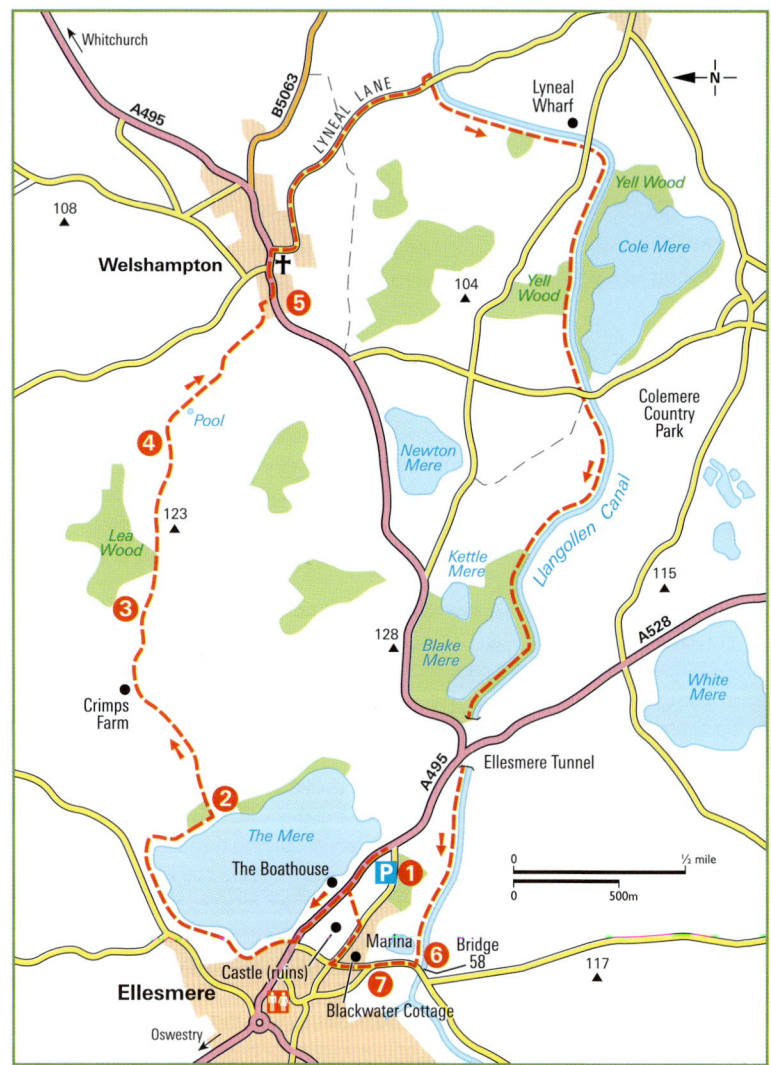

1. Cross to The Mere and turn left. Pass The Boathouse and walk towards town, until you come to Cremorne Gardens. Join a path signed 'Woodland Walk' that runs through trees close by the water's edge for about 0.75 miles (1.2km).

2. Ignore paths going left until you meet one signposted 'Welshampton'. The fenced path soon joins a track. Ignore a turn to the right, marked 'Private Road'. Just before Crimps Farm turn right on another track.

3. The track leads into pasture. Go straight on, guided by waymarkers and gates. Go through a field with a vegetation-choked pool in it and then aim for three prominent trees close together at the far side. As you approach them, bear left into the field corner.

4. Go through a gate and descend by the right-hand hedge. When it turns a corner, go with it, to the right. Skirt a marshy pool then keep right to a kissing gate in the hedge (easily missed). Follow the hedge left and soon join a clear track. This leads to a farm where you join a road.

5. Turn left into Welshampton. Go past a church and turn immediately right on Lyneal Lane. Follow it to a bridge over the Llangollen Canal. Descend steps to the towpath and turn right, passing under the bridge. Pass Lyneal Wharf, Cole Mere, Yell Wood and Blake Mere, then go through Ellesmere Tunnel. Beyond this are three footpaths signposted to The Mere. Take any of these short cuts if you wish, but to see a bit more of the canal, including the visitor moorings and marina, stay on the towpath.

6. Arriving at Bridge 58, further choices present themselves. You could extend this walk to include the signposted Wharf Circular Walk (recommended) or to explore the town (also recommended): just follow the signs. To return directly to The Mere, however, go up to the road and turn right.

7. Fork right on a road marked 'Unsuitable for HGV'. Turn right at the top, then soon left at Rose Bank, up steps. Walk across the earthworks of the long-gone Ellesmere Castle and follow signs for The Mere or the car park.

Where to eat and drink

There is plenty of choice in Ellesmere. Special mention goes to Vermuelen's bakery/deli where you can buy the ingredients for a picnic. Or there's The Boathouse by The Mere, an attractive, large café with a good range of snacks and drinks on offer, and dogs are welcome in the garden, which borders The Mere. Afternoon tea (booked in advance) can be enjoyed overlooking the breathtaking Mere.

What to see

Many bird species can be seen, but one of the most endearing is the great crested grebe. This distinctive diving bird is nearly always present on the larger meres. You can recognise it by the crest on top of its head. In spring it has cute, stripy chicks which it sometimes carries on its back to give them a rest from all that paddling.

While you're there

While The Mere is the highlight of Ellesmere, it would be a shame not to explore the town, especially the refurbished canal wharves and basin. There's lots to see, including the offices from which Thomas Telford directed the construction of the canal. Ellesmere was the headquarters of the Llangollen Canal (originally called the Ellesmere Canal) and so there are former workshops, warehouses and dry docks, while British Waterways still has an office and maintenance depot here.

WHITTINGTON CASTLE TO LLANGOLLEN CANAL

DISTANCE/TIME	6 miles (9.7km) / 2hrs 30min
ASCENT/GRADIENT	Negligible
PATHS	Tow path, lanes and field paths, some overgrown, many stiles
LANDSCAPE	Low-lying farmland, pastoral and arable, attractive canal
SUGGESTED MAP	OS Explorer 240 Oswestry
START/FINISH	Grid reference: SJ325312
DOG FRIENDLINESS	Can run free on towpath, probably nowhere else
PARKING	Car park next to Whittington Castle
PUBLIC TOILETS	At castle when open

The name Llangollen Canal is relatively recent; originally it was called the Ellesmere Canal, and later became part of the Shropshire Union system. The earliest stretch to be built was the one running southwest from Frankton to the important limestone quarries at Llanymynech, which was opened in 1796. This was later linked to the Montgomery Canal, and that name was applied to the entire 35-mile (56km) stretch from Frankton Junction to Newtown, Powys, which was completed in 1819.

The Ellesmere Canal was extended to Llangollen, and a northern branch was planned via Ruabon, which would have ultimately linked the Dee and Mersey to the Severn at Shrewsbury, but this was never built. It was only when canal-boating for pleasure took off in the later 20th century that it was renamed the Llangollen Canal. Its most famous landmark is the great aqueduct at Pontcysyllte, which carries the canal in an iron trough 120ft (37m) in the air. Although the canal negotiates some hilly country, the only locks between Frankton and Llangollen are the two at New Marton.

You can hardly miss Whittington Castle, right at the start of the walk. Uniquely, it is owned and run by a local community trust, which acquired a 99-year lease in 1999. Castles are plentiful in these lands near the Welsh border, and though the site may not look particularly strategic at first glance, it was once largely surrounded by difficult marshes. Parts of the area are still poorly drained and remain susceptible to flooding; there's a glimpse of this in the later stages of the walk.

The castle began, like many others, as a Norman motte-and-bailey, built by William de Peverel. The fortress passed to his daughter and then by marriage to the Fitzwarine family, who rebuilt it in stone in the 13th century. After the defeat of the Welsh, the castle became neglected. Damage inflicted during the English Civil War was not repaired, apart from the 19th-century renovation of the gatehouse, until the Preservation Trust became active in the 1960s.

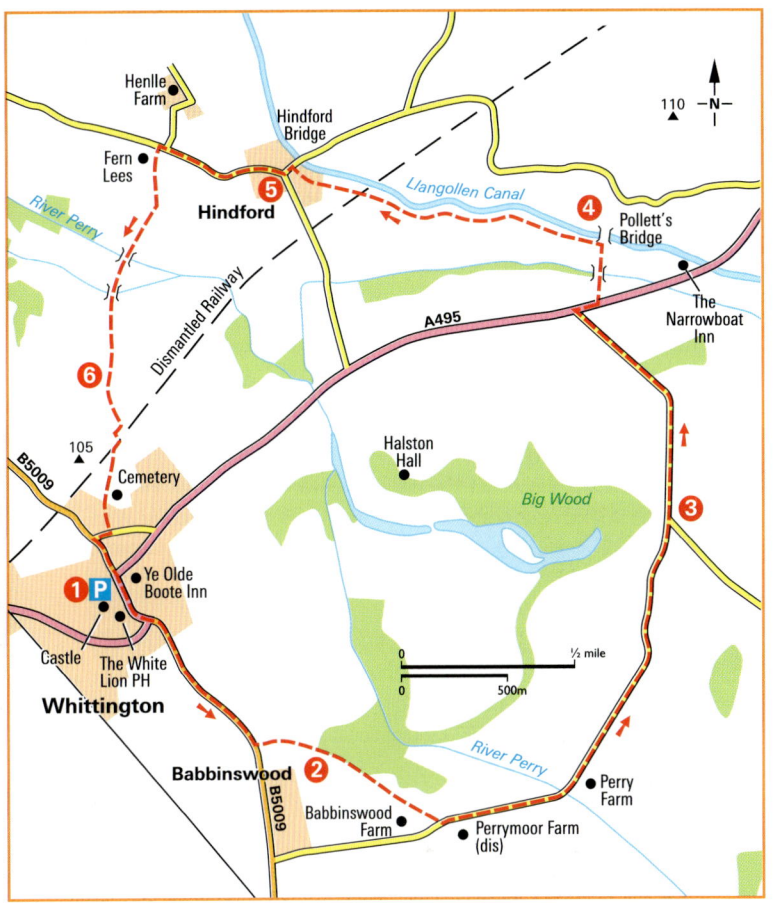

1. Cross a pedestrian crossing in front of the castle and follow the Shrewsbury road (B5009). Just before the Babbinswood speed limit signs, cross a stile on the left and follow a waymarked path across three fields to a corner by a copse.

2. Walk along a field-edge, with the copse on your left. Cross a gap in the corner, then go obliquely across another field as indicated by a waymarker. A prominent oak tree is a useful guide. There is a stile left of the tree, but you may have to fight through nettles to get to it. Cross the next field to a gate onto a lane and turn left.

3. Keep left at a junction and continue to the A495. Cross and turn right for about 70yds (63m) to a stile and footpath sign in the hedge. Go along the left-hand edge of a field to a stile and footbridge. Beyond these, keep going along the field edge until a gap in the hedge. Go through, then continue in the same direction as before, soon going up a bank.

4. Meet the canal at Pollett's Bridge (No. W6). Join the towpath and go under the bridge. Follow the tow path to Hindford Bridge (No. W11), then go up to a lane.

5. Turn left at Hindford Bridge, then right again, signposted 'Iron Mills and Gobowen'. After half a mile (800m), opposite a no-through road, go left over a stile. Walk down a paddock to the far end, then cross a stile on the right. Follow a fence to a footbridge, continue to another footbridge and keep straight on across marshy ground to a stile ahead. Cross the next field, aiming just left of a copse. Go through a gate and then left by a field-edge.

6. Join a track that soon bends right beside a dismantled railway. Look out for a stile giving access to the railway. Turn right on the former trackbed for a few paces, then up the bank on the left – watch out for the remains of steps concealed in the undergrowth here. Cross a stile to a field, turn right along a fence running alongside a track and cross another stile. Bear left to a large oak tree, then continue past the cemetery to a lane. Follow it to Top Street and turn right, then left to Whittington Castle.

Where to eat and drink

There is a small, simple but friendly tea room at the castle – kitchen@ thecastle; a shop nearby and two pubs, Ye Olde Boote Inn and The White Lion. Both offer real ales and menus featuring local and seasonal produce. The White Lion has a beer garden.

What to see

The dismantled railway met near the end of the walk was originally the Oswestry, Ellesmere and Whitchurch Railway, opened in 1863. In 1864 the line became part of the Cambrian Railway, which in turn was absorbed into the Great Western in 1923 and nationalised in 1948. The line closed in 1965.

While you're there

Oswestry, once the headquarters of the Cambrian Railway, was a hub for services to North Wales. One of the former engine sheds now houses the Cambrian Railways Museum, which chronicles Oswestry's railway history. The Cambrian Heritage Railways regularly steams up one of its locos on site and there is plenty of railway memorabilia.

FRANKTON AND THE MONTGOMERY CANAL

DISTANCE/TIME	5.3 miles (8.5km) / 2hrs
ASCENT/GRADIENT	289ft (88m) / ▲
PATHS	Field paths, quiet lanes, canal towpath (rough and narrow in parts), many stiles
LANDSCAPE	Low-lying watery pastures and slight, partly wooded ridge
SUGGESTED MAP	OS Explorer 240 Oswestry
START/FINISH	Grid reference: SJ368310
DOG FRIENDLINESS	Can run free on towpath, probably nowhere else
PARKING	Lockgate Bridge car park on minor road south of Lower Frankton
PUBLIC TOILETS	None on route
NOTES	Very steep canal bridge immediately north of car park; long vehicles risk grounding. If in doubt, use the approach from the south.

The waterway that we now call the Montgomery Canal runs for 35 miles (56km) from the Llangollen (formerly Ellesmere) Canal at Frankton Junction to Newtown, Powys. Originally, it was three canals – the Ellesmere, and the eastern and western branches of the Montgomery – built by three different companies over 25 years. The Ellesmere (Frankton to Llanymynech) section opened first, in 1796. The Montgomery Canal was not completed through to Newtown until 1819.

The Monty became part of the Shropshire Union Railway and Canal Company (the Shroppie), in turn taken over by the London and North Western Railway Company. In 1923, it came into the ownership of the London, Midland and Scottish Railway Company (LMS). In 1936, the canal burst its banks by the River Perry below Frankton Locks. The LMS made no effort to repair it; the canal was simply left to its fate. Legal abandonment came in 1944 with the LMS Act of Parliament, which closed many miles of waterway. Under the 1948 Transport Act, the Monty passed into the ownership of British Waterways. Restoration work began in 1968; for more information turn to Walk 31.

Frankton Junction became the hub of the Ellesmere system. There are actually two junctions, forming an H-shape, both of which you'll see on this walk. From these, the waterways radiated out to Ellesmere, Pontcysyllte and Llanymynech. The limestone quarries at Llanymynech provided one of the canal's most valuable cargoes. The Weston arm of the canal was intended to continue to Shrewsbury, but got no further than Weston Lullingfields, rather less than half the distance. It's derelict today, but its course can mostly be traced across the ground and on OS maps.

Many renowned engineers were involved with the Monty, including father-and-son teams William and Josias Jessop and John and Thomas Dadford, as well as Thomas Telford. In engineering terms it's an unusual canal; it first descends by 11 locks from Frankton to the Severn, then climbs again, with 14 locks taking it up the Severn Valley to Newtown. As you'll see, there are four locks in quick succession at Frankton itself, and the first two of them are combined, forming a lock staircase.

Staircase locks are more complex to operate than simple locks and can cause novice boaters a few headaches. With single locks, the system is most efficient if ascending and descending boats alternate, but staircase locks are more efficient if successive boats travel in the same direction. Staircase locks are usually supervised and boats are often required to book passage in advance, as is the case at Frankton, where a maximum of 12 boats per day are normally allowed through in each direction.

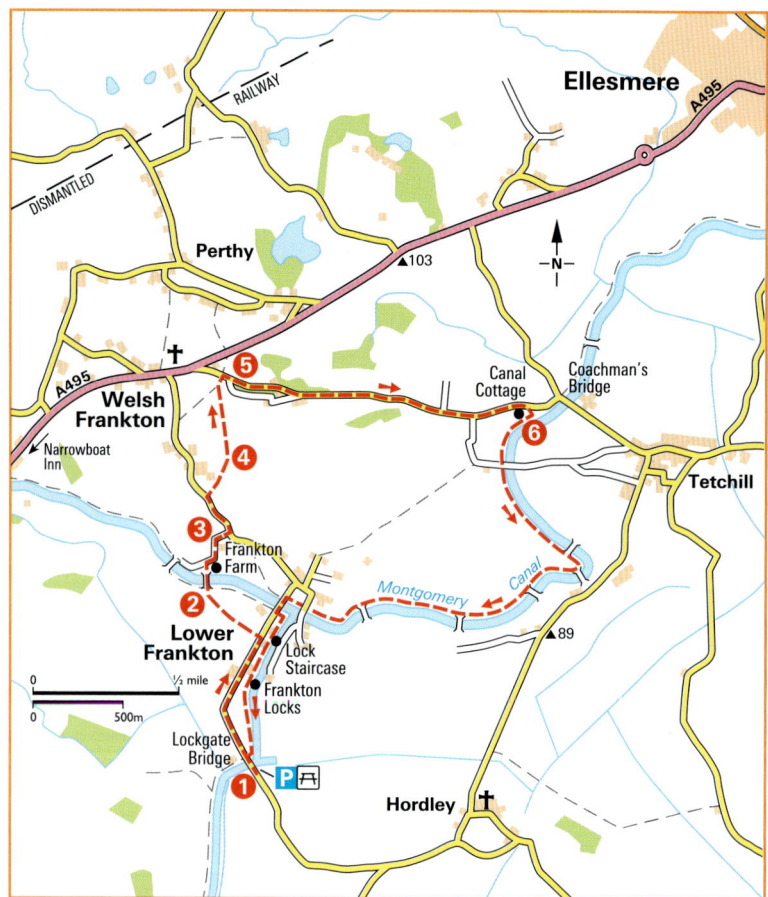

1. From the car park, walk over the steep Lockgate Bridge and continue along the lane for 0.5 miles (800m) to a stile and footpath sign in the hedge on the left opposite farm buildings. Go straight across a field to the next stile and

continue through more small fields over a series of stiles. You're effectively following the same hedge-line, though you do switch sides a couple of times.

2. Cross a plank bridge between two stiles then bear half-left to a canal bridge. Don't cross the stile onto the towpath but go over the bridge (you may need to go round a section of fence to access it). Go through a gate, or use the stile on the right if not blocked by barbed wire, and along a short green track to a yard (Frankton Farm). Go right a few paces then walk between the buildings to a lane.

3. Go up the very quiet lane to a T-junction and turn left. After a couple of bends you'll reach steps and a stile on the right, with a footpath sign on the other side of the road. Go up a field to cross a track just left of a large oak.

4. Go through a metal gate and continue up the next field. As you go over a slight rise you'll see two gates ahead. Cross two stiles in the hedge between these gates and go straight up another field to a gate onto a lane.

5. Turn right along the quiet lane for almost a mile (1.5km). It runs along a slight ridge and there are intermittent views to the south. It descends gradually. After Canal Cottage, and just before Coachman's Bridge, you can join the towpath. Turn right, almost doubling back on yourself.

6. Follow the towpath for almost 2 miles (3.2km) to Frankton Junction. Pass under Bridge 69 and continue to the next, which is not 70 but 1W. Cross this bridge then turn left to join the towpath (and the Shropshire Way), following the canal down past Frankton Locks to Lockgate Bridge. Cross the bridge to return to the car park.

Where to eat and drink

There are no sources of refreshment either at Lower Frankton or Welsh Frankton. The nearest opportunity is The Narrowboat Inn, on the A495 0.75miles (1.2km) southwest of Welsh Frankton. There is a picnic site at the Lockgate Bridge.

What to see

In places the banks of the lane between Points 5 and 6 support a profusion of Arum maculatum, a very unusual plant whose common names include lords-and-ladies and cuckoo pint. In spring its flowers form a purplish poker-like structure (the spadix), which is shielded by the hood-like, pale green spathe. In late summer this withers and the spades form a cluster of bright red berries. Beware – these are highly toxic.

While you're there

Take a look at the first section of the Weston arm on the canal, which runs east from the Lockgate Bridge car park. There's a short stretch of open water, and a service point for boaters, but then it's blocked and increasingly choked with vegetation. It now forms a nature reserve.

OSWESTRY RACECOURSE TO OFFA'S DYKE

30

DISTANCE/TIME	4 miles (6.4km) / 1hr 30min
ASCENT/GRADIENT	459ft (140m) / ▲
PATHS	Undefined across fields but not hard to follow, excellent paths in woodland and on common, many stiles
LANDSCAPE	Woods, commons and pasture
SUGGESTED MAP	OS Explorer 240 Oswestry
START/FINISH	Grid reference: SJ258305
DOG FRIENDLINESS	Can run free on common, but not in sheep pastures
PARKING	Car park/picnic site at south end of Racecourse Common, off B4580 west of Oswestry
PUBLIC TOILETS	None on route

Its Welsh name is Cyrn y Bwch (Horns of the Buck) which sounds less prosaic than Racecourse Common, but there really was a racecourse here where the local squirearchy, from both sides of the border, held race meetings from the early 1700s until 1848. Apparently, the main event was the impressive-sounding Sir Watkin Williams Wynn Cup. You can still see traces of the course, which was returfed by French prisoners during the Napoleonic wars. It's sometimes loosely described as a 'Figure 8' shape, but this is misleading as the tracks did not actually cross – the potential dangers of which are only too obvious!

Apart from the grassy traces of the course itself, the most significant relic of the sporting past is the ruin of the grandstand, which lies not far from the car park and is easily visited towards the end of the walk. It was evidently a substantial stone structure and is believed to have been built in 1804. A board nearby gives more information about the grandstand and the general history of the racecourse.

There's also a view indicator at one end of the ruins – but no view! Clearly the trees have grown up since. Still, there is a chance, mainly as you follow a quiet lane after the second crossing of the B4580, to take in a wide prospect to the east. Perhaps the most striking aspect of this view is the contrast between the north Shropshire plain and the south Shropshire hills, and you can identify the locations of many of the other local landmarks. The view indicator may be some help with this, but you're bound to notice that the vertical dimension has been greatly exaggerated, making the Clee Hills, Caer Caradoc and Stiperstones look like something from the Lake District.

Later in the walk you follow the line of Offa's Dyke through beautiful Candy Wood, above the steep slopes of Craig Forda. The wood is dominated by oaks, but there are some superb beech trees too, which must have been planted, as beech is not native this far north.

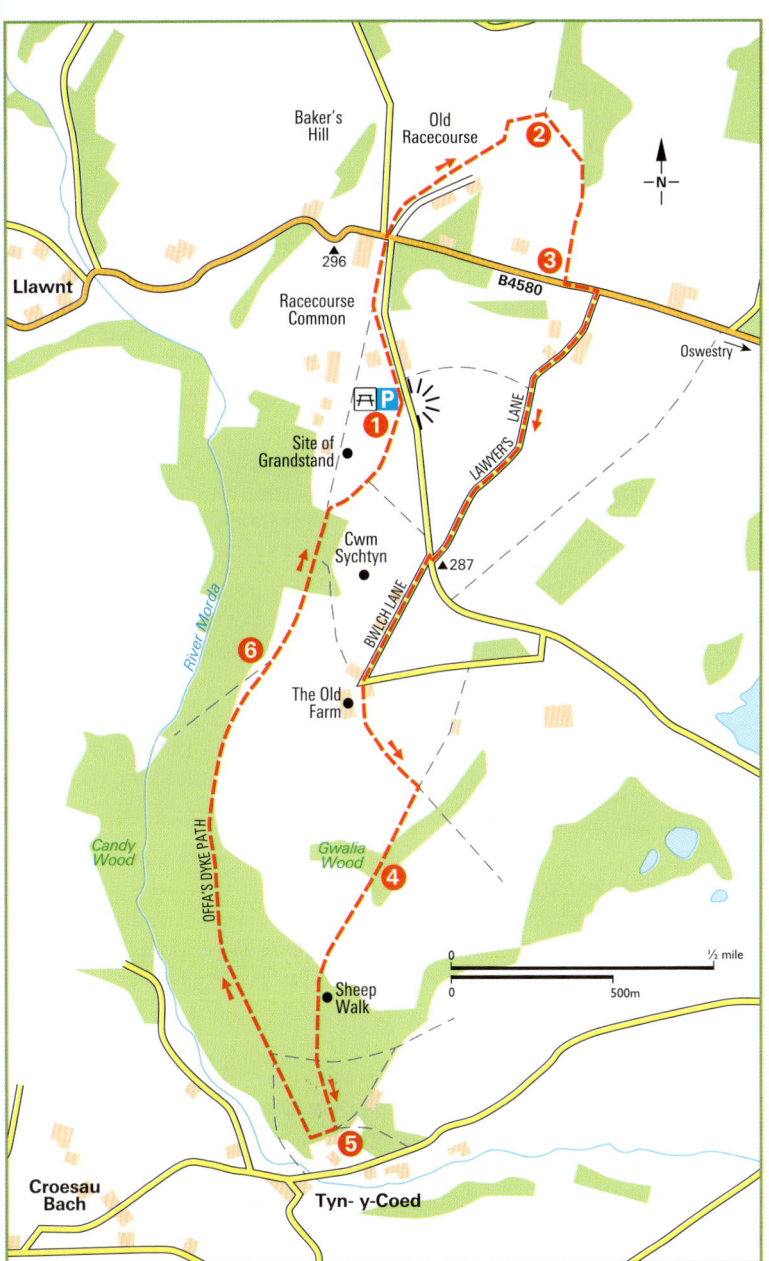

1. At an explanatory board near the car park, turn right on a wide green path – part of the old racecourse – which runs parallel to the road. Follow this, crossing several access tracks. Cross the B4580 to access the northern part of the common. The path forks immediately: keep right. As you approach the far end of the common, take a worn path on the right at a Shropshire Way signpost. The path is narrow but well trodden, with bracken to the right of it and gorse bushes and rowan trees to the left.

2. The path soon leaves the common by another Shropshire Way sign. Continue for a very short distance, keeping your eyes open for a path going off to the right at a stile. Walk across a brackeny pasture, with scattered trees. Power lines give a rough guide to the far corner where you find a stile. Cross this, continue to another and then go straight on to the B4580.

3. Turn left on the footway then first right on a quiet lane. Follow it to a junction, where you turn right, then immediately left on Bwlch Lane. Pass the turning to Cwm Sychtyn and continue until the lane bends abruptly left. Go forward on a footpath that uses the driveway of The Old Farm, then bears left across a lawned area to a stile. Cross a track to enter a field and go diagonally to the far corner. Use the plank bridge as a pointer across the next field to a stile leading into Gwalia Wood.

4. Follow a path through the wood and into a field. Go diagonally towards the far corner, guided by a group of tall sycamore trees, and then across the next field to a stile giving access to woodland at Sheep Walk. Turn left, soon crossing a track and going straight on as indicated by a waymarker. The downhill path is narrow, but clear enough. Another waymarker guides you left alongside a cleared (but rapidly regrowing) area to meet a grassy path.

5. Turn right, keeping the cleared area on your right, then right once more to join Offa's Dyke Path, recognisable by the acorn logo that signifies a National Trail. Follow the path beside the prominent earth- and stoneworks of Offa's Dyke through Candy Wood.

6. Switch to the other side of the Dyke at a waymarked junction, pass a pasture and continue through the adjacent Racecourse Wood until a gate gives access to Racecourse Common. Fork left here to visit the old grandstand or go right, soon joining the racecourse again, to return to the car park.

Where to eat and drink

There's nowhere along the route, but Oswestry has plenty of tea and coffee shops. The Griffin on Leg Street is recommended, as is the Oak public house in Church Street. Bailey Head is well placed for visiting what remains of Oswestry Castle.

What to see

Racecourse Common is basically acid grassland, but on the north common there's heathland that supports heather and whinberry. Look for drifts of beautiful blue harebells in the late summer. The south common has some magnificent rowan trees which are best seen in October.

While you're there

Hen Dinas, also known as Old Oswestry, is an impressive Iron Age fort that was first occupied about 300 BC. It's multivallate (has several ramparts) and dominates the northern edge of town. It's one of the finest forts in the country and there are great views from the top.

ALONG THE MONTGOMERY CANAL

31

DISTANCE/TIME	6.5 miles (10.4km) / 2hrs 30min
ASCENT/GRADIENT	92ft (28m) / ▲
PATHS	Towpath, quiet lanes and field paths, many stiles
LANDSCAPE	Level, low-lying farmland by Montgomery Canal
SUGGESTED MAP	OS Explorer 240 Oswestry
START/FINISH	Grid reference: SJ338268
DOG FRIENDLINESS	Good, but keep close at heel along Woolston Road
PARKING	Car park opposite Queen's Head PH, between A5 and B5009
PUBLIC TOILETS	None on route

Comedians sometimes joke about the bizarre British propensity for grim roadside picnics, but an official picnic site has been provided, ear-shatteringly sandwiched between Holyhead Road and the A5 Oswestry bypass. But despite this testament to poor imagination, at least the Queen's Head is a convenient place to begin this delightful walk along the Montgomery Canal.

This walk explores a restored section of the Monty, so it's worth saying a few words about the restoration work, which was started by the Shropshire Union Canal Society in 1968. One of the remarkable things is that most of the work has been done by volunteers. The Welshpool stretch was the first to benefit, followed by the locks at Carreghofa (near Llanymynech), while the Inland Waterways Association's Waterway Recovery Group restored the four locks at Frankton Junction, with the aid of volunteer groups from all over the country.

Frankton Locks reopened in 1987. Since then, restoration has continued apace. South of Frankton, a new lock and aqueduct had to be built, but by 1996 the canal was open all the way from Frankton to Queen's Head, where a new bridge was also required. South of Queen's Head, volunteers restored Aston Locks and developed a nature reserve, on the opposite bank to the towpath, as some small compensation for the valuable wildlife habitat that is lost when an overgrown canal is restored. The seven-acre Aston Lock nature reserve is now designated as a Site of Special Scientific Interest (SSSI) and included in this wetland area is a number of rare aquatic plants and different species of dragonflies.

The section south of Queen's Head was reopened in the late 1990s and a highlight of this stretch is Maesbury Marsh, the best surviving canal village on the Monty. It's hard to imagine that this quiet place was once a busy port, but it was the nearest wharf to Oswestry, so trade was brisk. There used to be a factory, warehouse, coal and grain stores and flour mill, as well as workshops and offices. Most of the buildings remain, though converted to other uses.

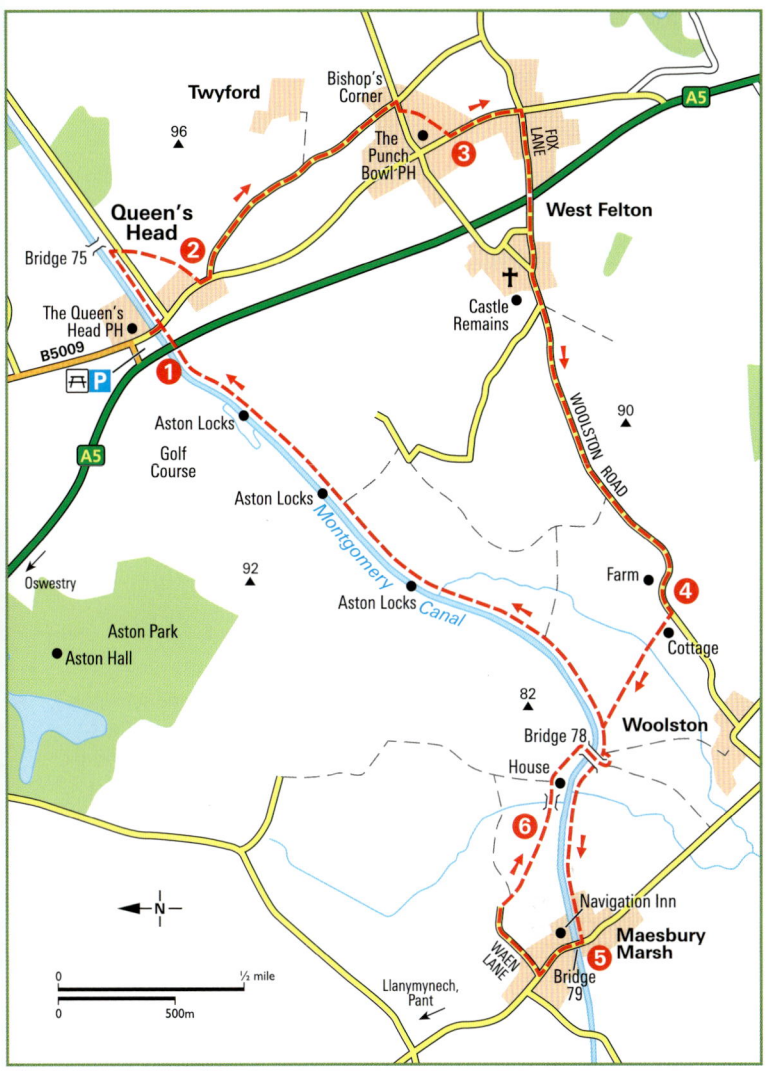

1. Leave the car park, cross the bridge, join the towpath on the far side of the canal and head northeast, away from the A5. Within a few minutes you will approach Bridge 75. About 50yds (46m) before it, look for a gap in the hedge across the road. Bear right across a narrow, damp meadow to a stile, then continue, heading over a rise and down the other side. Pass through a gappy hawthorn hedge, then continue in the same direction to a gate in the corner of a field. Turn right along a tractor track to the road.

2. Turn left, then left again, signposted 'Twyford'. Ignore the Twyford turn a little further on and instead continue to a crossroads (Bishop's Corner). Turn right on School Road, then immediately left on a grassy path called Hicksons Lane.

3. Turn left on Old Holyhead Road, then take the third right onto Fox Lane, soon crossing the main A5 road on a footbridge. Go straight on through West Felton, then turn left onto Woolston Road. Continue along Woolston Road, past the church, for about a mile (1.5km).

After an obvious double bend and just before a small cottage, cross a stile on the right. Follow the line of the garden hedge, straight across the field to a footbridge and two stiles. Cross the boggy corner of the next field and continue straight on to a wobbly stile giving access to the canal towpath. Turn left, soon passing under a small bridge (No. 78) continue for 0.5miles (800m).

4. Cross Bridge 79 at Maesbury Marsh, and walk through the village. Take the first turn right along Waen Lane. This becomes a stony track at a cattle grid. A few paces further on, leave the bridleway at a gate on the right (footpath waymark). Head diagonally across a large field to the furthest corner.

5. Cross a footbridge and continue over the next field, then across a stile to join a bridleway. Keep straight on, passing to the left of a house and along field edges until an unsigned but trodden path goes right, to cross the canal at the small bridge (No. 78) you passed under earlier (see Point 4). Descend some steps on the right and go under the bridge to join the towpath. Follow it back heading northeast to Queen's Head.

Where to eat and drink
You can choose from The Queen's Head (open Wed–Sun) at the start, The Punch Bowl at West Felton or the attractive Navigation Inn (open Thu–Sun) by the canal at Maesbury Marsh. All do food, offer veggie options and welcome children. The first two have large gardens, with a play area at The Punch Bowl.

What to see
Go to the rear of the churchyard at West Felton and look across a track to the tree-covered mound rising above a moat. This is the remains of a Norman motte-and-bailey castle, typical of hundreds that were built in the borders. The castle would have been built of timber and stood on top of the motte, with wooden bailey walls surrounding the site.

While you're there
Visit Llanymynech and Pant, border villages with a wealth of industrial remains, particularly a lime-processing works at Llanymynech, where you can see the old bottle kilns and a rare rotary kiln. Best of all is the Shropshire Wildlife Trust reserve at Llanymynech Rocks, with its spectacular disused quarries, wonderful views, Offa's Dyke Path and profusion of lime-loving wild flowers in the spring and summer.

HOPE VALLEY AND STIPERSTONES

DISTANCE/TIME	9.5 miles (15.3km) / 4hrs
ASCENT/GRADIENT	1,279ft (390m) / ▲ ▲
PATHS	Some boggy areas, streams to ford, route-finding skills required, very many stiles
LANDSCAPE	Pastoral scene of hills and valleys on the Welsh border
SUGGESTED MAP	OS Explorer 216 Welshpool & Montgomery
START/FINISH	Grid reference: SJ350017
DOG FRIENDLINESS	Mostly on lead, particularly in nature reserves
PARKING	Hope Valley Nature Reserve, signposted from A488
PUBLIC TOILETS	None on route

Hope Valley is an ancient woodland of sessile oak, but in the 1960s much of it was felled and replanted with conifers. However, the oaks regenerated from their mossy stumps and Shropshire Wildlife Trust, recognising the potential for restoration, bought the long, narrow wood in 1981. Most of the conifers have now been removed and Hope Valley is recovering.

The Trust installed nest boxes for birds and in the 1980s a naturalist checking one of them was startled to discover a dormouse. This was an exciting find because dormice were known to be in serious decline. Since then, much research has been done to find out exactly where dormice do occur in the county. One way to detect their presence is to look for discarded hazelnut shells. Dormice nibble them in a unique style, leaving a perfectly smooth oval hole with an inner rim.

The good news is that over 30 dormouse colonies have been discovered, several of them in the valleys round Stiperstones. The bad news is that coniferisation, hedge removal, flail cutting and other modern practices have left these colonies isolated and vulnerable. The Trust is working with local landowners to restore hedgerows linking woods, to maintain mature hedgerows and to carry out appropriate woodland management. You're not likely to see any of Hope Valley's dormice, shy and famously sleepy as these endearing mammals are, but it's good to know they're there.

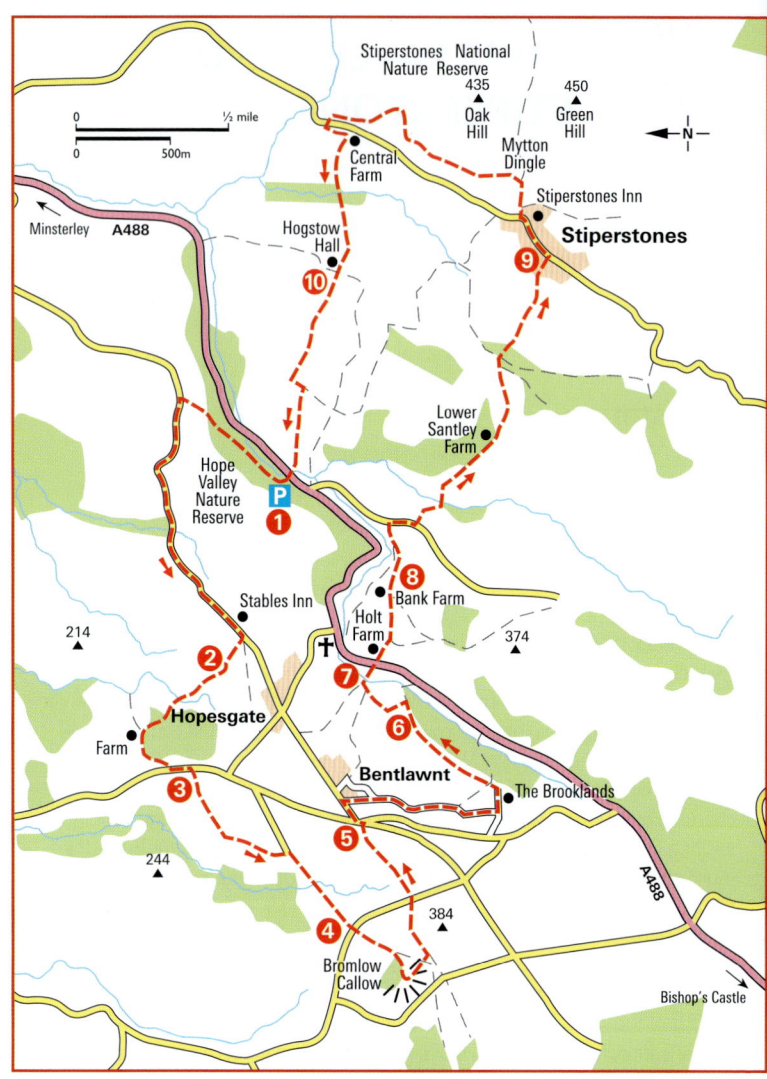

1. Follow a bridleway through the reserve. Ignore all branching paths and eventually meet a lane. Turn left. After passing the Stables Inn you'll see two footpaths together on the right. Take the right-hand path to a hedge corner and then follow the hedge to the field corner.

2. Follow the left edge of the next field until a stile leads to a terraced path going down a pasture. Skirt woodland, cross a brook and follow a track towards a farm. Cross a stile, turn left and follow waymarkers to a lane.

3. Turn left, then first right on a track as far as a stile. Turn right along a field-edge, pass a cottage, then bear left and up to a stile/gate. The path continues across a track and two more fields, then goes through a plantation to a drive-way. Turn left to a lane, then right, keeping straight on along a track.

4. Cross a lane and climb up Bromlow Callow. Enter the fenced Scots pines on the summit. Leaving the trees again, turn sharp left and descend, soon bearing right through gorse to a marshy saddle. Go left to a gate and signboard. Descend rightwards to a lane and go a few paces right to a footpath. Follow this along field-edges and out to a lane.

5. Descend through a crossroads, towards Hopesgate. Turn first right on a track and follow it to a T-junction, then go left. When it runs out into a field, bear left, roughly following power lines. The track soon becomes clear again.

6. When you come to an old quarry turn left down a bank (the ground is uneven) and across a field. Twenty yards (18m) left of a power line pole, a path descends to ford a brook. Go right to a stile then walk down the lovely little valley to a footbridge.

7. Walk to the A488 and cross to a path opposite. Go past Holt Farm and follow a fenced path past Croft Cottage to a stile. Go left and climb a steep jungly slope on a clear narrow path. At the crest, bear left and follow frequent waymarks to Bank Farm.

8. Cross a lawn (waymarks) and follow the access track out to a lane. Turn right, then first left on a bridleway. Bear half-right across a field to find a metal gate and then cross a footbridge. Climb up to another field. Bear right and cross the field to another metal gate and footbridge. Skirt Lower Santley Farm then join a green track. Climb between fields then enter a wood. Turn second right on a path, descending steeply at first. Join a track then keep straight ahead as it bends left, and meet a road in Stiperstones.

9. Turn left, past the pub and shop, then right at Mytton Dingle. After passing through a gate, turn left and climb very steeply into Stiperstones National Nature Reserve. Follow the path round Oak Hill, then down to a road. Cross and turn sharp left on a track to Central Farm. Turn right at a T-junction, through the farmyard, then along a track.

10. At Hogstow Hall, turn left for a few paces, then right on a footpath. Cross two fields, a belt of trees, and another field, then go left on a track. Pass through a gateway, then turn right, following the right-hand hedge to a gate. Switch sides and continue down to the A488 and cross to the Hope Valley Nature Reserve.

Where to eat and drink
The Stables Inn is homely with home-cooked meals available. Open Tue–Sun, check opening times. No dogs inside but there is a garden. The Stiperstones Inn is also recommended.

What to see
Wild flowers struggle to survive in conifer woods because insufficient light gets to the floor in spring. Now that the conifers have mostly been removed, Hope Valley overflows with bluebells in spring, as well as species considered indicative of ancient woodland.

While you're there
The Vale of Montgomery, overlooked by this walk, has much to see, including a lowland section of Offa's Dyke. Montgomery itself (Trefaldwyn in Welsh) is a charming town with a fine Georgian square and some striking castle ruins that survived Owain Glyndwr's attacks but not the firepower of Cromwell's forces in the Civil War.

33 STIPERSTONES NATIONAL NATURE RESERVE

DISTANCE/TIME	4.5 miles (7.2km) / 2hrs
ASCENT/GRADIENT	951ft (290m) / ▲ ▲
PATHS	Good paths across pasture, moorland and woodland
LANDSCAPE	Shropshire's second highest hill, with great views
SUGGESTED MAP	OS Explorer 216 Welshpool & Montgomery
START/FINISH	Grid reference: SJ374023
DOG FRIENDLINESS	On lead in nature reserve and near livestock
PARKING	Car park at Snailbeach
PUBLIC TOILETS	At car park

At first sight it looks as though this walk will be all about industrial archaeology, for it begins at Snailbeach, formerly an important lead mine. The derelict landscape has been transformed into one of the most fascinating post-industrial sites in the Midlands, complete with engine houses, loco sheds, compressors, crushers and tramways.

There's another sort of transformation going on near by, on the rugged moorland ridge of Stiperstones, one that aims to restore the landscape to its full glory. The quartzite rock was formed 480 million years ago. During the last ice age the ridge stood out above the glaciers and was subjected to constant freezing and thawing, which shattered much of the rock into a mass of scree surrounding several residual tors and leaving the top of the ridge jagged as a dragon's or dinosaur's crest. Subsequent soil formation has been so slow that much of the scree remains on the surface, largely unvegetated. Where soil has formed, it is thin, acidic and nutrient poor, sufficient only to support a limited range of plants. Over much of the summit area the vegetation is dominated by heather and whinberry, with some crowberry and cowberry. At one time, this meant that in summer most of Stiperstones, except the very crest, turned a glorious purple.

Part of Stiperstones is protected, but modern agriculture and silviculture have encroached, fragmenting the ridge with areas of improved grassland and conifers so that it no longer turns so purple. However, for several years it has been the subject of the ambitious Back to Purple initiative. Thousands of conifers have been felled, including the unsightly Gatten Plantation, which lay just below the summit ridge. On the southern part of the ridge, further conifers have been cleared to reveal the jagged outline of Nipstone Rock, hidden for many years. Thousands of heather seedlings have been planted in these areas to supplement natural regeneration.

Work is also being undertaken to restore and protect other habitats which lie below the summit ridge such as herb-rich grasslands, hay meadows, wet flushes and woodland. The flora of these areas includes bog cotton, heath bedstraw and the increasingly scarce mountain pansy.

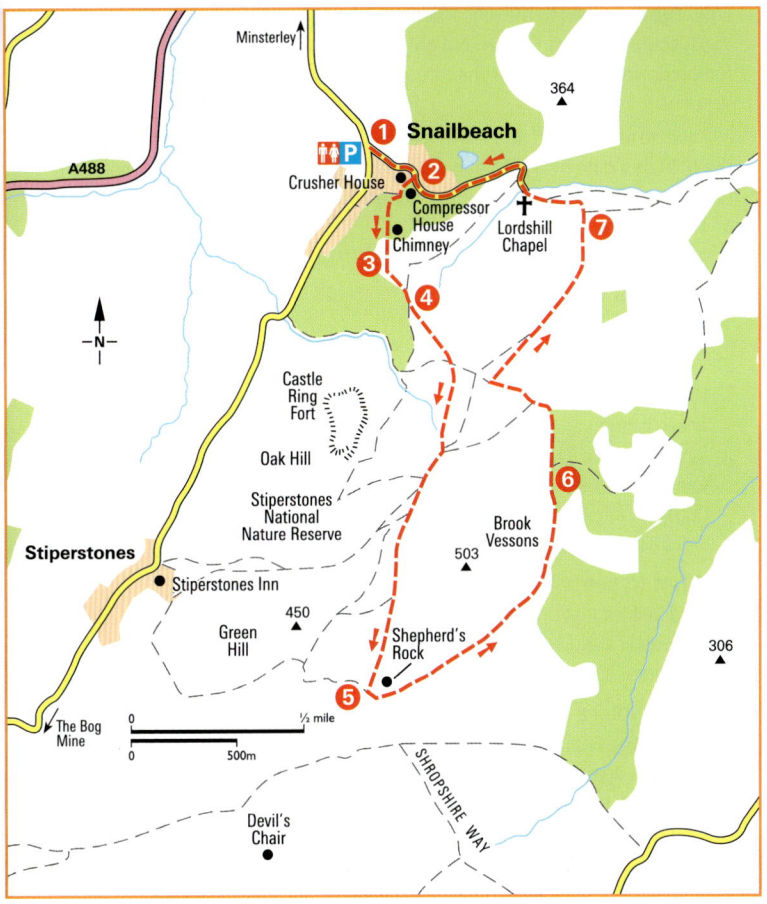

1. Take the Lordshill lane opposite the car park, then join a parallel footpath on the left. Rejoining the lane, cross to the site of the locomotive shed, then continue up the lane, noticing the green arrows directing you to the main sites.

2. Turn right on a track between the Crusher House and the Compressor House. A few paces past the Compressor House, turn left up steps. At the top, turn right, then soon left up more steps. Turn left to the Pumping Engine House, then right, and continue through woodland. A detour left leads to the smelter chimney, or it's uphill all the way.

3. A sign indicates that you're entering Stiperstones National Nature Reserve (NNR). The woods give way to bracken, broom and bramble before a gate leads to the open hill. A path climbs the slope ahead to a gate at the top.

4. Two paths are waymarked. Take the left-hand one, which runs between a fence and the rim of the spectacular dingle on your right. Climbing away from the dingle, bear right on a grassy ramp before meeting a stony track. Turn right. As the path climbs you can see the rock tors on the summit. The nearest, isolated from the rest, is Shepherd's Rock.

5. Just beyond Shepherd's Rock is a junction marked by a cairn. Turn left and after about 50yds (46m) fork left again. Descend to leave the NNR at a gate/

stile. The path runs to the left, shortly bordered by a hawthorn hedge. You'll soon see that this is an old green lane, variously lined by trees or a tumbledown stone wall. It runs through the tiny local nature reserve of Brook Vessons.

6. Keep straight ahead at an NNR sign. At the next junction, fork right to leave the NNR at a gate by a plantation. Go diagonally across a field to a track; turn right, going back across the field, through the plantation, then across pasture on a bridleway.

7. Fork left at a bridleway junction and continue past Lordshill Chapel to a lane. Turn right and stay with it as it swings left to Snailbeach.

Where to eat and drink

There is nothing along the way, but you are not far from the Stiperstones Inn, open from 11.30am, with food served noon–9pm. It also acts as a tourist information point, sells maps and walks leaflets and offers B&B. Dogs are allowed in the bar, but not the lounge bar. There are also shops and pubs in Minsterley, north of Snailbeach.

What to see

Lordshill Baptist Chapel was built in 1833 and enlarged in 1873. It has been carefully restored and Sunday meetings are held here most summers. It also appeared in the film of Mary Webb's *Gone to Earth*.

While you're there

Explore the Snailbeach site, then visit The Bog Mine, a little further south. There's a seasonal visitor centre, waymarked walks and mine workings. At dusk you'll see bats – they live in one of the mine tunnels (known as The Somme) which has been blocked by a grid for their protection.

THE DEVIL'S CHAIR AT STIPERSTONES

DISTANCE/TIME	4.8 miles (7.8km) / 2hrs 30min
ASCENT/GRADIENT	640ft (195m) / ▲▲
PATHS	Clear paths throughout, but some are extremely rocky, 4 stiles
LANDSCAPE	High moorland with rocky outcrops flanked by rough pasture
SUGGESTED MAP	OS Explorer 216 Welshpool & Montgomery
START/FINISH	Grid reference: SO357978
DOG FRIENDLINESS	Dogs must be on leads at all times in the Nature Reserve
PARKING	Large parking area above The Bog Mine
PUBLIC TOILETS	At The Bog Visitor Centre during opening hours
NOTES	Some optional scrambling required to reach the top of outcrops.

Good things come in small packages, they say, and this short walk certainly bears out the saying. There's a wealth of history around The Bog – although the name is, admittedly, unenticing. But if the weather's good when you arrive, you might want to save that till later and get straight on with the walk, as Stiperstones on a clear day is irresistible. There's an air of wildness about the broad ridge with its abrupt, jagged outcrops, and perhaps an atmosphere of mystery, too. As Shropshire's second-highest point, and well to the west of the county's other main hills, it's no surprise that Stiperstones has far-reaching views, especially into Wales.

As the highest point of all, Manstone Rock is the best place to take in the full 360-degree view. However, it takes a bit of scrambling to reach the crest. The easiest route starts on the west side, but it needs care and a modicum of agility by any route. There's not much room around the trig pillar on the summit, so you may have to take turns too. Of course all this is entirely optional and you can get much the same views from elsewhere along the ridge – though even here, the paths are so rough that walking and gazing at the same time can be slightly tricky! If you want to flex your scrambling muscles beforehand, the ascent of Nipstone Rock is considerably easier.

While the heights of Stiperstones are quartzite, the western flank, and specifically the area around The Bog, is composed of rocks known as the Mytton Flags (Mytton Dingle is a little to the north, east of Stiperstones village). These contained some rich veins of lead, which were first mined commercially in the 1730s. A tunnel, known as the Boat Level, was dug to drain the mines, thereby making The Bog rather less boggy too. Vertical and inclined shafts reached down to over 1,200ft (366m). Lead-mining ceased late in the 19th century, but another mineral, barytes, was extracted until 1922.

Lead, of course, is highly toxic, and the spoil from the mines still contained enough lead to make it inhospitable to most plant species. Even today, well over 100 years after lead-mining ceased, the area around the mine still has an unusually bare appearance. The presence of lead also means, however, that the area is not tempting for agriculture and gradually it has become an important haven for wildlife.

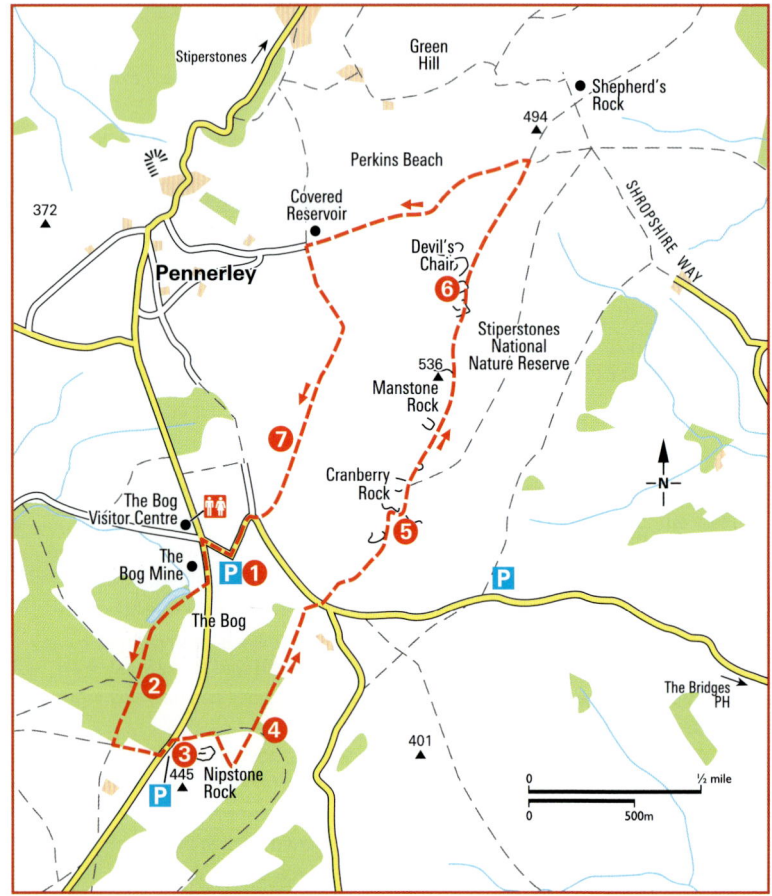

1. Walk down the road towards The Bog Visitor Centre. Turn sharp left before reaching it and walk past The Bog Mine. Bear right at a footpath sign and follow a pleasant level track. Note, however, that its far end can be quite muddy after a wet spell, in which case it can be avoided by walking along the lane instead.

2. Keep straight on along the track to a crossing track: go straight ahead again (waymark) on a smaller path to the end of a wood. Go over a stile on the left and up to the top left corner of the field to find a gate and stile onto a lane. Turn left for 200yds (183m) then turn right into Nipstone car park.

3. Follow a track through two gates then go right, over a stile. Take a rough little path through bracken, heather and bilberry, passing to the left of the first

outcrop then bending right behind it. If you want to scramble up Nipstone Rock it's easiest at the far end, otherwise just bear left to a broader track along the ridge and turn left.

4. Cross a stile and recross the track from the car park. Continue, now following Shropshire Way signs, through a plantation then on in the same line across a large field to a road. Go straight across through a couple of gates to a National Nature Reserve (NNR) sign. Follow the waymarked footpath up the broad ridge. When Cranberry Rock comes into view, the paths begin to multiply, but the easiest and widest one keeps to its right.

5. Continue climbing to reach Manstone Rock with its prominent trig pillar. Continue north along the almost-level but still very rough ridge path to the Devil's Chair, arguably the most impressive of the Stiperstones outcrops and the one whose summit is hardest to reach.

6. Descend gradually to a cross-tracks with a cairn and waymark post. Turn left on a smoother bridleway. Pass a small covered reservoir then turn left on another good track along the edge of the NNR. This climbs slightly then gently descends. After two gates, reach another NNR sign by a third.

7. Beyond this the track becomes narrower and greener but is still easy to follow. Descend more steeply then swing right and down to a gate. Turn left a few paces to a lane. Follow this down to the car park, or use the permissive bridleway just the other side of the fence for the first bit.

Where to eat and drink

The Bog Visitor Centre has a fantastic selection of delicious home-made cakes as well as hot and cold drinks. For full meals, however, you'll have to travel a short distance, either north to the Stiperstones Inn or east over the hill to The Bridges (formerly The Horseshoe Inn) near Ratlinghope. This is family owned and run, their priority is to serve good honest food, either homegrown on their farm or locally sourced from one of the Marches' many talented producers, check the meal times.

What to see

Legend has it that if you visit Stiperstones on a dark night you will see the Devil and his cronies gathered at the Devil's Chair, while witches congregate at Manstone Rock on the longest night each year. And if you should see an army on the move you will know that England is in danger, for that is when Wild Edric and his men will emerge from the lead mines to tackle the enemy.

While you're there

Allow time to visit The Bog Visitor Centre, March – November (closed on Mondays). It's full of background information about this important and fascinating locality, and the friendly staff are both knowledgeable and enthusiastic. If you want to investigate more deeply, the centre's resources include census records and school registers. Local crafts are also on sale. As many visitors are walkers, the centre is completely accepting of muddy boots and dogs. Light refreshments are available; drinks, cakes and other snacks.

STAPELEY HILL AND MITCHELL'S FOLD

DISTANCE/TIME	3.6 miles (5.7km) / 1hr 30min
ASCENT/GRADIENT	476ft (145m) / ▲
PATHS	Faint field paths at start, then clear moorland tracks, 6 stiles
LANDSCAPE	Mostly wide-open moorland with extensive views
SUGGESTED MAP	OS Explorer 216 Welshpool & Montgomery
START/FINISH	Grid reference: SO303981
DOG FRIENDLINESS	Livestock usually present so on leads throughout
PARKING	Car park for Mitchell's Fold Stone Circle at end of rough track off minor road west of A488
PUBLIC TOILETS	None on route

Although a short walk, in terms of value, it's one of the best. Most of the walking is over close-cropped turf, which is one of the kindest surfaces to walk on, gradients are gentle too, and yet there is more to see and enjoy than on most walks of twice or three times the length.

The walk is entirely in Shropshire, but to get to the start, unless you take a roundabout route, you will have to pass through a small corner of Wales (a hamlet with the un-Welsh sounding name of White Grit). Nearby is Cwm Dingle – 'cwm' is the Welsh word for a valley cutting back into a hill, and Dingle a Shropshire dialect word meaning exactly the same thing. So it could be translated as 'Valley valley'.

Stapeley Hill's most obvious 'attraction' is the Mitchell's Fold Stone Circle, and indeed that's what the car park sign directs you to. Thought to be at least 3,500 years old, it's Shropshire's best-known stone circle. However, it's not exactly in the league of Stonehenge or Castlerigg, with only 15 stones still in place, and the tallest of those barely shoulder-high. This shouldn't matter; it's a lovely spot, and the lack of the crowds that often besiege grander circles gives more scope for your imagination.

Ideally, bring an OS Explorer map to refer to as your eyes roam across the landscape; there's an ancient tumulus on lumpy Lan Fawr just to the south, several burial cairns on hulking Corndon Hill next to it, and a hillfort just to the north at Castle Ring. There are also a couple of cairn sites on Stapely Hill itself, as well as some enigmatic 'Pillow Mounds', all of which are close to the walk route. One lies less than 50yds (46m) past the first modern 'summit' cairn on the ridge; it's now visible as a low circular bank.

The 'Pillow Mounds' shown on the Explorer map are a sign of later habitation, probably medieval. Pillow mounds are a form of artificial rabbit warren, mostly found in areas where the ground is predominantly rocky. The thin topsoil would be gathered and piled up into heaps or mounds, often rectangular and therefore resembling a pillow, to give enough depth for the rabbits to burrow into. It's worth recalling that rabbits are not native to Britain but were introduced by the Romans and remained a very important food source through the Middle Ages. The Stapeley Hill mounds may well be allied to the fish ponds in the valley just below; these are now marked by three squarish blocks of trees, easily visible if you walk a little further along the ridge at Point 4.

The stones of Mitchell's Fold are a close-grained volcanic rock called dolerite, and would have been quarried close by. In fact, as you walk up the start of the ridge you can see a line of dolerite outcrops jutting up from the ground. These mark an intrusion, where molten rock forced its way between two layers of older rock. Because the dolerite is harder than the rocks around it, it now stands out proud of the hillside.

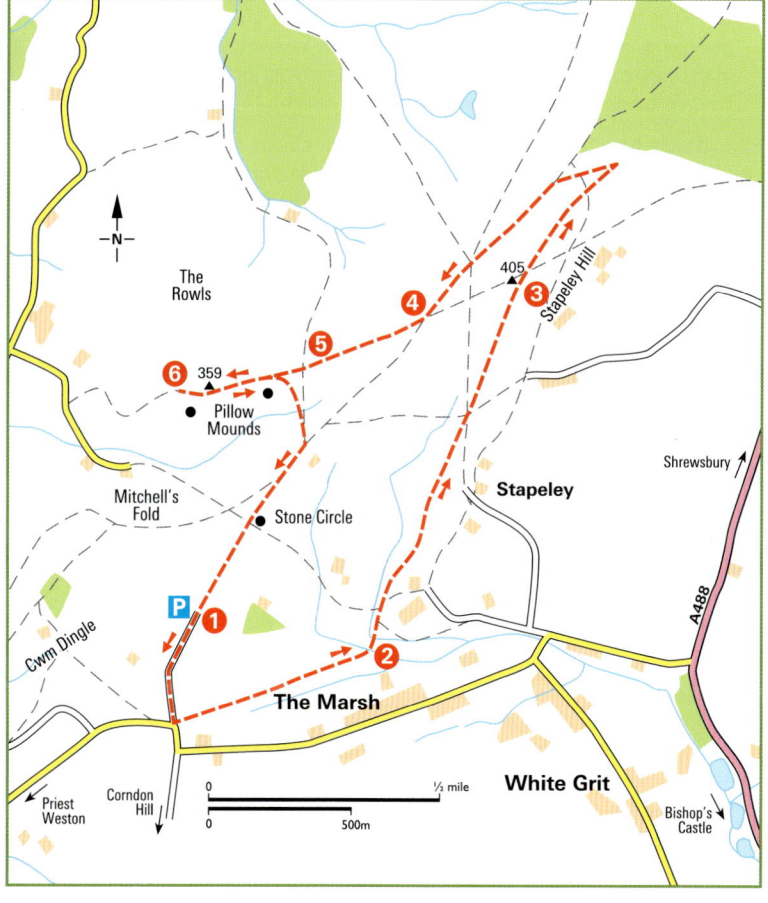

1. Walk back down the track and just before the road turn left over a way-marked stile. Walk straight on through a series of fields by a succession of stiles. Stiperstones fills the horizon. Cross a garden to another stile then continue to a gate in the far corner of the next field.

2. Bear slightly left, cross a track and go straight up the low-angled ridge ahead, dotted with gorse and rocky outcrops. Continue more easily along the gentler ridge then climb to the first 'summit', marked by a cairn. Continue along the ridge to the main summit, with another cairn.

3. Keep following the ridge, over another slight rise and then generally down, until a green track cuts across. Turn left on this and keep left again at the next junction by a waymark post. Continue along the track, passing another post liberally plastered with waymarks, on a slight rise.

4. Soon there are three more waymark posts in quick succession, keep right at the second of these, following a green track through bracken. It bends right and descends to a broad, slightly marshy saddle.

5. Keep generally ahead here, crossing other tracks, then keep to the left side as you go up the facing slope. Continue to the corner of a fence. It's worth going on a little further down the fence to get even more depth of foreground in the view over Wales. Perhaps you'll be able to spot some of those pillow mounds too (it's hopeless when the bracken is high).

6. Double-back to the fence corner and down the slope, but keep right at a fork and curve around the right side of the saddle onto a broad grassy ridge, with trees to your left. Walk along here to the stone circle and continue down the main track back to the car park.

Where to eat and drink

The nearest pub is the traditional, if slightly eccentric, Miners Arms in Priest Weston. Hours are limited but when open you'll find a warm welcome, well-kept ales, and a garden. Wednesdays and Fridays are Pizza nights and very popular.

What to see

Stapeley Hill is liberally scattered with 'lumps and bumps', not all of which have been investigated by archaeologists. The easiest to spot, as you walk along the ridge, are some long, very obvious earthen banks or dykes. These are thought to be remnants of a prehistoric field system.

While you're there

It's in Wales, but that shouldn't stop you from climbing nearby Corndon Hill (you could even do it from the same car park). It's quite a bit higher and steeper than Stapeley Hill, but the views are more extensive as a result – and they're mostly Shropshire views, as the county surrounds the hill on three sides. When the wind is right (especially from the east), its steep regular slopes also make it a very popular spot for launching paragliders.

36 A CLIMB UP EARL'S HILL

DISTANCE/TIME	4 miles (6.4km) / 2hrs
ASCENT/GRADIENT	984ft (300m) / ▲ ▲ ▲
PATHS	Easily followed, may be boggy by Habberley Brook, 8 stiles
LANDSCAPE	Hills, oakwoods and plantation above deeply cut valley
SUGGESTED MAP	OS Explorer 241 Shrewsbury
START/FINISH	Grid reference: SJ408057
DOG FRIENDLINESS	Can run free in forests, but keep under close control around livestock and in nature reserve
PARKING	Earl's Hill Nature Reserve car park off narrow lane to Pontesford Hill: turn off A488 just southeast of Pontesford
PUBLIC TOILETS	None on route

This is a shortish walk, but it's second to none in terms of steepness. This isn't only true on the ascent of Earl's Hill itself, but also as you descend into, and climb out of, the deep, lush valley of Habberley Brook. Take your time on the steep bits and the effort will be well-rewarded as this walk packs plenty of variety and interest into its short length. Earl's Hill is composed of Precambrian rocks, formed about 650 million years ago, and is volcanic in origin. Iron Age people built a fort on top in about 600 BC, and there are intriguing local legends and customs attached to the hill, one of them involving a search each Palm Sunday for a golden arrow, a story that was the inspiration behind Mary Webb's novel *The Golden Arrow*. Mary lived in nearby Pontesbury for a time and made long walks into the hills.

Earl's Hill is often said to resemble a sleeping dragon or lion and, from certain angles, you can just about see the lion. More prosaically, it is both a Scheduled Ancient Monument (because of the Iron-Age fort) and a Site of Special Scientific Interest (SSSI) for its wildlife value. It became Shropshire Wildlife Trust's first nature reserve back in 1964; an auspicious start, given the quality of the site. The adjoining Pontesford Hill, where the walk begins, is leased and managed by Forest Enterprise.

Ecologically, Earl's Hill is most valuable for its great variety of habitats, and you can see most of them from here, ranging from fast-flowing Habberley Brook through mixed woodland, anthill meadows, scrub, scree and cliffs to the acid grassland that surrounds you on the summit. The anthills, made by yellow hill ants, are composed of well-drained, sandy soil which heats up quickly in the first sunny days of spring, supporting flowers which appreciate a little extra warmth, such as wild thyme, heath bedstraw and heath speedwell. In this way, each anthill forms a distinct microhabitat with a different range of flowers than the surrounding meadowland.

In 2006 Shropshire Wildlife Trust acquired a further 25 acres (10ha) of meadows on the Habberley Valley side of the hill to extend the nature reserve. The Trust continues its long-term plan to restore floristic diversity to these meadows, partly through careful grazing by rare-breed sheep.

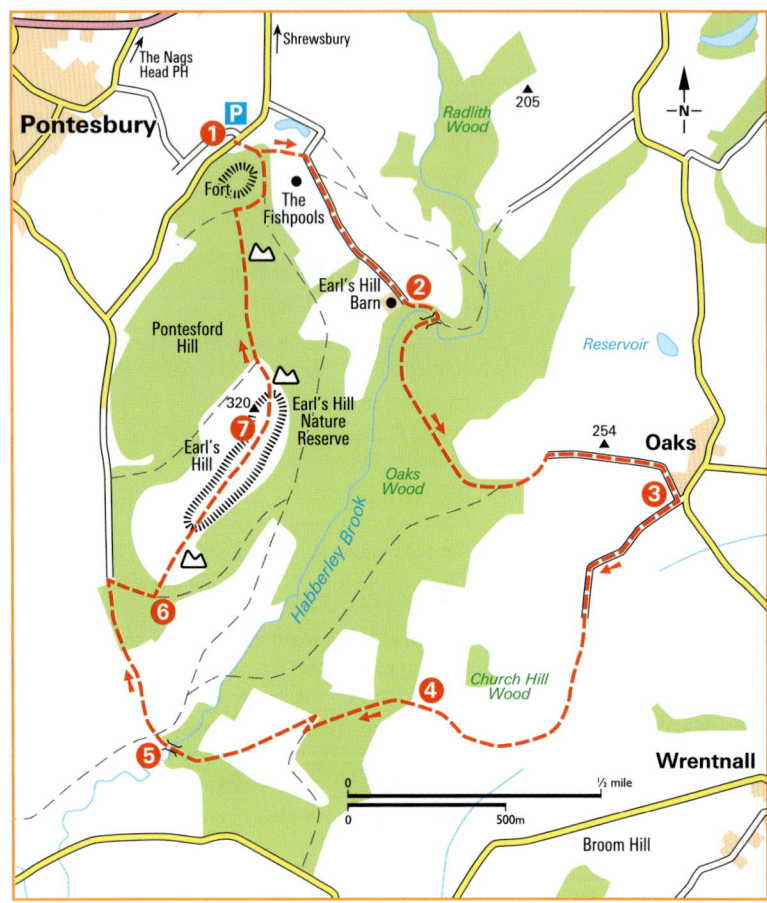

1. Take a bridleway that runs beyond the timber vehicle barrier. Go left at a fork and in a few paces descend to a gate half-hidden below the bank on your left. Bear right across a field to join a track. Turn right, following the bridleway past The Fishpools and on through farmland.

2. Turn left by Earl's Hill Barn and descend through oakwoods above the steep valley of Habberley Brook. Turn right to cross the brook at a footbridge. Bear right uphill, through mixed woodland and plantations to a T-junction and track (bridleway marker). Turn right and follow the main track, soon curving left. Follow it until there's a field on the left. Where the main track makes a sharp turn back right, leave it to continue along the (sometimes muddy) bridleway, following a hedged track towards the hamlet of Oaks.

3. Don't join the lane at Oaks, but turn right, on another track. This fades in an open field with tree-crowned Church Hill above on your right. Follow the left edge of this field and then follow a cattle-track through the next to meet the corner of a fence which descends from the summit. Continue along the fence ahead to enter plantation once more.

4. Descend to a waymark post and bear left down a newer track (the bridleway has been re-routed here) to meet a clear track. Go right a few paces, then left over a stile. Walk diagonally down three fields to the far corner of the third. Cross into forest again. Go right and then descend leftward, in lush surroundings, to find a footbridge and cross Habberley Brook.

5. Go up a slope to a bridleway junction at a gate/stile; keep straight on, just right of a hedge, towards the south end of Earl's Hill. Go through a gate then continue along the edge of a wood until another gate gives access into it. Go straight on to pass through another gate, then turn right and start climbing steeply across the southern end of the hill.

6. Take the second path on the left, which climbs very steeply to the top of the hill, passing through the Iron Age fort to reach the summit.

7. Descend from the top in a northerly direction, across the top of Pontesford Hill (with more prehistoric earthworks on your left – outworks of the main fort) and down through the conifers to meet a wide sunken path by another prehistoric fort at the northern end of the hill. Turn right, then keep left to rejoin the bridleway by which you originally left the hill. The car park is just beyond.

Where to eat and drink

The Nags Head on the A488 is the closest to the walk and has a large car park and beer garden. In Pontesbury there is very popular Horseshoes Inn, a small pub with a conservatory. The Plough on Chapel Street has a quiet, pleasant location and a friendly reputation. Pontesbury also has shops, a chippy and a Chinese restaurant.

What to see

Earl's Hill and Habberley Brook are rich in all kinds of wildlife. Rarer species include the grayling butterfly, which inhabits the bare top, and the common lizard, which is no longer at all common. A good place to see a lizard is the exposed scree below the summit to the east, but you would have to approach very slowly and quietly to have any chance of sighting one. Dormice live in the woods on the west side of the hill, but they're even more elusive than lizards.

While you're there

Wroxeter is a hamlet by the Severn, southeast of Shrewsbury, which would be unremarkable but for its superb Roman remains. It was the site of Viroconium, the fourth largest city in Roman Britain. English Heritage looks after the site, which includes a high basilica wall and the excavated remains of municipal baths, an exercise hall, market hall and forum. There's a small on-site museum too.

37

BISHOP'S CASTLE AND INTO WALES

DISTANCE/TIME	7 miles (11.3km) / 2hrs 30min
ASCENT/GRADIENT	738ft (225m) / ▲
PATHS	Generally good, undefined across some fields, 20 stiles
LANDSCAPE	Gently hilly and mostly pastoral, with great views
SUGGESTED MAP	OS Explorer 216 Welshpool & Montgomery
START/FINISH	Grid reference: SO324886
DOG FRIENDLINESS	Can run free on track between Bankshead and Shepherdswhim, livestock elsewhere
PARKING	Bishops Castle Auction Yard Car Park off Station Street
PUBLIC TOILETS	At car park and by Market Square

Bishop's Castle is one of the smallest towns in the country. If it was in the southeast it would be smaller than many a neighbouring village. But a town it is, and one of enormous charm and fascination. There is nothing ordinary about Bishop's Castle. Its documented history began in Saxon times when Egwin Shakehead, grateful for having been miraculously cured of the palsy at St Ethelbert's tomb in Hereford Cathedral, gave what is now Bishop's Castle to the Bishop of Hereford. The castle was built around 1100 by another Bishop of Hereford, but very little remains of it today. What does survive can be viewed from Castle Street.

In the early Middle Ages, the parish of Bishop's Castle was partly in England, partly in Wales, so territorial dispute was a way of life. In later years, after peace came to the Marches, Bishop's Castle acquired notoriety as the smallest and rottenest of rotten boroughs, a term which denoted electoral corruption. From 1585 this tiny town returned two MPs to Parliament. Local landowners (including Robert Clive, better known as Clive of India) expended vast sums of money on buying voters and seats to increase their power. In 1726, one rejected candidate was able to prove that of the 52 people voting for his rival, 51 had received bribes. The Reform Act of 1832 put an end to this kind of thing, and Bishop's Castle was disenfranchised.

It has attracted artists, writers, musicians and craftspeople and has reinvented itself as a town of fairs, festivals and fetes. Dozens of colourful, hand-painted banners are hung along the main street for events such as the Michaelmas Fair. It must surely be the most colourful place in Shropshire, with buildings painted in all colours of the rainbow. The Six Bells Inn looks magnificent in yellow, and the violin maker's house at the top of the town is a delightful bluey-purple. Rather more eccentric is the house painted white with green circles – but after a while it starts to look almost normal, such is the effect of Bishop's Castle.

The town is also home to a group called the Knitwits, who have taken delight in 'yarn-bombing' the town, adorning bollards, doorways and other features with colourful knitted and crocheted decorations. There's even a child's bicycle completely encased in yarn. One of the group explained, 'We want to brighten up the town and make people smile.'

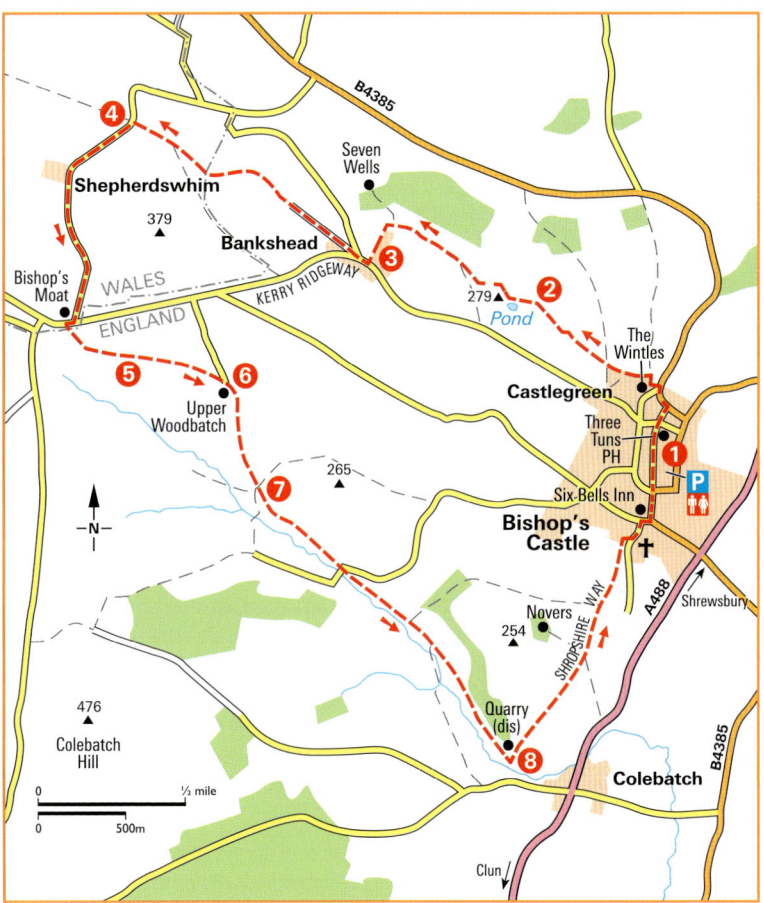

1. Walk from car park past The Kings Head onto Church Street, High Street and Bull Street, then go left along Bull Lane. Continue almost straight ahead into a new development of eco-homes, the Wintles. Pass between two granite obelisks and 50yds (46m) further on go up steps on the right, with wooden railings (ignore the first path on the right). Go left on a green path, near the road, then keep on ahead, following footpath signs. Cross a track into a green lane.

2. Follow the right edge of the next field, cross a stile at the top and go slightly left to a fence corner. Follow the fence/hedge past a pond to a stile. Go slightly left across the highest point of the next field, then down to a gate halfway along the far hedge. Go diagonally right across another field to meet a hedge and follow it through fields to a lane. Turn left to meet a road.

3. Turn right, immediately right again and then left on to lane, which soon becomes a track. It descends into woodland, crosses the border into Wales and eventually meets a lane.

4. Turn left and walk up to meet a road, the Kerry Ridgeway, at Bishop's Moat, where you cross back into England. Turn right, then over the first stile on the left. Go diagonally left to the end of a line of hawthorn trees, then continue in the same direction over another field to meet the far hedge where there's a kink in it.

5. Go diagonally across a third field to meet a line of trees which leads to a gate. Continue down the next field to the far corner, walking through one of those scrap metal collections that so many farmers seem to love.

6. Meeting a farm lane, turn right. Go through the farmyard at Upper Woodbatch and continue on down the sunken track to a stile on the left.

7. Descend a little further, now with the hedge on your right, then go left across the field to a gate at the far side below the steeper slope. Continue across two more fields to meet a lane. Join the Shropshire Way opposite, following it along the bottom of several fields, quite close to the brook.

8. After passing an abandoned quarry, turn left uphill opposite a gate and track on your right. Join a track, then a green path which leads to Field Lane. Follow this to Church Lane, which leads to Church Street and the beginning of the walk.

Where to eat and drink

The Six Bells and The Three Tuns are both famous for their on-site breweries producing traditional ales. The food's good too: the sausage and mash at The Three Tuns is out of this world. There are several other pubs, and a range of coffee houses, such as the wonderful Yarborough House, where they also sell second-hand books, records, CDs and Fair Trade goods, such as tea, coffee, chocolate and a range of gifts, cards and clothes. Poppy House is great too, with home cooked food and a south facing, partially covered courtyard.

What to see

The tree-covered mound at Bishop's Moat is all that remains of a Norman motte-and-bailey castle which was a more important defence than the castle at Bishop's Castle. It was originally called Bishop's Motte and was probably built between 1085 and 1100. It commands an extensive view of the Welsh Camlad Valley from its border position on the Kerry Ridgeway, once a prehistoric trading route and later a drove road.

While you're there

Learn about local history at the House on Crutches Museum, the timber-framed building overhanging the cobbles at the top of High Street. Or find out about the Bishop's Castle Railway at the Rail and Transport Museum. The Three Tuns is a must for real ale enthusiasts, the UK's oldest licensed brewery.

38

THE LONG MYND FROM CHURCH STRETTON

DISTANCE/TIME	7.5 miles (12.1km) / 3hrs
ASCENT/GRADIENT	1,545ft (471m) / ▲ ▲ ▲
PATHS	Mostly moorland paths and tracks
LANDSCAPE	Moorland plateau with extensive views
SUGGESTED MAP	OS Explorer 217 The Long Mynd & Wenlock Edge
START/FINISH	Grid reference: SO453936
DOG FRIENDLINESS	On lead between March and July on the Long Mynd
PARKING	Easthope Road car park, Church Stretton
PUBLIC TOILETS	At car park

The Long Mynd derives its name from mynydd, a Welsh word for mountain. It's not a mountain, though, but an undulating plateau cut by steep-sided valleys known as batches or hollows, forming one of the most distinctive and individual upland ranges in Britain. Clothed in heather, whinberry, bracken and wiry moorland grasses, with a scattering of stunted, wind-contorted hawthorns and the occasional holly or rowan, it constitutes our most southerly grouse moor. While the grouse skulk in the heather, exploding into a frenzy of alarm calls and occasional flight if you venture too close, the skies above are regally patrolled by species such as raven, buzzard and kestrel.

The Mynd is a wonderful place, sometimes referred to as the last wilderness in the Midlands. However, this is no wilderness. It has been subject to human use and, to some extent, human occupation, since the earliest times. It is liberally dotted with prehistoric remains, including Bronze Age tumuli and dykes, with an Iron Age fort on Bodbury Hill. The Portway runs along the top of the Long Mynd and has been in use for at least 4,000 years. There are more than 40 tumuli beside it or close to it, and stone tools have been found. It was probably a trading route ('port' means market) and part of it was later used by cattle drovers coming from mid-Wales.

The Mynd is an upland heath today and this may be how it was when Neolithic people first came here. During the Bronze Age, upland oak forest spread across the plateau, but this had been cleared by the Iron Age, when the Mynd was the home of a pastoral community practising transhumance – the movement of stock into the hills for the summer months. By the Middle Ages, parts of the Mynd had become permanent sheepwalk and this pattern of land use persists. Most of it is common land, owned by the National Trust, and farmers in surrounding villages retain rights of common, allowing them to graze sheep and ponies on the hill. Nowadays, there are few ponies, but very many sheep. The Mynd is seriously overgrazed, which means the glorious mosaic of heather, whinberry and other heathland plants were in retreat before a tide of bracken. The Trust, long concerned about this, has finally secured what may be a solution. In 2002, the government announced grant assistance to compensate farmers for reducing the numbers of sheep on the Long Mynd. The Trust has also closed car parks that shouldn't have been there in the first place, and is helping to fund shuttle buses. The car parks are already returning to heath.

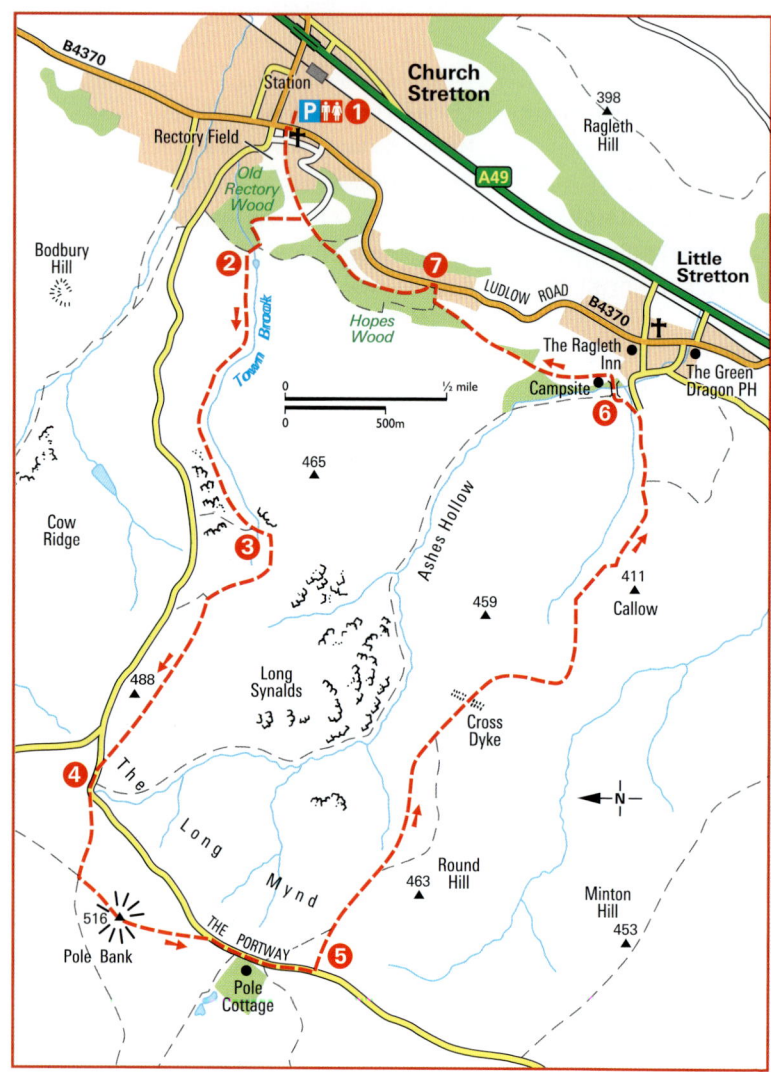

1. Walk up Lion Meadow to High Street and turn right. Turn left at The Square, go past the church and straight on into Rectory Field. Walk up a broad swathe of green then turn right near some houses and enter Old Rectory Wood. The path descends to a junction, where you turn right, soon crossing Town Brook. Turn left and climb to a gate on to the Long Mynd.

2. Go forward beside the brook to meet iron railings around a pool, then continue in the same direction with the brook on your left. After an almost

imperceptible height gain, the path begins to climb more steeply before curving leftward around the head of the valley.

3. At a Pole Bank Way marker post, bear right. Just follow these posts now, gaining height very gradually again. Ignore branching paths and, after ascending a slight rise, you'll see the summit ahead on the left.

4. Meet an unfenced road. Turn left, ignore a path to Little Stretton, and go straight on when the road bends left, joining an obvious stony track. Cross the Portway (just an indistinct groove here) and continue to clear cross-tracks. Turn left to the summit then straight on down to the road. Bear right and follow it past trees surrounding the site of Pole Cottage.

5. About 100yds (91m) further on, turn left on a wide green path. Soon bear left again, joining an even clearer green track. In a dip, fork left to follow a narrower path contouring around Round Hill. Go straight on at a junction, then descend to Cross Dyke (a Bronze Age earthwork). After the dyke the path ascends briefly, but soon levels out, then begins its descent, eventually following a brook. Pass some houses and a campsite.

6. Cross a footbridge by a ford. Keep on down the lane to visit Little Stretton and its pubs; otherwise after a few paces take the footpath on the left over a stile. It climbs by a field-edge to the top corner, then turns left, following the top of a steep slope to a pasture. Follow the right-hand edge of this until the path enters woodland. Descend to Ludlow Road.

7. Turn left and immediately left again on a bridleway. It climbs into woodland, emerging at the far side to meet a wider track, which soon becomes a road. As it bends to the right, go left through a car park to Rectory Field. Descend to The Square, turn right on High Street and left on Lion Meadow to the car park.

Where to eat and drink

Both The Green Dragon and The Ragleth Inn at Little Stretton are very popular. The Green Dragon is a free house with a beer garden, and does food daily, including a children's menu and veggie dishes. The Ragleth Inn welcomes grubby boots and wellingtons, children under 14 and dogs of the well-behaved variety in the bar. It does snacks and meals and has a large garden and children's play area.

What to see

The ring ouzel, or mountain blackbird, was mentioned in previous editions of this book as a species you might see on the Long Mynd. Sadly, ouzels no longer breed here and even passage sightings are rare. If you do see one, count yourself lucky: it looks very like a blackbird but with a white half-moon just below the throat. Other birds you may see and hear include the curlew, with its long, down-turned beak and distinctive rippling call.

While you're there

The walk bypasses the village of Little Stretton, but it's worth a detour if you like period architecture. Several charming buildings include the picturesque Manor House, built around 1600. However, the timber-framed, thatched church is from 1903.

39

THE STRETTON HILLS

DISTANCE/TIME	6 miles (9.7km) / 3hrs
ASCENT/GRADIENT	1,060ft (323m) / ▲ ▲
PATHS	Good paths through pasture and woodland, many stiles
LANDSCAPE	Beautiful range of hills overlooking the Stretton Gap
SUGGESTED MAP	OS Explorer 217 The Long Mynd & Wenlock Edge
START/FINISH	Grid reference: SO453936
DOG FRIENDLINESS	Under close control near livestock
PARKING	Easthope Road car park, Church Stretton
PUBLIC TOILETS	At car park

Squeezed between the heathery bulk of the Long Mynd and the enticing Stretton Hills lies Church Stretton. This small market town makes an ideal base for a few days of quality walking. If you've explored the Long Mynd you may have looked across the Stretton Gap at Caer Caradoc and its neighbours and thought you'd like to know them better. Until recently, a glance at an OS map would have suggested that there was limited access to these hills, but in fact there has been permissive access for many years and this is now guaranteed by law.

The Strettons may well be the shapeliest hills in the county. Or, at least, three of them are: Ragleth Hill, Caer Caradoc and The Lawley, which run in a north-south alignment to the east of Church Stretton. Basically, they are hog's-backs, very much like The Wrekin. But, also like The Wrekin, catch them from the right angle (end-on is best, or check out Caer Caradoc from The Cwms) and they look almost conical, with an alluring mini-mountain shape that screams 'Climb me'. If you do climb one of them, for instance Caer Caradoc, and look north, you will see The Wrekin, lying on exactly the same alignment, and taking much the same form as Caer Caradoc and The Lawley.

The Strettons are also of volcanic origin, like The Wrekin; long, narrow ridges of resistant Precambrian rock, which was thrust up from the earth's core by movements along the Church Stretton fault. This break in the earth's crust has been traced from Staffordshire to South Wales, but it is here in Shropshire that its effects are most noticeable, where the hard Precambrian rocks are brought up against much softer rocks, such as limestones. If you look at the OS map you will notice a line of springs marked along the western slopes of Caer Caradoc. This marks the line of the fault. If you walked along the footpath that runs below the springs, you would see some small quarries where earlier generations of farmers dug out the soft limestone to make agricultural lime to sweeten the acidic soils that prevail in the area.

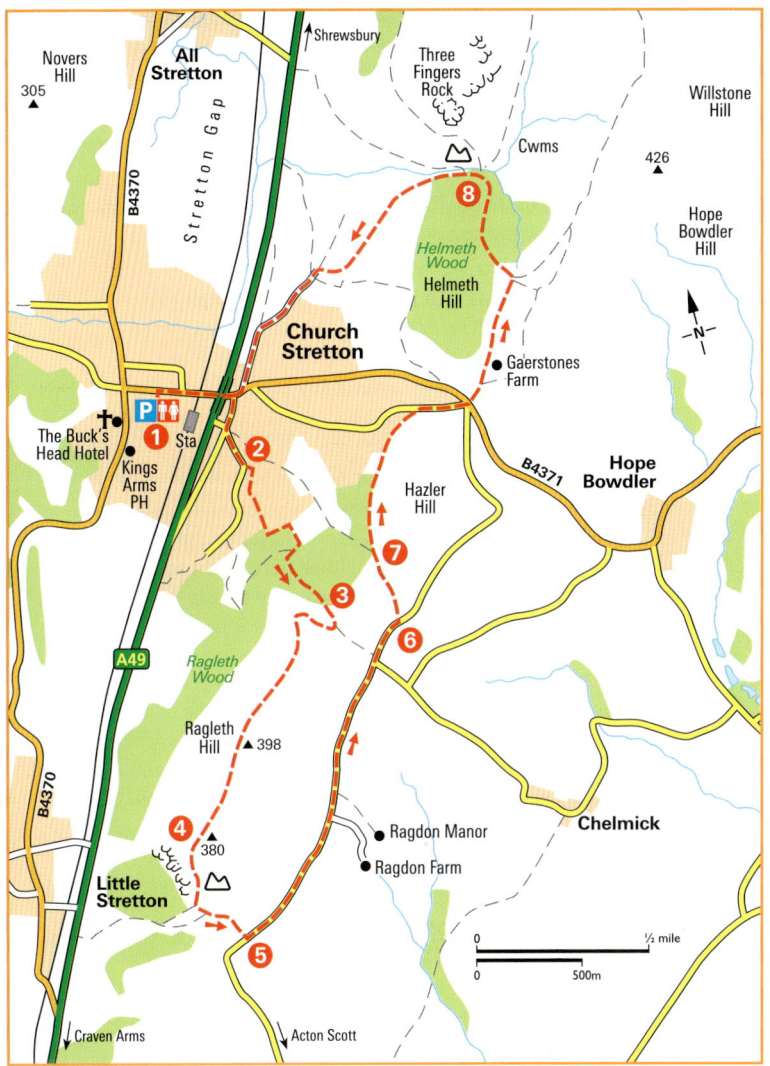

1. Walk along Easthope Road to Sandford Avenue, turn right and walk past the train station. Cross the A49, proceed along Sandford Avenue, then turn right on Watling Street South. Turn left by a postbox, fork right and shortly left on Ragleth Road.

2. Turn right into a Woodland Trust reserve, through a 5-bar gate into Gough's Coppice. Keep left at a fork, climbing by the edge of the wood, and left again at the next junction. Leave the wood at a stile and turn right on a footpath. After a level section, the path climbs steeply to a stile. Turn right for a few paces, then fork left to follow a higher path, which goes by the left-hand fence through woodland.

3. When the path emerges on to the open hillside, keep straight on as far as a stile, but don't cross it. Turn your back on it and follow a trodden path up Ragleth Hill, then walk along the spine of the hill.

4. A pole marks the southern summit. Descend the steep well-worn path past rocks then follow a fence down to a stile. Drop left to another stile and climb to the top left corner of the next field. Follow the left-hand hedge down another field and join a lane.

5. Turn left and follow the lane, with its wide green verge, for about a mile (1.6km), passing the turn for Chelmick and Soudley.

6. Just past a timber clad house (Clemcroft) turn left on a bridleway signed to Church Stretton. Follow this to a gate and down through woodland.

7. Approaching a second gate, don't go through, but turn right to contour round Hazler Hill for 0.4 miles (65m). Turn right at a lane, walk to a junction and cross to a bridleway opposite, which passes Gaerstones Farm. After Caer Caradoc comes into view, go through a gate then look for a bridleway branching left to a gate/stile about 40yds (37m) away. The bridleway descends past Helmeth Hill to meet another bridleway at the point where this is crossed by a brook.

8. Turn left, soon emerging from woodland into pasture. Keep on in much the same direction, with a fence on your left. The path becomes a sunken track, which can be very muddy. Reaching a lane, turn left. Turn right on Helmeth Road bearing immediately left into Watling Street North, right again at a T-junction onto B4371, and retrace your outward route back to the car park.

Where to eat and drink

Church Stretton has a number of cafés as well two public houses in the town centre – the Buck's Head and the Kings Arms. The Kings Arms is an attractive timber framed building dating from 1593. It has recently undergone restoration revealing original beams of authentic character. It now serves local craft beers, home-cooked food and welcomes well behaved dogs.

What to see

If you are unconvinced by the power of sheep to shape a landscape, take a look at Helmeth Wood. It's easy to visit from the bridleway round Helmeth Hill. While the other Strettons are mainly covered in short, springy turf, this one is entirely wooded, and there's only one reason for that – the fence that keeps sheep out.

While you're there

Take the kids to Acton Scott Historic Working Farm, south of Church Stretton, which recreates daily life on an upland farm in the late 19th century. There are rare breeds too, such as Longhorn cattle, Tamworth pigs and Shropshire sheep. It is due to reopen in Spring 2024, check their website for updates.

CAER CARADOC

DISTANCE/TIME	6.6 miles (10.6km) / 3hrs
ASCENT/GRADIENT	1,282ft (391m) / ▲ ▲ ▲
PATHS	Generally excellent though steep in places, many stiles
LANDSCAPE	Steep ridges with rocky outcrops, rolling farmland
SUGGESTED MAP	OS Explorer 217 The Long Mynd & Wenlock Edge
START/FINISH	Grid reference: SO506952
DOG FRIENDLINESS	Mostly grazing land, limited scope for dogs to run free
PARKING	Cardington Village Hall; if in use for an event, use great consideration when parking elsewhere in the village
PUBLIC TOILETS	None on route

Caer Caradoc is not the highest hill in Shropshire – most lists put it at no. 6 – but many people rate it the best. It has a compelling outline from any direction; when approaching from the north, for instance, it completely outshines the Long Mynd, though the latter is both higher and far more extensive. The steepness of its slopes makes the summit probably the best all-round viewpoint in the county, and the jagged, occasionally bizarre, rock outcrops which encrust the ridge make great foregrounds for your photos.

Caer Caradoc is, not surprisingly, most often climbed from Church Stretton. There's absolutely nothing wrong with this approach and it has the great advantage that you can arrive by train, but it's steep nearly all the way and almost feels too short to do justice to this splendid hill. The alternative approach from Cardington makes the build-up more gradual, and gives you a 'bonus' top on the return leg. This is Willstone Hill, which has its own stark outcrop, the Battle Stones, just north of the summit.

The ramparts of a hill fort, around the summit, can be seen from afar when the light is right, and are very obvious as you climb through them on your way to the top. Unlike other hill forts such as Bury Ditches on Sunnyhill, the area is small and the ground rocky and uneven; it seems unlikely ever to have accommodated a permanent 'civilian' population but is a commanding defensive position.

Some say it was the last stronghold of Caradoc, whom you may remember from school history lessons as Caractacus (a Latinised form of the name). He is a real historical character, one of the last British chiefs to hold out against the Roman invasion. He was defeated in AD 50 and, though he evaded capture for a while, was eventually betrayed to the invaders and taken to Rome in chains. However, there is no hard evidence to link the Battle of Caer Caradoc with the hill which now bears the same name. There's even less evidence to explain the name 'Battle Stones' for the outcrop on Willstone Hill.

Cardington is a very ancient village, mentioned in the Domesday Book. The general layout of the village can be traced back at least to the 14th century. Its most significant building is the Church of St James, which has a Norman nave. Most of the rest is medieval and even the 'new' timber porch dates from 1639.

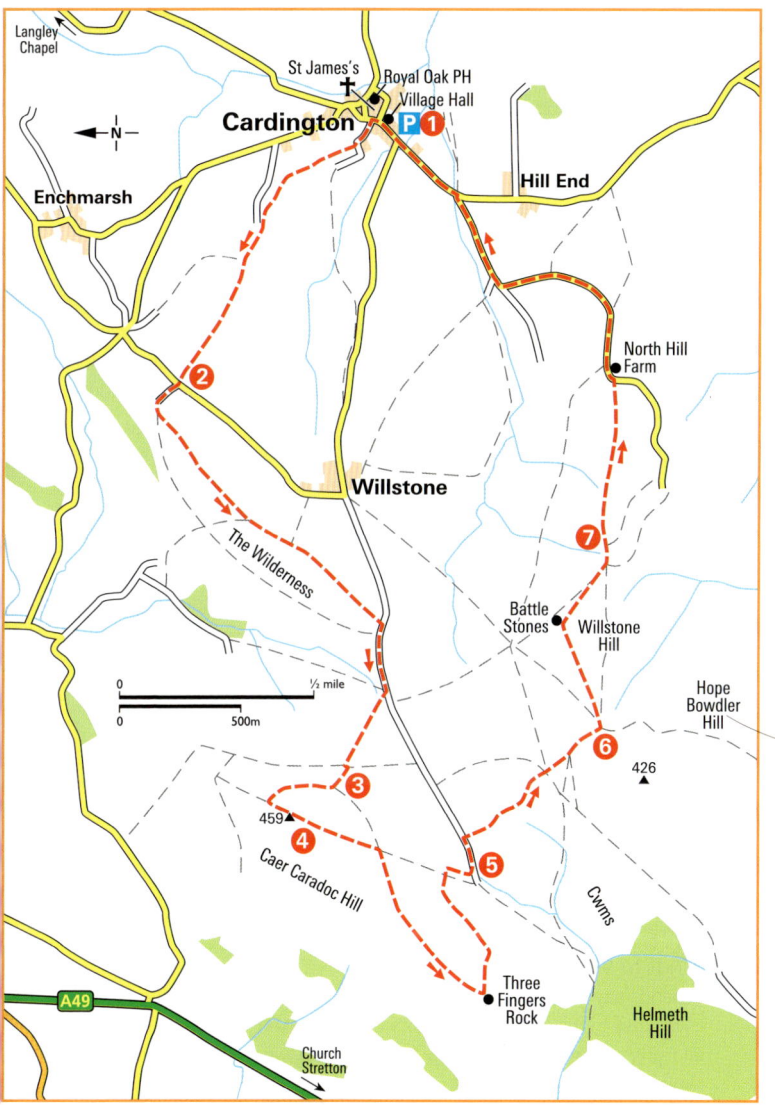

1. Turn left out of the car park, then right and left on a street with a 'Sat Nav Error' sign. It becomes a track, passing right of the Old Vicarage. As it bends left go straight ahead into a field. Go through a gate at the end, bear left in the next field then follow the right hand hedge through several fields. Switch sides at a stile and keep on in the same direction to a road.

2. Go straight across into a short track. When it opens out go left along a ridge with a fence on your left. Follow the ridge over several stiles then bear slightly

right to its highest point. Descend to a small gate and turn right on a clear track. Pass an Access Land sign and continue to two fingerposts by a stile. Cross and go straight up a steep bank, soon easing. Continue straight ahead to a field gate and kissing gate below the steep upper slopes.

3. Go ahead a few paces then turn right above the bracken. Follow sheep trods across the slope, forking left to avoid losing height. Keep traversing round until you meet an obvious path going straight up the ridge. Follow this through the ramparts of the hill fort to the summit.

4. Descend past gnarled outcrops and then along a more level section to Three Fingers Rock, overlooking Church Stretton. Double back about 40yds (37m) to a metal gate. Follow a faint path down the grassy slope, swing left to a fence corner then continue along a clear green track until this zig-zags down to join a stony track.

5. Go left for 150yds (137m), then bear right into the gap between two small rounded hills. Find a metal gate in the fence running down the gap, go up the slope a few paces, then bear right on a level sheep trod, which becomes clearer as it curves around the hill. As the slope opens out go right to a metal gate with bridleway markers, then straight ahead up a steep path through bracken to a saddle.

6. Turn left over a stile and follow the fence along the ridge. Pass a defunct gate then bear left to the summit of Willstone Hill. Return to the fence then follow the path down a steeper section to a cluster of gates. Go through the leftmost of these, skirt round a marshy little dip, then gradually return to the left-hand fence.

7. Cross a stile in the corner and continue along the fence-line to North Hill Farm. Follow a concrete track downhill and continue down a tarmac lane. Go left at the next junction and soon re-enter Cardington.

Where to eat and drink

The Royal Oak in Cardington claims to be the oldest continuously licensed pub in Shropshire. It has certainly retained a very traditional character, with low beams and a great inglenook fireplace. There's real ale on tap and good value home-made food; the speciality is the famous 'Royal' dish, the Fidget Pie, gammon cooked in spiced cider and apples with a puff pastry top.

What to see

Legends say that after the battle, Caradoc/Caractacus took refuge in a cave close to the summit. This story can be verified, but the cave is there all right, on the west side below the summit. However, it's not large and takes a bit of finding.

While you're there

Take a look at Langley Chapel, an English Heritage property a few miles north of Cardington. It stands alone in peaceful countryside and the interior contains a remarkably well-preserved collection of 17th-century timber furnishings. Admission is free, daily 10am–6pm in the summer and 10am–4pm in winter.

41

LUDLOW BONE BED AND WHITCLIFFE COMMON

DISTANCE/TIME	5.25 miles (8.4km) / 2hrs 15min
ASCENT/GRADIENT	820ft (250m) / ▲ ▲ ▲
PATHS	Good but one sometimes turns to shallow stream
LANDSCAPE	Historic town, quiet lanes, pasture and forest
SUGGESTED MAP	OS Explorer 203 Ludlow
START/FINISH	Grid reference: SO510746
DOG FRIENDLINESS	Ideal for dogs, but must be on lead between Priors Halton and Mortimer Forest
PARKING	Car park off Castle Street, Ludlow
PUBLIC TOILETS	At car park

Ludlow is often hailed as one of the most perfect small towns in Britain. Not only is it beautifully situated, but it has a total of 469 listed buildings, an astonishing number for such a small place. One of the oldest is the 11th-century castle, built on a superb defensive site high above the confluence of the rivers Corve and Teme. As you start the walk, descending to the river, look out for Dinham House, an imposing brick mansion with a long list of illustrious past residents, including Lucien Bonaparte, banished to England by his brother Napoleon for making an 'unsuitable' marriage. Further down Dinham is the 12th-century Chapel of St Thomas of Canterbury, one of Ludlow's two oldest buildings (the other is the castle).

In recent years, Ludlow has also gained a reputation as a 'foodie' hotspot. Factors which have drawn restaurateurs here include the quality of life and beauty of the surroundings, as well as the exceptional quality and variety of produce available. The Ludlow Marches Food and Drink Festival was the first of its kind in the country and has inspired many similar events elsewhere. Castle Square is home to a thriving market four days a week.

Whitcliffe is an ancient common over which Ludlovians have held common rights since at least 1240. They no longer exercise their grazing rights, nor do they quarry stone, and probably very few even bother to gather firewood. But they do come here to walk their dogs and admire the view from the top of the cliff of their incomparable town, set against its backdrop of the Clee Hills. Below the cliff, our walk follows the path known as the Breadwalk, which was laid out in 1850, the previously unemployed workmen being paid in bread.

At Ludford Corner, a small plaque adorns a low, rather overgrown bit of cliff on your right, behind a bench. This small chunk of Ludlow rock is a Site of Special Scientific Interest (SSSI) which geologists refer to as Ludlow Bone Bed. It's packed with bones, fish scales, spores, plant debris and tiny mites – fossil evidence of the first plants and animals to colonise the land. These rocks were laid down as sediments in a shallow tropical sea about 400 million years ago.

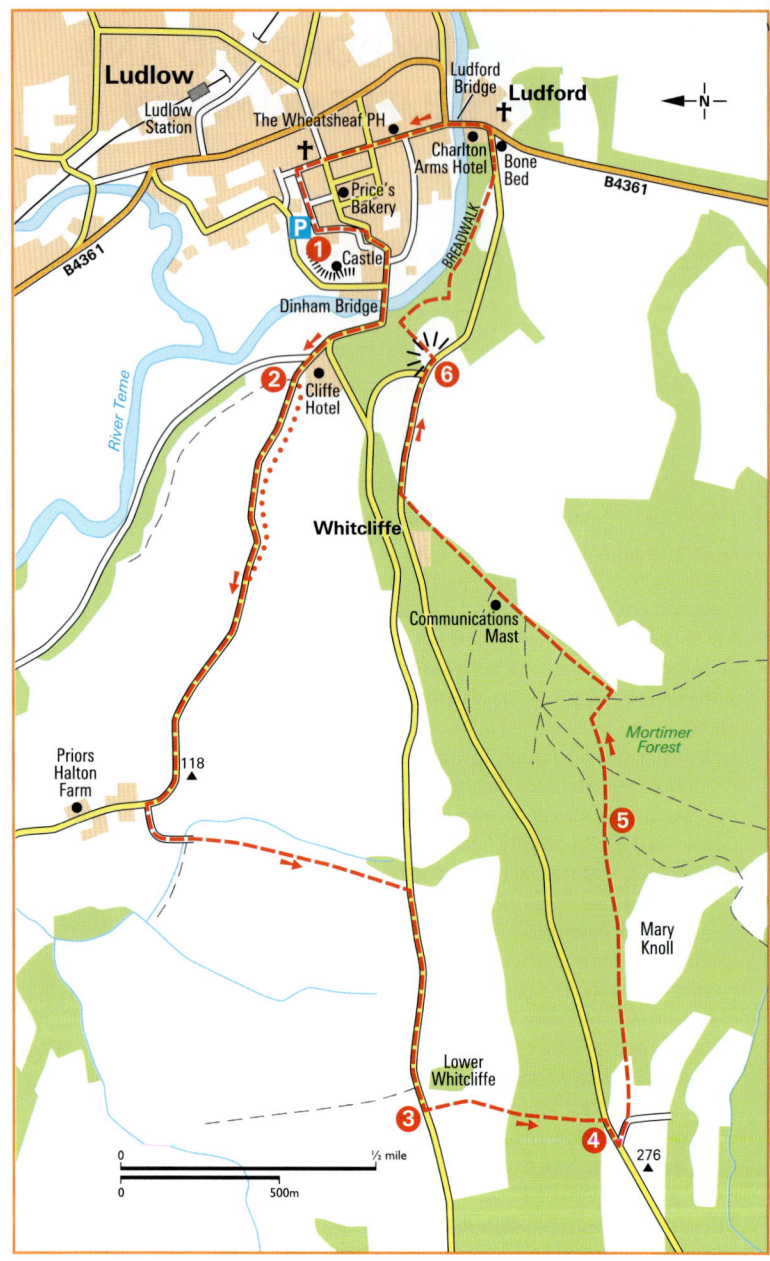

1. Turn right through Castle Square, then follow Dinham down to the River Teme. Cross Dinham Bridge to Whitcliffe. Follow the lane round to the right. At a junction go straight on along a no through road signposted to Priors Halton, soon passing the Cliffe Hotel.

2. Here you can take a footpath left of the road, first running past allotments then along field-edges, rejoining the lane further on. If you prefer to avoid

stiles, you can stay on the lane instead. When you reach Priors Halton farm, take the track on the left, which soon swings left towards Mortimer Forest. Ignore a path on the right and continue ahead to meet a road. Turn right. After passing a prominent stony track on the right, start looking for a less conspicuous track on the left, with a bridleway gate alongside a field gate.

3. Go straight up sheep pasture, following power lines, then through a gate into Lower Whitcliffe (Mortimer Forest). Cross a track and keep climbing, soon crossing a second track, after which the gradient eases as you continue up to a road. Turn right for 100yds (91m), then cross to a bridleway.

4. Take the right-hand of two tracks by a barn, then switch to the left track. Continue straight ahead until waymarks direct you onto a narrower path, still almost directly ahead, to the left of a field-gate. Continue, now descending steadily on a sunken track. Keep straight on, ignoring branching paths, including colour-coded forest trails. The path is high-banked and worn to bedrock in places, and obviously an ancient highway, so unlike the bland, modern forest paths.

5. When you reach a junction with a forest road, take the middle path of three directly ahead. It's hard to spot at first but it's the continuation of the one you've been on. Mossy, ferny and often wet, it descends steadily, eventually swinging left near a communications mast, through a gate in a deer fence and down a narrow funnel to meet a short track. Turn right to a road and follow this down right, past a junction, to a viewpoint with a good view of the castle.

6. Descend towards Dinham Bridge, but only cross the Teme here if you want a short cut. Otherwise, turn right beside the Teme, along the Breadwalk. Eventually you'll climb again on steps carved from the bedrock. Join a lane and continue in the same direction to Ludford Corner. Turn left to descend past the Charlton Arms Hotel to cross Ludford Bridge. Go up Lower Broad Street, through the Broadgate, and on up Broad Street, then turn left to High Street and Castle Square.

Where to eat and drink

Ludlow has a great choice, from humble chippies to top-notch restaurants. The 13th-century Charlton Arms by Ludford Bridge is a popular place and the 17th-century Wheatsheaf, right by the Broadgate, offers great-value pub food and real ale. Prices Bakery has a huge range of breads, cakes and pastries.

What to see

Many of the larger trees that grace Whitcliffe's slopes are hornbeam, an uncommon species this far north. You can recognise hornbeam by its distinctive smooth, fluted trunk and winged seeds. Hornbeam mast (the fruit of the tree) is a favourite food of the shy hawfinch.

While you're there

Don't miss the Castle. Norman in origin, it was held by the de Lacy and Mortimer families before passing to Richard Plantagenet. Abandoned in 1689, its ruins are still one of the finest medieval castles in Britain. It's open every day, apart from special events and in winter, when it's open at weekends only.

42

STOKESAY CASTLE AND VIEW EDGE

DISTANCE/TIME	6.25 miles (10.1km) / 2hrs 30min
ASCENT/GRADIENT	909ft (277m) / ▲ ▲
PATHS	Mostly excellent, short stretch eroded and uneven, byway from Aldon to Stoke Wood occasionally floods, many stiles
LANDSCAPE	Woods and pasture in unspoiled hills above River Onny
SUGGESTED MAP	OS Explorers 203 Ludlow; 217 The Long Mynd & Wenlock Edge
START/FINISH	Grid reference: SO437819
DOG FRIENDLINESS	Under control on Brandhill, Aldon and livestock
PARKING	Lay-by on A49 immediately north of Stokesay turn-off
PUBLIC TOILETS	At Stokesay Castle (English Heritage, check times)

This is an exquisite walk, with wonderful views from the aptly named View Edge, mostly west to Clun Forest, but also east and south to the Clee Hills, Wenlock Edge, Mortimer Forest and Ludlow. Brandhill Gutter and Aldon Gutter are highlights of the walk, and considerably more salubrious than they sound – a gutter is a local name for the sort of narrow, steep-sided valley more commonly known in Shropshire as a dingle.

But, however gorgeous the landscape, it has a rival for once, in the shape of the picturesque Stokesay Castle, which isn't really a castle at all. It's a fortified manor house, which might sound like a pedantic distinction, but isn't. A true castle was defensive in purpose, and therefore strictly practical. Stokesay Castle, however, could not have resisted prolonged assault. It was part fashion statement, part status symbol, and is today the best preserved and probably the oldest example of its kind in England.

In the mid-10th century, the manor of Stoke was held by Wild Edric, a Saxon nobleman, but after the Norman Conquest it was given by William I to Picot de Say – hence the name Stokesay. ('Stoke', a common English placename, means enclosure.) Picot built a house and a church some time after 1068, but in 1280 Stokesay was sold to Laurence of Ludlow, a wool merchant, who set about rebuilding and fortifying the house. Ten generations of Laurence's descendants lived at Stokesay, but in the reign of Charles I it came into the ownership of the Craven family and was used as a supply base for the King's forces when they were based at Ludlow in the early stages of the Civil War. It was surrendered to the Roundheads, without a siege, when it came under attack. By the 19th century it had fallen into decay, and was being used as a barn. Happily, in 1869 it was sold to John Darby Allcroft, a Worcester glove manufacturer and MP, who set about restoring it. Today, Stokesay Castle is in the care of English Heritage. Stokesay's great hall is a particularly rare survival, almost untouched since medieval times and containing its original staircase, open octagonal hearth and innovative timber roof. There is also a fine solar (an upper living room), containing Elizabethan panelling and a sumptuous fireplace, accessible only by an exterior stair. Across the courtyard is a timber-framed gatehouse decorated with wonderful carvings.

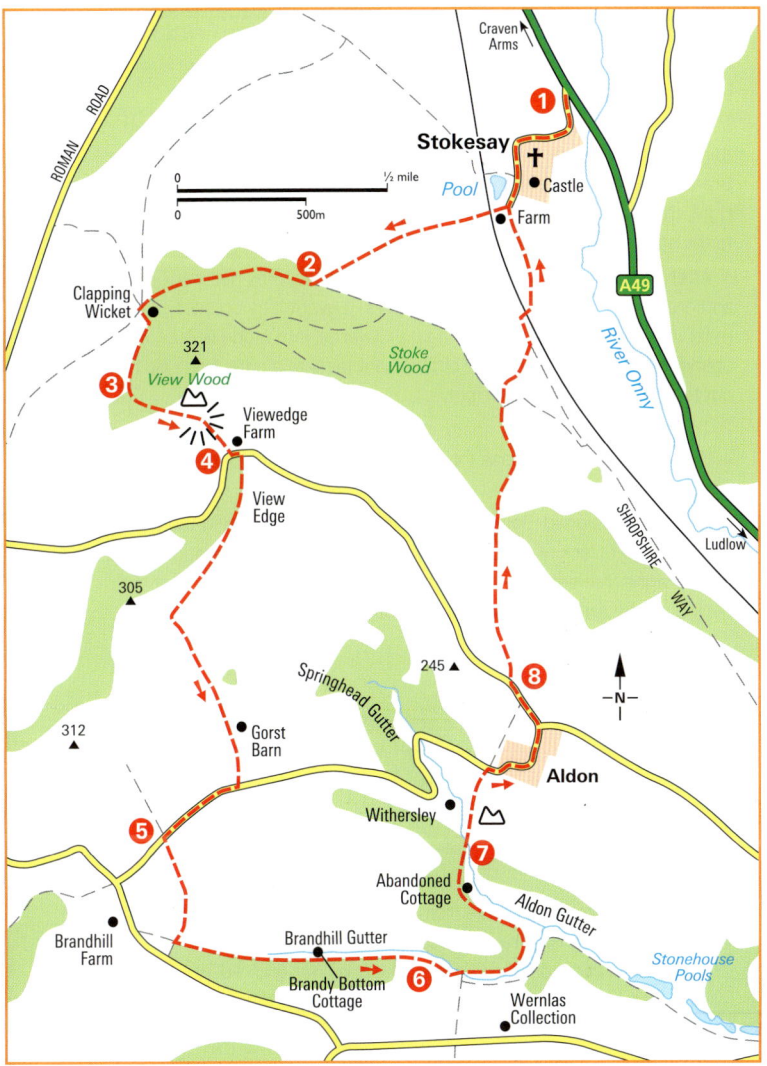

1. Take the footway from the lay-by to the lane that leads to Stokesay Castle. Walk past the castle and take the second footpath on the right, at the far side of a pool. It skirts a farm, then crosses the railway. Keep straight on through three meadows on a worn path, with stiles providing further guidance.

2. Enter Stoke Wood, proceed to a track and turn right. Turn left at a gate marked 'Clapping Wicket' and walk past the house before turning sharp left up the field in front of it. Turn right at the top, walking by the edge of View Wood.

3. Join a track that leads into the wood, then emerges from it to run alongside the edge. Where it seems vague, locate a sunken track just inside the wood, which climbs to a stile, then meets a lane by Viewedge Farm

4. Turn left for a few paces, then join a footpath on the right. Turn right by a field-edge and walk to the top of a rise, continuing in the same direction across fields until you come to a waymarker that sends you sharp left across an adjacent field. Join a track at the far side and continue past Gorst Barn to a lane. Turn right.

5. Turn left on a footpath, crossing three pastures. Go right and down in the third to a concealed stile, which gives on to a bridleway. Turn left down Brandhill Gutter. Opposite Brandy Bottom Cottage, go through a gate on the right, then immediately turn left to continue in the same direction. Keep close to the stream (often dry).

6. After passing through a gate, the bridleway becomes narrow, uneven and eroded for a while but soon improves. It eventually crosses the stream (next to a stile) and starts to swing northwards, into Aldon Gutter. Beyond an abandoned cottage, keep right of pheasant pens to a gate. Don't go through but follow the hedge to the right.

7. The path becomes clear again, climbing the steep valley side to meet a lane at the top. Turn right to pass through the hamlet of Aldon, then left at a T-junction.

8. Join a track signed 'Byway' on the right at a slight bend in the lane. This lovely hedged track leads between fields, then descends through Stoke Wood. Ignore signs that seem to suggest you should leave the track here. Stick with it back over the railway to the lane past Stokesay Castle.

Where to eat and drink

There is a tea room and toilets at Stokesay Castle (English Heritage); there also several options in Craven Arms on the A49. If you're heading northward after your walk, its also worth considering is Affcot Lodge on the A49 at Upper Affcot. It offers food throughout the day, as well as hand-pumped ales.

What to see

The view of Stokesay Castle from the adjacent churchyard is superb, and St John's Church is a rare example of Commonwealth style. The Norman church was badly damaged during the Civil War and rebuilt between 1654 and 1664 under Cromwell's Commonwealth, a time when very few churches were built.

While you're there

Hopesay Common, northwest of Craven Arms, is a fine expanse of upland heath grazed by 'wild' ponies. They all have owners and are carefully monitored but left to their own devices for much of the year. Unploughed for centuries, the open common has fine views and a stile carved with a verse by Omar Khayyam.

43

WART HILL AND THE ONNY TRAIL

DISTANCE/TIME	6 miles (9.7km) / 3hrs
ASCENT/GRADIENT	918ft (280m) / ▲ ▲
PATHS	Generally good, some muddy patches, steep, sometimes slippery descent from Wart Hill, careful route-finding needed, many stiles
LANDSCAPE	Wooded hills, pastureland and varied terrain by River Onny
SUGGESTED MAP	OS Explorer 217 The Long Mynd & Wenlock Edge
START/FINISH	Grid reference: SO430843
DOG FRIENDLINESS	Mostly permissive paths so keep on lead
PARKING	Car park for Onny Trail, next to railway bridge on unclassified road from A49 to Cheney Longville
PUBLIC TOILETS	None on route

Craven Arms is a young town, though possibly a very old settlement. It owes its present form to the coming of the railways, before which it was little more than a huddle of cottages at the hamlet of Newton, near the former Craven Arms Hotel. The Shrewsbury and Hereford railway was built through Craven Arms in the 1840s, followed by the Knighton line to Wales, the Buildwas line to the coalfields and the Bishop's Castle line, making The Arms, as it was known, a major railway junction. The cattle and sheep that had formerly travelled the drove roads now came by train, and other business opportunities were opened up. Local landowner Lord Craven recognised the potential and built a new town. For a while it seemed as though it might mushroom, but it never quite happened. Two of the railway lines have gone, but the Shrewsbury-to-Hereford line is still busy. The Knighton line is now part of the Heart of Wales line and runs through gloriously remote countryside to Swansea.

The line that inspired most affection has long gone. This was the Bishop's Castle line. The plan was for a link from the Shrewsbury and Hereford line to the Oswestry and Newtown (later Cambrian) line near Montgomery, with short branches to Montgomery and Bishop's Castle. Financial problems dogged the railway company, but they went ahead with an official opening in 1865, using a borrowed locomotive and coaches. Regular traffic started the next year, but only from Craven Arms to Bishop's Castle, via a junction at Lydham Heath. The rest of the line was never finished. Locomotives had to uncouple at Lydham and run around their carriages to recouple in reverse for the last few miles. Not surprisingly, the railway was never profitable. It is said that it was so slow that people would get off to pick blackberries or mushrooms, then stroll along the line to reboard. The easternmost stretch of the line is now the Onny Trail, open for public access under the Countryside Stewardship scheme. It makes a delightful walk along the banks of the River Onny. It also forms the return leg of this beautiful walk.

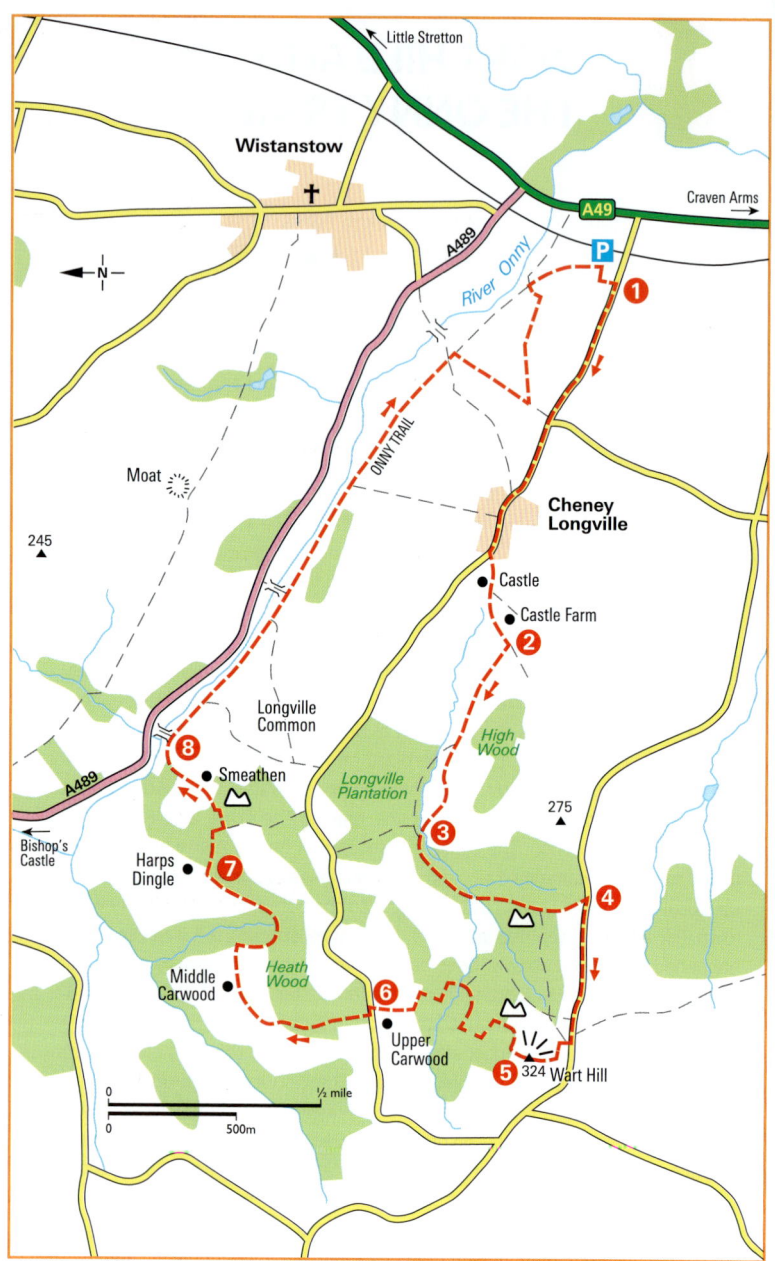

1. Walk to the lane and turn right. Keep straight on at a junction and pass through Cheney Longville. At the far side of the village, fork left at a sign for Castle Farm. A track climbs through the farm and enters pasture.

2. Walk along the right edge of the fields. In the next field, go straight on up a slope. The path soon levels out and, after a large oak, a waymarker sends you diagonally down to the bottom right field corner.

3. Climb a stile into woodland, walk to a T-junction and turn left. Soon fork left on a level track which runs past a pool then continues through plantation, soon swinging left and climbing. Go straight on at a waymarked junction and keep climbing to a lane.

4. Turn right, then right again after 600yds (549m) at gate and stile. A few paces further on, turn left at a tree-hidden signpost. A steep climb now takes you through woodland to the top of Wart Hill, covered in bracken, gorse and a scattering of pines.

5. Keep going in the same direction, past the trig point, then begin a steep, mostly waymarked descent. At an unmarked junction go straight downhill to a T-junction and turn left. Follow the level track to a sharp turn back right. At the next junction turn left, down-hill, and then zigzagging up again. Waymarks are present but often hidden by summer vegetation.

6. Meet a lane, turn left, then immediately right on another track into Heath Wood. At the far side of the wood, the track bends right. The track passes a house (Middle Carwood), becoming vague as it climbs a field then clear again at the top left corner. Follow it through more woodland. Turn right at a T-junction near a house.

7. A brief climb through woods leads to a junction. Turn left on a footpath, descending steeply. Leaving the trees, take a narrow path through bracken to pass to the left of a shed and house, then keep going down, following waymarks. The path hairpins down to meet the Onny Trail.

8. Turn right, following the old railway. At a break in the embankment keep left, then find a stile in a hedge ahead. Turn right up the narrow track until a gate on the left allows you to return to the railway route.

Where to eat and drink

The Station café in the centre of Craven Arms is a handy place to grab a tea or a coffee, or a hearty breakfast before your walk. The Ragleth Inn, situated in the lovely village of Little Stretton 6 miles away, dates back to 1663. The Ragleth Inn offers all you would expect from a family run English country inn with a large garden and serving delicious food and a good range of drinks.

What to see

The Onny Trail is notable for scenery and wildlife, but railway buffs will enjoy it too. The trail begins on the site of Strefford Junction, just north of Craven Arms, where the Bishop's Castle line left the Shrewsbury and Hereford main line. An interpretation board in the car park provides some useful information and access details.

While you're there

The Bishop's Castle Railway, despite (or perhaps because of) its deficiencies, inspired lots of affection and has generated reams of documentation. If you'd like to know more, or if you just enjoy looking at interesting old photos and memorabilia, check out the Rail and Transport Museum which occupies a 15th-century building in Bishop's Castle.

44

FLOUNDER'S FOLLY ON WENLOCK EDGE

DISTANCE/TIME	6.5 miles (10.4km) / 2hrs 30mins
ASCENT/GRADIENT	817ft (249m) / ▲ ▲
PATHS	Mostly good, not always clear between Quinny Brook and Halford, muddy in places, 12 stiles
LANDSCAPE	Pasture and woodland on scarp slope of Wenlock Edge
SUGGESTED MAP	OS Explorer 217 The Long Mynd & Wenlock Edge
START/FINISH	Grid reference: SO4433828
DOG FRIENDLINESS	Off lead in woodland, on lead in pasture
PARKING	Car park off B4368 Corvedale Road, Craven Arms or small car park/picnic area on same road on outskirts of town
PUBLIC TOILETS	None en route

In the 18th and 19th centuries, follies were the height of fashion. The focal point of this walk is Flounder's Folly, a stone tower on top of Callow Hill, the highest point of Wenlock Edge. Like so many follies, it has an entertaining tale behind it, which may or may not be true. The story goes that a wealthy merchant called Benjamin Flounder ordered the tower to be built in 1838 so he could admire the view across Corve Dale to his fine house at Ludlow. But he got a nasty surprise when he first climbed to the top of the newly completed tower. His mansion was not to be seen – there was a hill in the way. 'Take it down' he roared, and it's unclear if he meant the hill or the tower. Both were spared, however, when a watery gleam on the horizon was pointed out to him. Benjamin was placated by the suggestion that it was the Mersey, and that he would be able to watch his ships leaving Liverpool. The initials BF are carved into the stonework and, perhaps that says it all.

Why did he have the tower built? It may have been for the view, a fashion choice or because he was a generous landowner who wished to provide work at a time of high unemployment.

The first follies appeared in the 16th century, but it wasn't until the 18th century that the craze took off, partly reflecting a new enthusiasm for all things classical. Wealthy young men were educated in the classics, then sent off on the Grand Tour. They came back full of the glory that was Greece and Rome and set about building temples on their country estates. This developed into a romantic search for the ideal landscape and people would enhance, as they thought, the view from their country seats with all manner of towers and castles, preferably ruined.

Flounder's Folly is a tall plain tower built from local stone, it has been restored and can be visited between 11am and 3pm or 4pm on days when a Cross of St George's flag flies from the top.

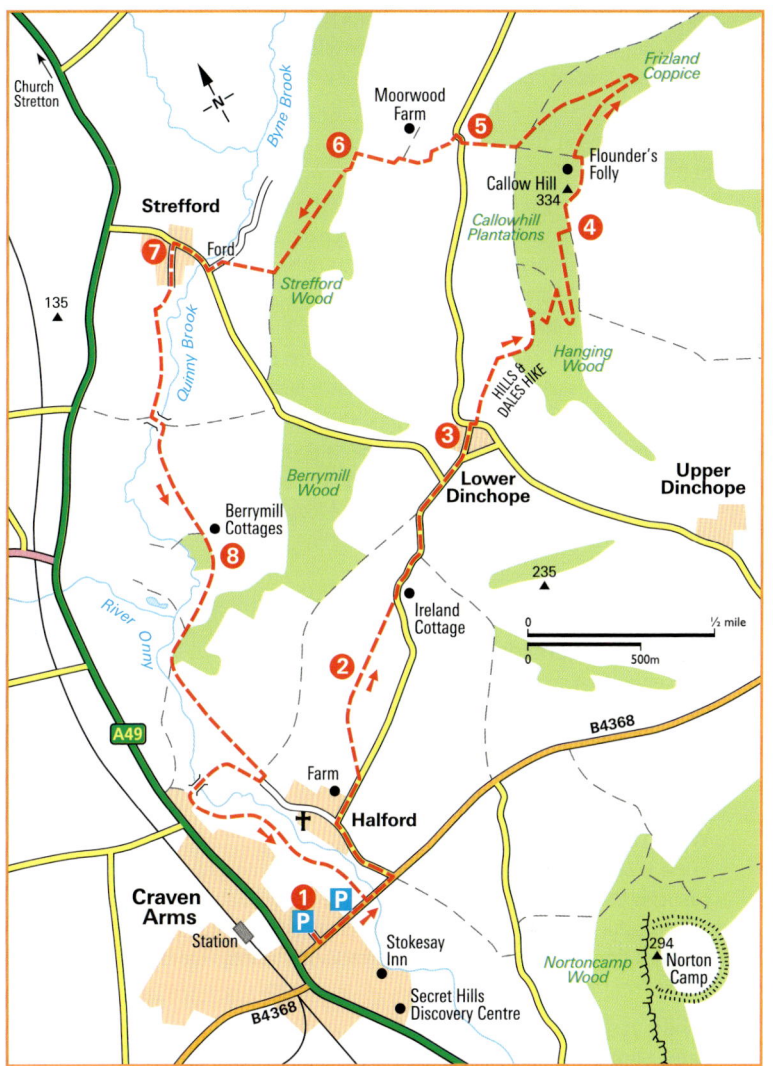

1. Walk down Corvedale Road, cross the River Onny and turn left into Halford. At a junction with a view of the church, turn right towards Dinchope. Pass a farm, then take a footpath on the left. It climbs to the far corner of a field, then along the left-hand edge of another.

2. When the hedge turns a corner, continue across the field to a stile by a power line pole, then up the next field to a concealed stile, near the top left corner. Turn left along a lane. Pass a turning for Strefford, then fork left and walk up to a T-junction.

3. Go a few paces right to a stile below a fingerpost confirming that you're following the Hills and Dales Hike. Just follow the frequent waymarkers, which guide you across fields and into woodland, before sending you zigzagging up graded and stepped paths to the top of Callow Hill.

4. Turn left at the top, skirt round Flounder's Folly, then return to the edge until you are forced to descend sharp left on a forestry track. The slope eases and the track swings right then passes a barrier to meet the Lower Dinchope–Westhope road.

5. Go straight ahead, then left at a triangular junction. Where the lane bends right (to Moorwood Farm), bear left on a bridleway.

6. Follow the track round as you enter Strefford Wood. Keep right at a fork, on the descending bridleway. Lower down it is sunken and muddy. Follow it out between fields to a lane. Turn left, then right, crossing Quinny Brook at a foot-bridge next to a ford into Strefford.

7. Turn left on a no through road, which becomes a track. Bear left through fields to a foot-bridge over Quinny Brook. Cross the bridge and go forward to another. Cross this and go ahead again to a stile just beyond three large oaks. Keep straight on, past Berrymill Cottages and through a copse into a field.

8. Follow the trodden path the length of the field. Go through a wood, then across fields towards Halford, keeping left of a fence. Turn sharp right on a track by School House, then left on a concrete footpath to a bridge across the River Onny. A permissive path on the left runs near the river back to Corvedale Road.

Where to eat and drink

You can enjoy home cooked food in The Stokesay Inn, which has a traditional pub feel. They offer a wide range of beverages and meals along with accommodation. Well behaved dogs are welcome and there is a car park behind or next to the pub. On Corvedale Road you'll find fish and chips plus Chinese and Indian takeaways.

What to see

In the 1960s and 1970s, our buzzard population plummeted because of pesticide poisoning. Since the banning of the worst poisons, it has staged a successful comeback. For years it was confined to Scotland, Wales and the West Country, but is now moving steadily eastwards across England, and is very common in Shropshire, especially round Craven Arms.

While you're there

At the Shropshire Hills Discovery Centre one can experience the Shropshire Hills Through Time exhibition. You can also meet their Mammoth and enjoy and explore their 30 acres of riverside meadows. There is a café on site as well as a shop with gifts and treats. They rely on donations alongside the income from the café, exhibition and shop to keep the Centre open for everyone to enjoy and to continue delivering their charitable aims. The Centre is open 7 days a week, 10am–5pm.

CRAVEN ARMS AND NORTON CAMP

45

DISTANCE/TIME	4.4 miles (7km) / 2hrs
ASCENT/GRADIENT	679ft (207m) / ▲ ▲ ▲
PATHS	Good field and woodland paths, but those around Norton Camp may be overgrown in high summer, 5 stiles
LANDSCAPE	Rolling fields and woodland
SUGGESTED MAP	OS Explorer 217 The Long Mynd & Wenlock Edge
START/FINISH	Grid reference: SO435825
DOG FRIENDLINESS	Good chance to run free in woodland
PARKING	Shropshire Hills Discovery Centre on outskirts of Craven Arms
PUBLIC TOILETS	In Discovery Centre

Craven Arms really does have hills on four sides: Hopesay Common and Wart Hill rise to the northwest, Callow Hill (the highest point of Wenlock Edge) to the northeast and View Edge to the southwest. Steepest of them all, and closest to the town, is Norton Camp. Given its commanding position, it's no surprise to find there's a hill-fort up there, just north of the highest point.

In fact, the Iron Age hill-fort at Norton Camp is one of the largest in Shropshire – the area within the ramparts being at least equal to Bury Ditches, for example – but it's harder to appreciate as there's no public access to the interior, which is used as farmland.

The dense growth of trees on and around the ramparts also obscures any view of their structure, but you can at least appreciate the scale by walking around it. Technically, it's a multivallate fort, with two complete ramparts, each with its associated ditch. Like Bury Ditches, it would have been a permanent settlement: the term 'fort' really doesn't do it justice; 'fortified village' would be closer to the truth.

An ancient legend relates that long ago the land hereabouts belonged to two giants, probably brothers, one living on View Edge and one at Norton Camp. They kept their riches in a locked chest in the vaults below Stokesay Castle, but there was only one key, which they shared by throwing it back and forth between their respective hills. However, one day, one of them muffed his throw and the key fell into the castle moat. They tried for a long time to find it, and many others have tried since, but to no avail. So the chest is still there in the vaults, but no one can get in: for some unexplained reason it is also guarded by a huge raven. So they say.

It's worth noting that one or two paths around Norton Camp can be rather overgrown in summer. Spring (for flowers) and autumn (for leaf colours) are often the best times for woodland walks anyway, but this would also be a good winter walk. There's more chance to enjoy the distant views, and it's much easier to see the earthworks of the hill fort when the trees are bare.

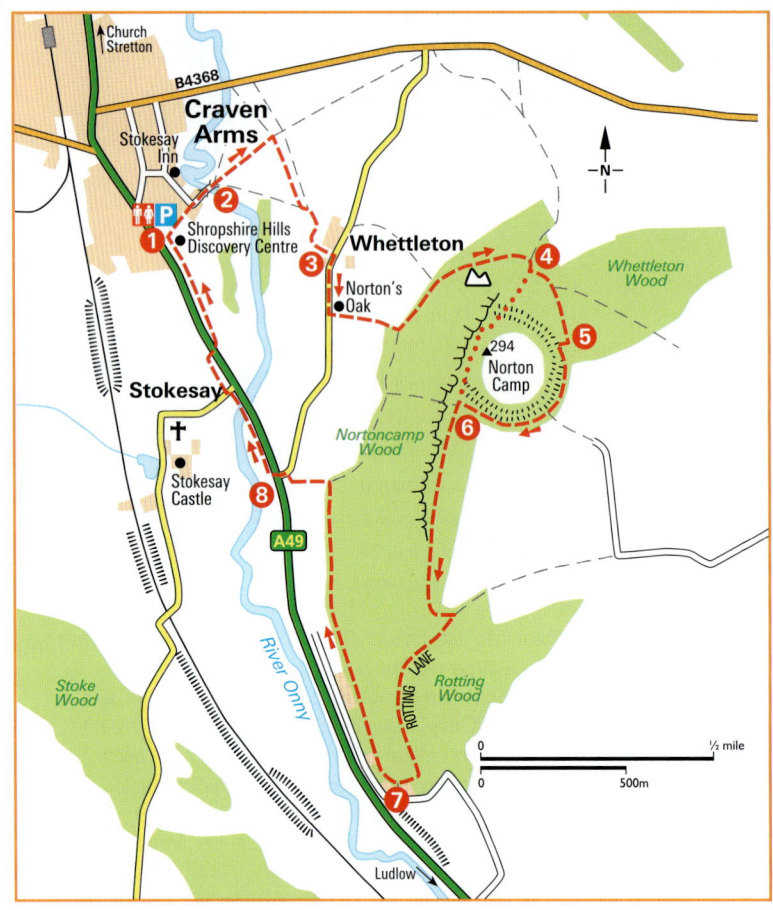

1. Walk past the left side of the Discovery Centre along a clear path into the Onny Meadows. Pass under wooden 'mammoth tusks' then, at a junction, turn left and shortly pass a community garden on your right. Join a tarmac lane, keeping straight ahead and then bearing right at a junction by a half-timbered house. At the end of the lane cross a footbridge over the River Onny.

2. Bear slightly right and pass right of two powerline poles. Just before the field corner turn right to cross a small footbridge then walk near the left edge of the next field, beside an old sunken track. Continue into a hedged track, which swings left around a farm and emerges into a lane.

3. Turn right. Pass the entrance to Norton's Oak then turn left at a footpath sign. Follow the path climbing gently at first, then more steeply. As you enter Nortoncamp Wood, bear left just inside the edge, then bear right, climbing more steeply again on a sunken track. This bends right, still climbing, then back left as it levels out.

4. Keep ahead then bear right. The path is soon lined by rhododendron bushes. Keep straight ahead at a junction and shortly the path becomes a track. There are inter-mittent views on the left towards the Clee Hills, while on the right are the remains of the earthworks of Norton Camp.

5. The track arrives at a renovated house. Continue virtually straight ahead, between the house and a red-brick building. The track (sometimes overgrown) curves gradually rightward, still following the perimeter of the hillfort, until it reaches a signpost and stile.

6. Cross the stile and go left along a clear path close to an obvious craggy edge. Follow the path down the ridge then bear left to meet a track (Rotting Lane). Turn right and follow this downhill. Join a wider forest track and turn left; follow this track down, bending right to reach a T-junction.

7. Go right, passing the backs of houses, with the A49 below them. Continue along the track until it bends right and starts to climb again. Leave it here for a footpath down a field to a lane. Go left a few paces to the A49, cross, and turn right along the footway.

8. Cross a bridge over the Onny, then turn left (signs for Stokesay Castle). Very shortly turn right by a postbox on a tarmac path to a lay-by. Just beyond this, at a sign-post, cross the A49 again to a waymarked path leading back to the Shropshire Hills Discovery Centre.

Where to eat and drink

The café at the Discovery Centre serves hot and cold food prepared, as far as possible, from local produce. It has indoor and outdoor tables overlooking a meadow. The adjacent Stokesay Castle Inn is open all day and serves home-cooked food, tea and coffee. It's pleasant and traditional, with a garden, a children's play area and a good reputation.

What to see

The rhododendrons in the woods are a notable feature of this walk, especially when in full flower (May–June). However, they are alien plants, having been first introduced from their native habitat in the foothills of the Himalaya in the 18th century. Tough and vigorous, they often crowd out native species, and their foliage is unpalatable to most herbivores. As a result they are an unwelcome but hard-to-eradicate invader in many places.

While you're there

Shropshire Hills Discovery Centre Hills began as part of an initiative to attract more visitors to Craven Arms. The grass-roofed building houses a shop, café and library as well as an interactive exhibition. Among its displays, one – appropriately for this walk – gives a flavour of life in the Iron Age. There's also a full-size replica of the Shropshire Mammoth, whose skeleton was found at Condover, near Shrewsbury.

46

THROUGH HOPTON WOODS TO BEDSTONE

DISTANCE/TIME	5 miles (8km) / 2hrs
ASCENT/GRADIENT	892ft (272m) / ▲ ▲
PATHS	Forest tracks and quiet lanes, some field paths
LANDSCAPE	Steep-sided hills between rivers Clun and Redlake
SUGGESTED MAP	OS Explorer 201 Knighton & Presteigne
START/FINISH	Grid reference: SO348777
DOG FRIENDLINESS	Bikes, livestock, roads: on leads at all times
PARKING	Forestry Commission Hopton Woods car park, off minor road west from Hopton Castle to Llanbrook and Obley
PUBLIC TOILETS	None on route

This walk takes you across the top of a hill called Hopton Titterhill, but most people know it as Hopton Forest or Hopton Woods now because it has been almost completely planted with conifers. Don't let that put you off, because there are also patches of beechwood, fantastic views, a Norman castle and two charming villages to enjoy.

In a small way, Hopton Woods is a magnet for mountain bikers. 'Trail centres' have sprung up all over the country, the first – and now one of the largest – being Coedy-Brenin in mid-Wales. Large trail centres may have cafés, bike shops and hire facilities, and see hundreds of riders on almost every day of the year. Hopton isn't on that scale, and may be deserted in midweek, but it does have a selection of trails aimed at all abilities.

Mountain bike trails are usually graded like ski-runs, from green (easiest) through blue, red and black. The one you'll be most aware of is the Pearce XC, usually called 'the Red'. It includes lots of narrow purpose-built trails, known as 'singletrack'. These are for bikes only and are also designed to be ridden in one direction. Linking the singletrack section, the route uses wide shared tracks, with ample room for walkers and cyclists. Hopton also has several black-graded downhill routes, though you won't see these from the walk route.

Leaving the forest, the walk descends to Bedstone. There's a lovely Norman church, with a timber-framed bellcote and a shingled spire. It was subject to 19th-century restoration, but retains some original windows and a Norman font. Nearby stand a few thatched cottages and a Victorian schoolhouse, while Manor Farm is a splendid timber-framed house, partly faced in stone in 1775. To the south of the village is Bedstone College, a flamboyant black-and-white mansion of 1884, now a junior, senior and 6th form college. It was designed by Thomas Harris for Sir Henry Ripley MP and the main school building is said to be a calendar house, with 365 windows, 52 rooms and 12 chimneys.

You'll reach Hopton Castle before the village which shares its name. Only the keep survives, but it's solid and substantial and enjoys a fine setting. It was built by the de Hopton family in the 11th century and rebuilt in the 14th century. During the Civil War it was held for Parliament, but taken by the Royalists after a three-week siege. Most of the defending garrison was killed and the bodies dumped in the moat.

Hopton Castle is another attractive little village. It has only a handful of houses, most notably the timber-framed former rectory. The church is Victorian, built in 1870–71, by the architect T Nicholson.

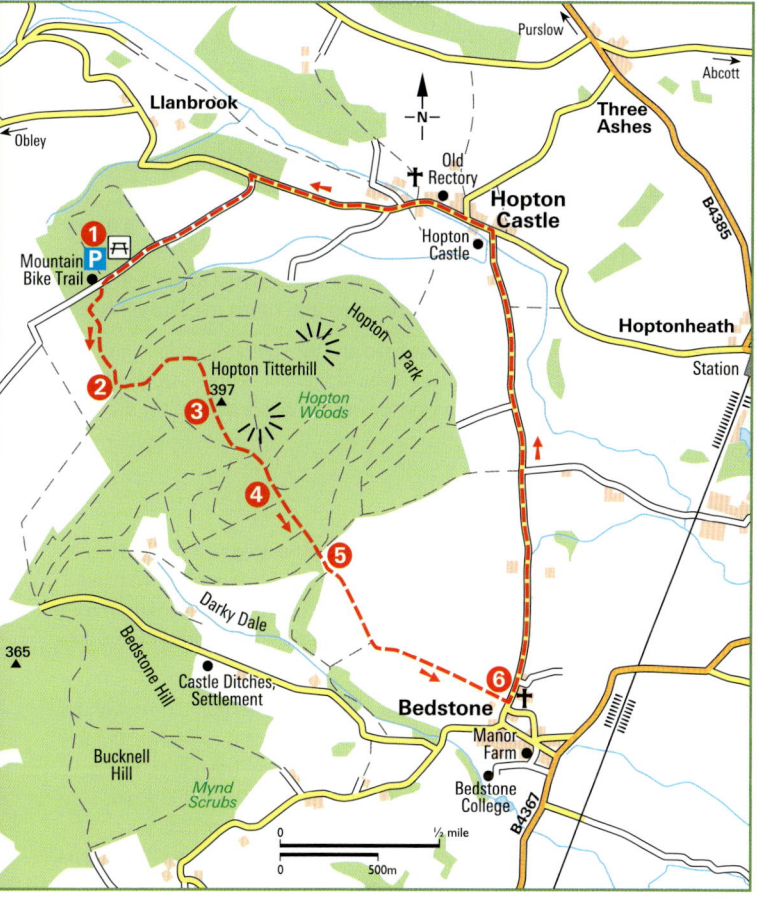

1. From the car park, return to the access track and take another stony track half-right, beyond a barrier and to the right of an information board outlining the bike routes. Climb steadily, soon crossing the Red for the first time. Continue up, with a field on the right, to a complex junction.

2. Take the path half-left, climbing steeply through beech trees and on along a mostly grassy path through mixed woodland and plantation. Turn left at a T-junction, then right at the next junction, by another Red marker. Reaching

open ground, fork left to climb the small, stony, conical summit, carpeted with heather and whinberry – the natural ground cover.

3. Enjoy the view, as far as encroaching trees permit, then turn sharp right to descend and rejoin the main track. Continue in the same direction as before, then fork right down a grassy path where the Red goes left. Meet a stony track by a pool and turn left. A little further on you'll come to a major junction; a track branching left is labelled 'downhill start'. Bear right here and continue along the stony track.

4. When the track bends left keep straight on instead, down a narrower path. The Red climbs up here, joining in from your right a little lower down. Continue straight on down a grassy path, enjoying fine views ahead. After crossing a forest road (final encounter with the Red), the path becomes a bit more overgrown for a short way, but soon you go through a gate at the edge of the forest.

5. Bear left to follow an intermittent hedge of hawthorn trees (and one oak) across a field. Go through a gate at the far side, to the right of another oak. Cross a cattle pasture, again to a gate at the far side. Turn left along the edge of the next field, on a track that becomes increasingly well defined as it descends to Bedstone. When you reach the road you need to turn left to return to Hopton Castle, but you may want to take a look round the village first.

6. Follow the narrow Hopton Castle road and turn left at a junction just after the castle. Walk through the village, keep straight on towards Obley, then turn left at the Forestry Commission sign for Hopton Woods and follow the access track to the car park.

Where to eat and drink
You'll find nothing along the route, but you're not that far from The Hundred House Inn at Purslow crossroads, which has a very traditional bar as well as a lounge and dining room, decked area and garden. The chef uses locally-sourced produce and there's a fine selection of real ales.

What to see
Look under the conifers in the forest and you will see that for most of the year almost nothing grows there because the shade is too dense. But for a couple of months in autumn you should see fungi. The most striking species is the fly agaric, the traditional toadstool of children's books – bright red with white spots. If you see one don't be tempted to take it home because it is highly toxic. The harvesting of wild fungi has become popular recently, but you really do need to know what you're doing.

While you're there
8 miles northeast of Craven Arms along the B4368 is Millichope Park. Here you'll find historic landscape gardens covering 14 acres with lakes and cascades dating from the 18th-century, woodland walks and wildflowers. The grounds feature many specimen trees and views into the surrounding parkland and the Clee Hill. Snowdrops feature in February, bluebells and daffodils in May, and autumn colours in October. The gardens take part in the National Gardens Scheme so check opening days.

BURY DITCHES HILL FORT

DISTANCE/TIME	5.4 miles (8.7km) / 2hrs
ASCENT/GRADIENT	804ft (245m) / ▲ ▲
PATHS	Field and woodland paths, lengthy stretch of quiet lane
LANDSCAPE	Hilltop woodland and plantation, mixed farmland in valley
SUGGESTED MAP	OS Explorer 216 Welshpool & Montgomery
START/FINISH	Grid reference: SO334839
DOG FRIENDLINESS	Off lead for much of way, but not round Acton
PARKING	Forestry Commission car park at Bury Ditches off minor road north from Clunton
PUBLIC TOILETS	None on route

It is impossible to spend much time in Shropshire without becoming aware of its hill-forts. The southwest corner of the county is particularly rich in these impressive monuments. The same is true of the neighbouring parts of Herefordshire and Montgomeryshire, so that there is hardly a hilltop in the area that doesn't provide a view of several forts. Some were built in the late Bronze Age, but most were constructed in the Iron Age; that is, after around 600 BC. They were built in stages, often over very long periods of time, possibly as much as 1,000 years in some cases.

This walk takes you to one of the finest of all, Bury Ditches, which crowns Sunnyhill (also called Tangley Hill), above the valleys of the Clun and the Kemp. Elliptical in shape, Bury Ditches is an example of a contour fort, which means that its Celtic builders took advantage of the topography, making the ramparts follow the natural contours of the landscape. Such construction wasn't always possible, but where the natural slope was sufficiently steep, it enabled them to get away with fewer ramparts, or even none at all. On the relatively gentle northern slope of Sunnyhill summit, three substantial ramparts were considered necessary, but there are only two on the south side, below which the slope plunges down steeply.

It's possible for archaeologists to tell approximately when a fort was built by the design of the ramparts. Bury Ditches' construction suggests a date somewhere around the 6th century BC (early Iron Age). All the local community would have been involved, including young children. Trees would have to be cleared first, using axes made from flint, stone or bronze, and then the ramparts and ditches would be dug with deer-antler picks and shovels made from the shoulder blades of cattle. Earth, turf and stones would have been carried away in hand baskets. It's a task of almost unimaginable proportions, especially when you consider that Bury Ditches covers a larger area than most hamlets and many villages in Shropshire.

It was thought that hill-forts were used only for defence at times of danger, but excavation and other archaeological techniques have revealed that the larger ones were more like defended villages, where people lived and farmed. Did they also appreciate the view, in purely aesthetic terms? The immense panorama visible from the top of Bury Ditches is one of the finest in Shropshire, but it was lost for several years, after the Forestry Commission planted conifers there. A timely gale in 1978 flattened many of the alien trees and the Commission took the hint, removing the rest.

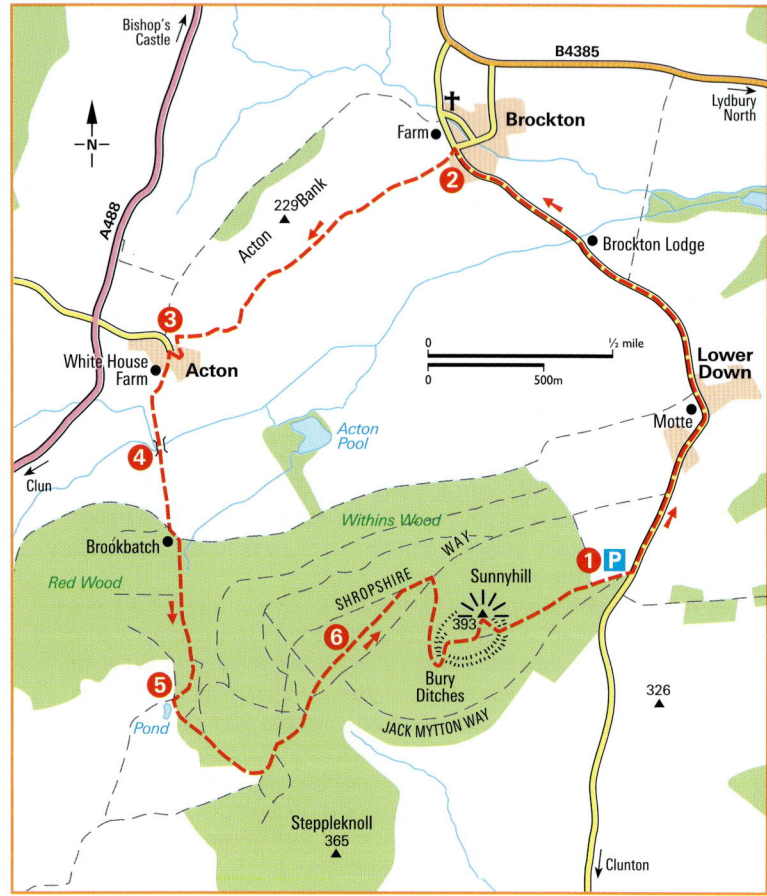

1. From the car park at Sunnyhill, walk back to the lane and turn left. Descend through the hamlet of Lower Down. There's access to a Norman motte in a field on the left. Continue down to Brockton. Pass Shropshire Highland Seeds, and some more large sheds, then a stone barn. Turn left immediately on a track (Blue Remembered Hills Bridleway).

2. Follow the track, climbing steadily at first. It can be a bit overgrown as it descends, but mostly it's just harmless cow-parsley. At a junction go left down an attractive slab by the track, then turn right to meet a lane at the hamlet of Acton.

3. Turn left, pass to the right of a triangular green and join a path running past White House Farm. Frequent waymarkers guide you past the house, across a small field, then left over a stile and along the right-hand edge of another field.

4. Cross a footbridge and continue straight across the ensuing field towards a building at the far side. Cross a stile in the hedge, turn left for a few paces on a track which passes by a house called Brookbatch. Swing right to a path rising into woodland. When the track eventually bends to the left, go forward over a stile instead and continue climbing.

5. Emerging on to a track, turn left and pass a pond. Cross a defunct cattle grid and leave the track, turning right on a footpath, scarred by motorbikes, through beech-woods. At an obvious crossroads of tracks turn left, then bear right on a forestry track by a Shropshire Way sign. Ignore all side turnings then keep left at a fork where there are distant views through the trees on the right.

6. Climb gently for a while. Where the main track levels off and starts to descend, turn right. The path leads to Bury Ditches hill-fort, then cuts through a gap in the ramparts and crosses the interior. At a waymarked post, a path branches left to allow a visit to the summit, with its toposcope and incredible views. Bear right to return to the main path and turn left to follow it to the car park.

Where to eat and drink

Bishop's Castle, Clun and Clunton are all near by. Or there's the Powis Arms at Lydbury North, a traditional Georgian coaching inn, the seasonal menu uses the finest local ingredients that the county has to offer. Worth a special journey is the marvellous Harvest Wholefoods shop at Lydham, north of Bishop's Castle, with a huge range of organic and GM-free goodies.

What to see

Here's a challenge – can you identify the entrances to the hillfort? Bury Ditches has two and they're more elaborate than is usual in the Marches. One is inturned with a straight corridor and indications of two guard houses. The other is out-turned and curving, with a barbican and an overlapping rampart truncated by a forest road. A big clue – one is at the northeast, the other at the southwest.

While you're there

Walcot Hall at Lydbury North was once the home of Robert Clive (Clive of India), and is a wedding venue and occasionally open to the public. Clive's son Edward was a keen arboriculturalist and the arboretum he created is open every afternoon except Saturday, April to November. The lake in the grounds was enlarged by French prisoners during the Napoleonic Wars.

EXPLORING OFFA'S DYKE FROM KNIGHTON

DISTANCE/TIME	8 miles (12.9km) / 3hrs
ASCENT/GRADIENT	1,542ft (470m) / ▲ ▲ ▲
PATHS	Excellent on ridge, undefined across fields, many stiles
LANDSCAPE	Steep hills overlooking the broad Teme Valley
SUGGESTED MAP	OS Explorer 201 Knighton & Presteigne
START/FINISH	Grid reference: SO287734
DOG FRIENDLINESS	Can run free in Kinsley Wood, but sheep present elsewhere
PARKING	Informal car parking in Kinsley Wood, accessed by forest road from A488 (or park in Knighton, Bowling Green Lane car park or at Offa's Dyke Centre)
PUBLIC TOILETS	In Knighton, near Bowling Green Lane car park and Offa's Dyke Centre

Knighton straddles the border, nine toes in Radnorshire and one in Shropshire. Its Welsh name is Tref-y-clawdd, which translates as 'town on the dyke', a reference to its position on the great earthwork known as Offa's Dyke. Offa was ruler of the English kingdom of Mercia between AD 757 and 796, and the eponymous dyke is the longest archaeological monument in Britain, an impressive structure consisting mainly of a bank, with a ditch on the Welsh side.

Nobody is certain why Offa ordered its construction. It used to be thought it was an agreed frontier, a way of defining the border or maybe even regulating trade. It's now thought that a period of instability, with constant cross-border raiding, led to Offa's decision to secure his frontier with a defensive boundary. It was formerly believed to have run all the way from Treuddyn (north of Wrexham) to Chepstow, but current thinking is that it may have been shorter than that. Recent work in Gloucestershire has suggested that the earthwork in the lower Wye Valley, previously accepted as part of Offa's Dyke, actually dates from a different period. The Shropshire earthwork is certainly part of Offa's Dyke, however. Most of the best-preserved sections are in Shropshire, particularly on remote Llanfair Hill, a little to the north of this walk, which is also the dyke's highest point (1,410ft/430m).

To date, nearly 200 archaeological digs have been carried out on the dyke system. As far as its purpose is concerned, the only thing that has been concluded with any reasonable certainty is that it was built in such a way as to defend Mercia from the raiding Welsh. It was probably not simply an agreed frontier or a boundary marker. But, then again, if it was defensive, why have no traces of fortifications or palisading been discovered? Clearly, there is still much to learn.

Offa's Dyke National Trail, opened in 1971, is a splendid walk that runs for 177 miles (285km) from Prestatyn to Chepstow, following the earthwork for 30 miles (48km). The dyke has survived for 1,300 years, but has never been under such pressure as it is today. It's damaged by agriculture, undermined by rabbits, threatened by development and now eroded by walkers. So walk alongside it where the route has been realigned, rather than on top. The paths are now managed by the Offa's Dyke Path National Trail Officer (NTO) who liaises with local councils and the Offa's Dyke Association to deal with any problems that arise anywhere along the Trail.

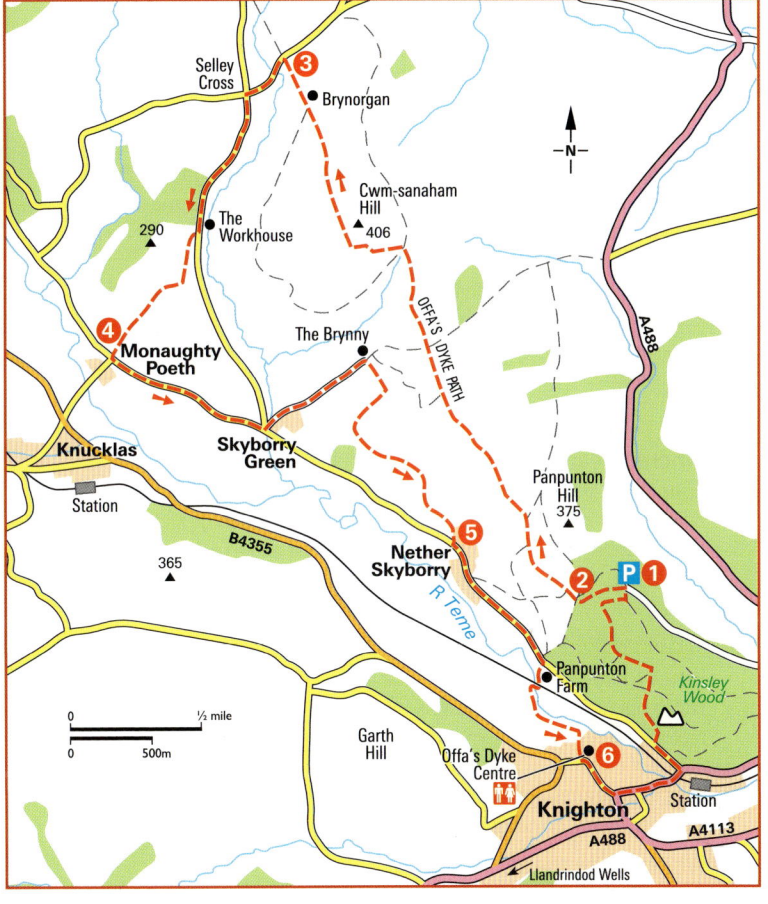

1. At the back of the car park, a gate leads into a meadow with a barn in it. Walk along the left-hand edge of this meadow. At the crest veer slightly away from the field-edge and descend through oak trees to a stile. Cross and join Offa's Dyke Path (ODP).

2. Turn right and follow the ODP for about 2.5 miles (4km). The path runs above steep slopes falling to the west, following the dyke all the way. After rounding a combe, it climbs to the top of Cwm-sanaham Hill (1,323ft/406m), then continues northwards, soon descending very steeply to a white house, Brynorgan.

3. Meeting a road, leave the ODP, turning left, then left again at Selley Cross. After 0.5 miles (800m) or so, just beyond The Workhouse, go through the next gate on the right. Follow a vague path along a field, then turn right, climbing steeply by a line of trees to a stile. Follow waymarks across several fields, to meet a lane at Monaughty Poeth.

4. Turn left for 0.75 miles (1.2km) to a junction at Skyborry Green. Turn left again, then immediately right, joining a bridleway that climbs to The Brynny. Turn right behind the house. Don't join the obvious track just above but follow a narrow footpath along the hedge. Take the lower option at all unwaymarked junctions. After three stiles in quick succession, join a track and descend to the road at Nether Skyborry.

5. Turn left for 0.5 mile (800m), then right on to the ODP just before Panpunton Farm. The path crosses the railway and the River Teme, then follows the Teme towards Knighton, soon crossing the border and turning right to the Offa's Dyke Centre.

6. Leaving the centre, turn left through Knighton, then left again on Station Road. After passing the station, turn left on Kinsley Road. Join the first path (steps) on the right into Kinsley Wood, opposite Gillow. Fork left after a few paces, then embark on a grindingly steep climb. The gradient eases a little before the path emerges from the trees to continue past picnic tables and across a forest road. Keep straight on to the top of the ridge, then turn left at a crossroads to walk across the summit. The path descends to a track. Turn right to return to the start.

Where to eat and drink

Prince and Pugh's is an excellent tea shop and only one of several in Knighton. There are plenty of pubs too, such as The George and Dragon, a 17th-century free house with home-made food and a beer garden. Near the station, the medieval, flower-bedecked Horse and Jockey with an outside courtyard is an attractive pub, and The Knighton Hotel has an internet café offering a variety of snacks and beverages.

What to see

Watch out for red kites, especially on the ridge. These magnificent raptors, all but extinct in Britain a century ago, have been successfully reintroduced in several areas and are now spreading naturally. They are roughly buzzard-sized but distinguished by their reddish colour, slimmer wings and most obviously by their prominent forked tail.

While you're there

The Offa's Dyke Centre is a must. There are interesting displays and a good range of tourist information. Behind the centre is a stretch of the dyke and an inscribed stone commemorating the opening of the National Trail by Lord Hunt (of Everest fame), who lived at nearby Llanfair Waterdine until his death in 1998.

49 THE CLUN VALLEY'S LITERARY CONNECTIONS

DISTANCE/TIME	5.5 miles (8.8km) / 2hrs 30min
ASCENT/GRADIENT	1,066ft (325m) / ▲ ▲ ▲
PATHS	Excellent, through mixed farmland (mainly pasture) and woodland
LANDSCAPE	Steep-sided, round-topped hills above valley of River Clun
SUGGESTED MAP	OS Explorer 201 Knighton & Presteigne
START/FINISH	Grid reference: SO302811
DOG FRIENDLINESS	Keep under close control near sheep and cattle
PARKING	Car park at Clun Memorial Hall, signed from High Street
PUBLIC TOILETS	At short-stay car park by castle on the B4368

Clun is enfolded by enticing green hills on all sides. It may have been settled as early as the Bronze Age; certainly by the Iron Age there was some sort of community there. But it was the Saxons who first settled in any numbers. Later, the Norman Picot de Say built a castle here around 1099 and laid out a new town in a regular grid pattern, which still survives. Clun was granted its town charter in the 14th century and is still, strictly speaking, a town, but it looks and feels more like a village. There is lots to see, including the substantial castle ruins, 12th-century church, 15th-century packhorse bridge, 17th-century almshouses, 18th-century town hall and many charming cottages.

Equally interesting, but not so well known, are the literary connections that abound in Clun. E M Forster visited the town, which subsequently featured as Oniton in *Howard's End*, published in 1910. One of his key characters, Margaret Schlegel, is totally captivated by the romance and magic of this corner of the Marches. The castle, with its great keep and commanding site, is said to have been the inspiration for Garde Doleureuse in Sir Walter Scott's novel *The Betrothed*, published jointly with *The Talisman as Tales of the Crusaders* in 1825. Scott is believed to have stayed at the Buffalo Inn while working on the book. More recently, playwright John Osborne lived near Clun and now lies buried in the churchyard. The best known literary link, however, is with A E Housman, the author of a timeless collection of poems called *A Shropshire Lad*. Housman famously described Clunton and Clunbury, Clungunford and Clun as 'the quietest places under the sun'. Clun also featured in *Valley With a Bright Cloud*, a ghost story written by Gareth Lovatt Jones in 1980, while nearby Clunbury became the adopted home of Ida Gandy in 1930. A writer and the wife of a country doctor, Gandy set out in an old Austin 7 to see rural England. On arriving in Clunbury she was so captivated that she decided to stay. The family settled in the village and Ida continued to write, and to broadcast too, with most of her work inspired by Shropshire. Her most famous book is *An Idler on the Shropshire Borders*, written in 1970.

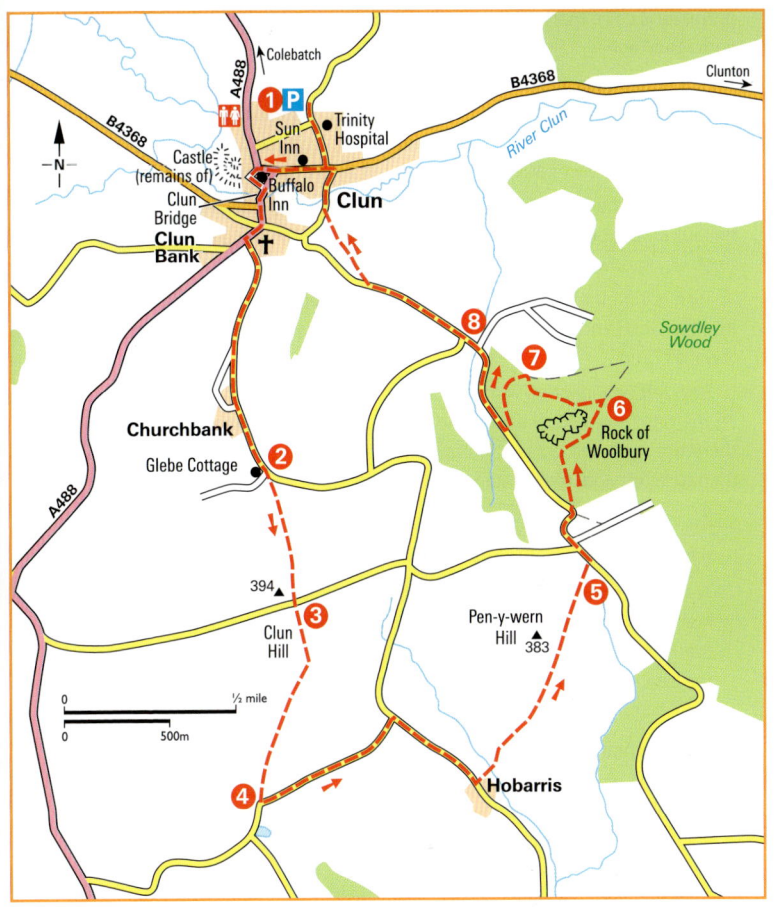

1. Walk down Hospital Lane turn right onto High Street and continue to The Square. Bear left and continue down Buffalo Lane and cross Clun Bridge. Go up Church Street, turn right on the Knighton Road, then left on Hand Causeway, signposted to Churchbank and Hobarris.

2. After 0.75 mile (1.2km), take a bridleway on the right, which leaves the lane on a bend by Glebe Cottage and immediately goes left into a field. Walk up the field, through a gate at the top, then straight on through two more fields to meet a lane running across the top of Clun Hill (part of the prehistoric Clun-Clee Ridgeway).

3. The path continues opposite, along the right-hand edges of two fields. At the end of the second one, go through a gate on the right and diagonally to the far corner of another field, then in much the same direction down the next.

4. Go through a gate and turn left on a byway, then right on a lane when you come to a T-junction. At Hobarris, just before the main farm buildings on the left, go left and through a gate on to a track, just before the main farm buildings. Soon after crossing a brook, branch left along a hollow way. When this bends right, go straight on instead, over a stile into a field. Go straight uphill, joining a field-edge track. To your left, three Scots pines and a

prehistoric cairn mark the summit of Pen-y-wern Hill. Turn left when you come to a lane.

5. At a crossroads, keep straight on, descending to the second of two bends in the lane. Ignore a signposted path on the right; instead take an unsignposted one a few paces further on. It leads into a plantation and soon bends right. About 200yds (183m) after this, branch left on a descending path.

6. After a further 100yds (91m) branch left again, descending through a beautiful oakwood, with scattered rowans and a ground cover of whinberries. Keep going down to meet a path at the bottom of the wood.

7. Turn left on the path, which almost immediately swings left, plunges back into the wood and winds through the trees to meet the lane. Turn right towards Clun.

8. Turn left at a junction with two tracks. Keep going along the lane until a stile on the right gives access to a field. Go diagonally left towards Clun. Join a lane, then turn right and cross a footbridge by a ford. Turn right meet the B4368 then turn left and immediately right onto Hospital Lane.

Where to eat and drink

The 16th-century White Horse has a micro-brewery on site and serves home cooked meals, it's dog friendly with a beer garden too. There is also the 15th-century Sun Inn on the High Street. The Maltings Café (next to the Sun Inn) and Post Card Café by the bridge are both recommended for their home bakes.

What to see

The wood on Black Hill has a ground cover of whinberry, or bilberry as it is called elsewhere. It produces delicious summer fruits. Some pubs and restaurants in southwest Shropshire still offer the local speciality, whinberry pie.

While you're there

Take a peek into the beautiful gardens of Trinity Hospital, in Hospital Lane, which are open to the public, but do respect the residents' privacy. The hospital includes almshouses from 1614.

ON THE BLACK HILL AND DOWN TO CWM

50

DISTANCE/TIME	5.7 miles (9.7km) / 2hrs 30min
ASCENT/GRADIENT	1,296ft (895m) / ▲ ▲
PATHS	Woodland paths, grassy track, quiet lanes and Forestry Commission paths
LANDSCAPE	Mostly forest, some pasture in steep, secluded valley
SUGGESTED MAP	OS Explorer 201 Knighton & Presteigne
START/FINISH	Grid reference: SO338805
DOG FRIENDLINESS	Mostly good for dogs, but check for livestock on leaving the forest
PARKING	Sowdley Wood car park near Clunton Coppice on Cwm Lane, which runs south from Clunton
PUBLIC TOILETS	None on route

Cwm, of course, is the Welsh word for 'valley', and more specifically for a steep-sided valley cutting into a hill or range of hills. It's related to the English word 'combe', which is common in some areas with a strong Celtic influence, like the West Country and the Lake District. In this particular case, Cwm is both an apt description of the landscape and a reminder that Welsh influence is strong in this area.

There's no shortage of Welsh placenames within a few miles of Cwm: Llan Farm, Llanhowell and Llanadevy just down the valley, Pen-y-cwm and Pen-y-wern just the other side of Black Hill. They're mixed, apparently indiscriminately, with distinctively English names – Rock of Woolbury, Fiddler's Elbow, Clunton, Clunbury. It should remind us that the Welsh were not just opportunistic raiders from beyond Offa's Dyke. Borders can be moveable, and often represent a zone of mingling and co-existence (peaceful or otherwise!) rather than a simple rigid barrier.

In 1982 Bruce Chatwin (perhaps better known as a travel writer) published his greatest novel, *On the Black Hill*, which won the James Tait Black Memorial Prize. In 1987 it was made into a film, directed by Andrew Grieve and starring Bob Peck. Variously described as 'brooding', 'poignant' and 'lyrical', it's essentially the story of two brothers, unbreakably bound to each other and to the land; great events and changes in the outside world impinge only occasionally.

The novel is set a little further south, on the borders of Herefordshire and Radnorshire, but owes much of its inspiration and atmosphere to the Shropshire Black Hill. Chatwin was friends with the owners of Cwm Hall and stayed several times in a cottage near the house. It was here, early in 1979, that he wrote the first chapters, and it's reported that one night in the Hall's kitchen, he said, 'I've got it, I will call my book On the Black Hill'. The looming presence of the Black Hill (just look to your left as you walk past Cwm Hall) and the confined, almost claustrophobic character of the valley, are strongly reflected in the novel. It's still easy, in Cwm today, to feel that the outside world is very far away.

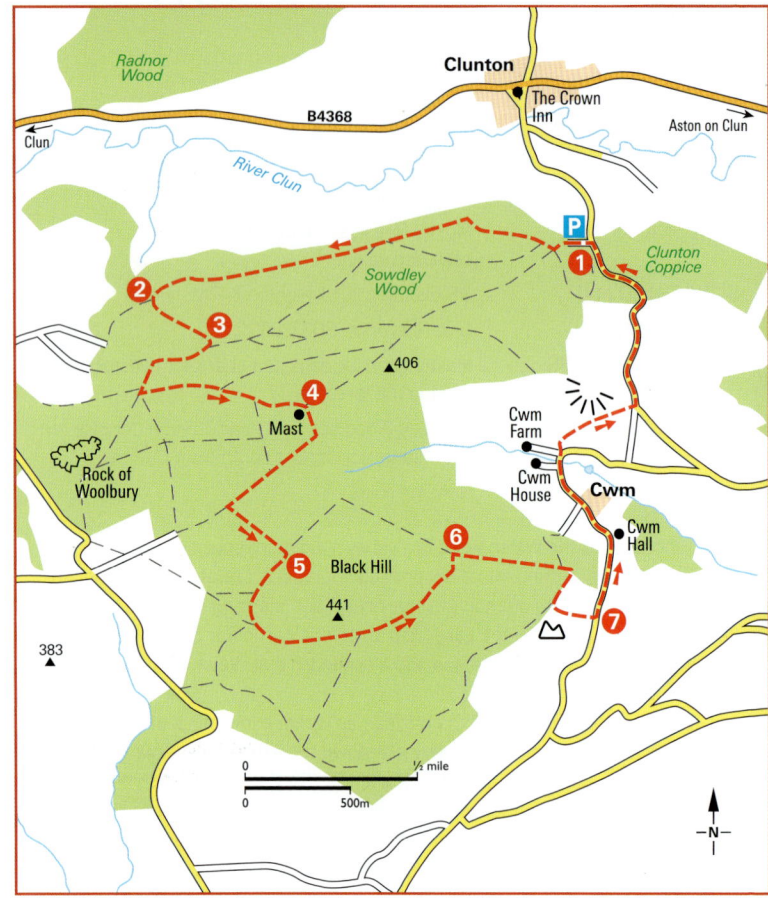

1. From the end of the car park, pass a barrier and follow the track. At the first junction go right, pass another track on the left, then descend to another barrier. Below this join another track and go left through Sowdley Wood. Follow this track, virtually straight and generally level, for almost a mile (1.5km) until it swings left into a small valley.

2. Just before the stream, which is sometimes dry, turn left up a neglected-looking track. Climb this quite steeply. Near the top it may be blocked by fallen trees and new growth – if so, simply go rightwards through the trees to join a clear track just above.

3. Go right on this, descending slightly, to a waymarked junction and go left uphill. Follow waymarks through the next junction and then again as you turn left onto a track which climbs steadily and almost straight. Take the middle way at a three-fold junction and keep straight ahead again at a cross-tracks. The gradient eases and you arrive at a junction by a transmitter mast.

4. Turn right (waymarked) past a barrier and at the next junction go right again on a stony track (byway) under power lines. Follow this, climbing gently, and as it levels off turn left; it's the first track on your left, and there's a bridleway sign just beyond the junction. Walk down here, with young trees on the left, to a T-junction and turn right.

5. Ignoring any fainter tracks, at the next clear junction, go left and then left again. Rise slightly and then start to descend, gradually curving left.

6. At a junction with a dilapidated waymark post, turn sharp right on a narrower green track and soon fork left on a descending footpath. (The right branch is currently overgrown, and could easily be missed). Descend to a gate, turn left and drop steeply into a field. Go down the left edge to a gate and exit onto a lane.

7. Turn left. Pass the entrance to Cwm Hall as the lane bends left, and walk through the tiny hamlet of Cwm. At a sharp bend in the lane, just past Cwm House, by the entrance to Cwm Farm, take a footpath that climbs diagonally up two pastures to meet the lane again. Turn left and descend through Clunton Coppice back to the car park.

Where to eat and drink

The Crown Inn at Clunton is recommended for its hospitality, with beer and food both earning praise, be aware, however, that opening hours for the bar and kitchen vary, check their website for details. There's a good choice in nearby Clun too.

What to see

Generally speaking, conifer woods are too dark for wild flowers to flourish, but on Black Hill the delicate wood sorrel proves an exception to the rule. Blooming in considerable numbers in very early spring, mostly on mossy logs or banks, its lovely flowers are white with mauve or pink veins and its bright green leaves, distinctively shamrock-shaped, are nearly as pretty.

While you're there

Explore Clunton Coppice, a fragment of native sessile oak woodland owned and managed by Shropshire Wildlife Trust. It's maintained by coppicing, a system of woodland management in which trees are cut close to the ground, then left to grow again. The cut stools quickly put out new shoots which can be harvested for small timber or left to grow on. Sessile oak is dominant, but small-leaved lime, yew and hornbeam also occur, while the shrub layer includes hazel, holly and rowan.

Explore
the UK at
RatedTrips.com

AA